SWORD AND SCALPEL

A Doctor Looks Back at Vietnam

Larry Rogers

Hellgate Press   Ashland, OR

Sword and Scalpel
©2014 Larry Rogers

Published by Hellgate Press
(An imprint of L&R Publishing, LLC)

Hellgate Press
PO Box 3531
Ashland, OR 97520
email: sales@hellgatepress.com

Editor: Harley B. Patrick
Interior design: Sasha Kincaid
Cover design: L. Redding

Library of Congress Cataloging-in-Publication Data

Rogers, Larry (Larry A.)
 Sword and scalpel : a doctor looks back at Vietnam / Larry Rogers.
   pages cm
 ISBN 978-1-55571-766-7
1. Rogers, Larry (Larry A.) 2. Vietnam War, 1961-1975--Medical care. 3. Vietnam War, 1961-1975--Campaigns. 4. Vietnam War, 1961-1975--Personal narratives, American. 5. Surgeons--United States--Biography. 6. Medicine, Military--United States--Biography. I. Title.
 DS559.44.R65 2014
 959.704'37--dc23
 [B]
                                2014012681

Printed and bound in the United States of America
First edition 10 9 8 7 6 5 4 3 2 1

Dedicated to:

Parker

Francie

Jane

Charlie Arch

Drake

and

Alex

And To the Memory of:

Major Albert G. Maroscher

First Lieutenant Randy G. Radigan

Sergeant Chuong

and

Cô Bay

True Heroes

CONTENTS

FOREWORD

Doctor Larry Rogers has written one of the most exciting books about war I have ever read. It is the fascinating true story of two wars in Vietnam—one about killing and destroying, the other about conserving human life. Saving lives under combat conditions demands great confidence and unerring performance. The author's spellbinding descriptions of managing medical challenges under enemy fire amount to a tumbling waterfall of medical maneuvers and procedures, each presented in a staccato style that will have readers scrambling to keep up. An example includes the amazing jerry-rigging of a device to convert a soldier's "dying heart" rhythm by connecting nearby scraps of wire and metal to a little-used generator. That episode proceeds with the tempo of a boxing match.

There is no pretentiousness here. *Sword and Scalpel* is full of stunning action in a do-or-die environment. Readers will find it difficult to control their emotions as lucid explanations of the actions of doctors, medics, and corpsmen fighting for life unfold and pile up. What could be more exciting than combat medics stealing life from death? This book is full of exactly that, told in a rapid-fire cadence.

—Brigadier General James E. Shelton, U.S. Army (Ret.), author of
   The Beast Was Out There

1.
SEARCH AND DESTROY

Beware the Ides of March.
Julius Caesar, Act I, scene ii

On March 15, 1968 I was pinch-hitting for the battalion surgeon of the 1st Battalion of the 16th Infantry Regiment (1/16) on a search-and-destroy mission somewhere north of Lai Khe, roughly half-way between Saigon and the Cambodian border. A "battalion minus" operation involved combining two of three rifle companies (typically approaching one hundred men per company) plus a weapons platoon (roughly two dozen infantrymen with machine guns, mortars, and RPGs, or rocket propelled grenades). Division policy dictated that a medical officer be part of any operation under direct command of the battalion's commanding officer as a means of enhancing troop morale. The thinking was that infantrymen would expect the same access to medical care as the CO. I was skeptical about what a soldier-doctor could do in the boondocks that an experienced combat medic couldn't, but nobody asked my opinion. Dust Off helicopters typically retrieved casualties to a fully equipped medical facility within twenty minutes from almost anywhere.

We moved out at 0830, single file, spaced five-to-seven yards apart to minimize casualties from a single incoming round. I was to stay within voice-communication distance of the CO, but instinctively I understood the danger of being too close to him. Generally the CO was immediately ahead of his RTO (radio telephone operator) in the column. Charlie was trained to search for the RTO's ten-foot radio antenna waving back and forth above what vegetation there was. That made the RTO as vulnerable as the point man, the fearless guy at the head the column. For Charlie to lob a grenade at the RTO could paralyze our entire operation. Plus, I understood that being too close to the CO or his RTO could be hazardous to my health.

"I hate this damn quiet," the guy in front of me growled at nobody in particular.

"Roger that, good buddy," somebody replied. "The birds always know where Charlie's at."

"Why don't you guys knock it the hell off," snapped somebody behind me."

I knew I was scared. I was on my first patrol. I had a right to be jumpy, but these guys were veterans at this shit.

We heard a bird or two over the next couple of hours but found no sign of Charlie. By 1100 we came onto a room-sized dugout nestled beneath a roof of limbs, brush, and dried mud. Its walls were reinforced by split saplings. It seemed to be an abandoned school, at least a classroom. But there was no sign of recent habitation. It was strange. We had to be miles from anything like a village.

Mildewed, hand-written booklets were stacked on a rough-hewn wooden table at one end of the room. Subject titles and owners' names were handwritten in Vietnamese on the covers. Inside were pages of lists of vocabulary words in neat columns, one in French, another in English, followed by a short phase in Vietnamese. The writing suggested a soft-lead pencil. The words were simple, like rice, water, rain, et al. Another booklet, presumably a math primer, was easier to understand. It listed multiplication and division tables, each figure and character precisely inscribed. The vocabulary lists seemed to be appropriate for persons of any age, but the arithmetic had to be aimed at nine- and ten-year-olds.

A reddish-brown carving of Buddha was perched on a miniature mantle projecting from a wall. It was almost a foot in height, of stunning workmanship. The statue had long, flat ears, a patrician nose, and delicate lips. The eyes were vaguely closed, and a tiny crack extended from above an eyebrow to one cheek, then reappearing briefly at the breast, and again across a clothed forearm, finally widening at the base. I could understand finding a religious relic in the middle of nowhere, but this seemed truly a work of art.

Finding tangible signs of culture, ambition, and belief deep in a war-torn forest got my attention. Who had lived here and when? The primers suggested multiple families, but where were they now, and why had they left?

With a sense of guilt I dumped two of the notebooks and the carving into my medical bag. Technically it was stealing, but I couldn't resist. To me they were abandoned property, amazing souvenirs.

When we stopped for chow I got the bright idea to back into the trunk of a tree and ease myself into a seat in the underbrush. It seemed reasonable enough so I ignored the looks of others as I dug into a can of pears with my pocket knife. Within minutes fire ants swarmed inside my fatigues and spread up my back and down my thighs. The guys around me broke into laughter as their doctor-for-the-week hopped up and down, slapping himself in the ass.

Hours later the column descended an overgrown bank toward a river twisting and turning in the sunlight. Soon water cooled my feet as I scanned the trees and vines ascending the opposite bank. I couldn't imagine a better spot for an ambush, with the command group wading and no cover in sight. They were sitting ducks for Charlie, and I wasn't far behind.

The current was gentle at knee-deep, leading me to loosen the shoulder webbing to let my medical bag float gently downstream. It was full of dressings, morphine and lesser analgesics, IV tubing, antibiotics, various topical ointments, a mini-surgical kit containing scalpels, hemostats, extra blades, sutures, and tracheotomy canulae. As I watched the soldier in front of me sink to his waist, though, I had a decision to make. He was a head taller than me, and there was no question I couldn't manage my weapon and the bag at the same time when I reached where he was.

As water reached waist-level I could still monitor the bank on the other side. So far there was no movement, but Charlie could be almost anywhere up there, high in the trees or prone in the underbrush.

When the point man made it across, the likelihood of an ambush would fall precipitously. Once in the stream though, monitoring the progress of forward elements amounted to little more than a guess. When the current picked up, I assumed I was almost a third of the way across. Then the water rose sharply, requiring more energy and focus to keep my balance and feel with my feet for river bottom holes and boulders. I cinched up the shoulder webbing, pulling the medical supplies closer to me. My weapon was now my number-one priority. For the fiftieth time since breakfast I made certain the firing mode was set to "semi" rather than "auto." I had never fired an M-16 on automatic and had no idea how quick the magazine could empty, a situation I would avoid whatever it took. I'd take my chances firing one round at a time over running the risk of carrying an empty weapon.

As I got deeper in the stream, it dawned on me that a single misstep could leave me swimming. I wouldn't lose any medical supplies—however soggy they got—but my M-16 could definitely become a casualty. Even glancing at the far bank was unthinkable.

Finally, just as water threatened to lap into my armpits, it began to recede. Seconds later I made out the RTO's antenna ahead as LTC Benedict began to make his way up an unseen trail. He was the tallest guy in the battalion, and he was carrying his helmet under an arm. I did a double-take as I watched the reflection of the sun from the top of his bald head. I felt enormous relief. I knew no sniper would pass up Benedict for a shot at me, and Benedict wasn't worried about a damn thing.

...

An hour later the pace slowed, then stopped. Word came back that we were about to enter a mine field. I didn't know the first thing about land mines, but I imagined a GI ahead sweeping a Geiger counter back and forth, with the rest of us playing follow-the-leader. I mumbled a prayer of thanks that I was nowhere near the head of the column.

I was sweating again. My fatigues, long since dried out from fording the river, were again soaked. We were on dry, hard-packed ground now, with little underbrush to hide a mine. I no longer dwelled on the broad shoulders ahead. Instead I focused on his boots, noting precisely where he set them down. I did the best I could to match his foot prints.

Some time later, when the "all clear" got back to us, I began to relax. I was weary of worrying. Eventually I calmed down and stopped imagining danger. But the guys around me were still quiet. I wondered what they were thinking.

•••

We returned to the NDP (night defense position) an hour before sundown with nothing to show for our day's work. We had seen not a single VC and no weapon had been discharged. Cooking fires blazed, and the smell of steak was in the air. Some guys climbed into the field shower contraptions but I planted myself at the front of my tent and peeled off my boots and socks. I sat there a long time, wondering what tomorrow would bring.

•••

At shortly past 1600 hours on March 16 we escaped the glare of the sun as we entered a stand of trees. The underbrush thinned out, making walking easy for the first time all day. It seemed a peaceful place, possibly even a safe place. Trees limited any sniper's fields of fire. That was always a plus. Soon we would be back at the NDP, ending my second day of patrol and still no contact with Charlie.

I had no idea where we were or why we were here. I concluded that contacting Charlie would be a matter of chance, pure guesswork. An infantryman's duty amounted to keeping on the move and dealing with whatever turned up.

The pace was relaxed for the first time all day, giving me the idea we were taking a break while continuing the march. We continued to maintain column integrity but even that seemed relaxed. My mind wandered as I searched out the treetops. It had become a habit. There was nothing new up there, and any VC on the ground had little cover and dozens of tree trunks between him and us. It was a reassuring thought.

The first shots rang out from deep in the woods to our left. Crack! Crack! Crack! Crack! Ungodly sounds. There were four: flat and crisp, like tree trunks split by unseen strokes of lightning. They were nothing like the sounds of firing down range at Fort Bragg.

The big guy ahead was down, six or seven paces away. His helmet tumbled then rolled toward the sound of the firing. He was flat on his face and perfectly still, his fatigues beginning to saturate with blood. Almost certainly he had a through-and-through chest wound, and dead already.

I heard a groan behind me. It was deep, guttural. On my belly, I twisted to face it. The soldier was face up, motionless, with blood spreading across his belly. He made not another sound. He was gut-shot, and miles from an operating room. I had heard the last sound he would ever make. If he wasn't dead, he would be in less than a minute. He was even closer than the guy ahead of me.

Hugging the ground, I twisted back toward Charlie, heartbeats pounding in my ears. Were those bastards on the ground or in the trees?

Voices around me were sporadic, urgent yet with thundering calmness. Some guys fanned out to the right, others in the opposite direction, their weapons discharging brief bursts. Nobody went directly at Charlie.

I was terrified. The bastard who knocked out the guys ahead of me and behind me could see me too, at least where I'd been standing. Was there more than one? There had to be at least two, real marksmen, and not shy about flaunting it. I was committed to staying alive, and that meant presenting no easy target. I pressed myself into the ground, hardly breathing, my heart pounding.

The soldier ahead remained frozen in place, still face down, awkwardly covering his weapon, his arms at weird angles beneath him. His fatigues were soaked in blood.

I inched my legs apart at an angle to Charlie's line of fire, my chin lightly touching the stubby undergrowth, then slipped my weapon into a firing position, fighting off terror. Finally I nestled my face into the dirt and lay there, blocking out everything. The shame would come later.

...

Later I was aware of LTC Benedict behind me, standing tall and straight, his steel pot again tucked under an arm, sunbeams streaming between the trees behind him, gleaming off his bald head. *Damn, Colonel, get down!* But I could not utter a sound. Was he out of his mind?

He was smiling, pure joy in his eyes. He had to be crazy. Did he think he was bullet-proof?

"You okay, Doc?" he said. "You hit?"

I struggled to my feet. I tried to answer him, but words would not come. "I'm fine, sir," I mumbled finally. "I'm just . . . It happened so fast . . ." I couldn't finish. What was I trying to say, anyway?

"You'll be okay, Doc," he said, slapping me on the back. "You'll be fine."

Maybe, I thought. I doubted it. I was no longer afraid, only ashamed of my fear, the paralyzing terror I had felt. It was behind me now, for a while.

It was the best and worst day of my life, the best because I was still alive, the worst as the realization sunk in that I was not who I had hoped I was.

...

A helicopter arrived, collecting our two dead. Benedict informed me we had killed two VC. Two? I'd missed it. I had been focused on the VC ahead of me. Had they been holed up somewhere and decided to take as many of us as possible before they were discovered? Or did their comrades withdraw as we approached, leaving two to face certain death? Charlie was brave and cunning, but he did not fight when the odds were against him. When I finally formulated a question, Benedict was gone.

•••

After chow I sat outside my tent, trying to make sense of my thoughts, replaying what had happened out there. I knew sleep wouldn't come for a while.

A young soldier appeared before me, the last rays of sunlight behind him. I could make out a single bar on his collar, but his face and name-tape were in shadow.

"I'm Lieutenant Peeler, Doc. I was behind you back there," he said calmly. "Second platoon." When I didn't reply, he continued, "You did good." Then he stood there, motionless.

What was he talking about? I got up, and faced him, trying to decide whether he expected me to shake his hand.

"I saw a new medic get himself killed once," the soldier said, "thinking about being a hero, trying to help a dead man."

"He must have been very brave," I said finally, forcing a grin.

"He was a fool. Your duty is to stay alive. We need you. We'll do the damn fighting."

"Thanks, Lieutenant," I said when it was clear he had nothing else to say.

He left, and I don't think I ever saw him again. In twenty minutes I was sound asleep.

...

The next day, at mid-morning, we came onto a tiny community of friendly Vietnamese in a wooded area. The surroundings were beautiful—dense jungle on one side but solid underfoot. Mangoes hung all around. I needed no engraved invitation. I suppose it could have tasted better if it wasn't so warm, but I doubted it.

There seemed to be several families, with kids of all ages. We stopped to speak to them. Through our interpreter, we exchanged greetings and began to quiz them about VC they might have seen or known about. They gave no useful information, but they pointed to an old man who hobbled behind them. His foot was grossly deformed.

He was short and hump-backed, but he possessed a beautiful toothless smile. He leaned on the club of a stick he had fashioned from a limb. His foot was wrapped in perfectly hideous, rotting rags. They were damp, almost black, and wreaked a wretched smell.

Gently I unwrapped the nasty dressing and began to examine the old man's foot. It was massively swollen, and covered by dark, weeping skin that extended to within inches of his knee. Swollen toes projected from a misshapen ankle. I'd never seen anything like it. It was thick and oddly firm, but I could feel nothing clearly bone-like anywhere.

There was little I could do. It wasn't just that we were in the middle of nowhere; I doubted this man's ankle would be salvageable anywhere in the world. He needed an amputation in the worst sort of way. Septicemia and death lay ahead, maybe within a week. His nutritional state promised he would not linger.

Carefully I cleansed his wound with several quarts of water from an earthenware vessel and cut away bits of dead and infected tissue, then slathered on a layer of antibiotic ointment. In my medical bag I was surprised to find a medium-sized tube of something that looked like Unna paste, had the same texture and scent anyway . I applied a thick layer of it, as I'd been trained to treat ulcerated wounds of venous insufficiency. The old man's neighbors watched in silence. Then I wrapped his extremity in layers of cotton pads and gauze, fashioning it into more or less a respectable dressing, topped off with an elastic Ace athletic wrap. Under ideal conditions it might keep the wound clean and almost dry for two or three days.

"You must keep this dressing clean and dry," I explained to him, then demonstrated how he should keep his foot elevated as much as possible. His family and neighbors listened in wonder, their looks suggesting I had performed a miracle. My treatment would be no more effective than what an ancient shaman might have rendered.

"This will take many months to heal," I went on. "You need to have another doctor do essentially what I've done today, in a few days, less than a week for certain. Without additional medical care this wound will not heal. It will get much worse."

They listened with dazed looks, as though everything I'd said was perfectly reasonable, like another American medicine-man would show up in a few days and others in succession. Many of the old man's family and friends stepped up to shake my hand, some holding it reverently, embarrassing me further for what little I had done. It was all I *could* do, but it would amount to nothing. I felt like a fraud.

•••

On March 18, at a little past 1100 hours, we took some mortar fire toward the rear but well wide of the column. No one suffered so much as a scratch. We promptly deployed into a defensive posture, shifting me to a platoon separate from the command group.

VC were spotted just over a hill some 150 meters away. The absence of trees and jungle gave us an excellent view for five hundred meters, all the way to the bend of a narrow stream. A sandy-haired lieutenant, his radio squawking for all to hear, pointed at the hilltop. "They're on the reverse slope, probably spread-eagled," he said. "No cover. They got no place to run."

He unfolded his map and spread it across my back, and studied it in silence. In a few minutes I felt him jot down a series numbers against my back. Then he was back on his radio, calling in the co-ordinates he'd calculated. I took a deep breath, imagining what was about to happen. The lieutenant seemed quite sure of himself, but I hoped he'd checked his calculations a couple of times. We weren't that far from the target. When he finished, his jaw muscles flickered briefly as he refolded his map. "Ordnance on the way." he said.

Four or five minutes later, a jet—an F4 Phantom, I was informed later—gleamed in the sunlight at a high rate of speed. He was high in the sky, moving from right to left. Minutes ago another twenty-three-year-old kid had converted the blond lieutenant's eight-digit coordinates to a point on his Air Force map, and now he was comparing the landmarks on his map with what he could see from four- or five-thousand feet. In less than a minute he was gone.

Some time later—it seemed a long time—the F4 reappeared, this time screaming from the treetops behind us. The noise was deafening.

The pilot bore in on the target and released his ordinance, ascending directly over the hill. His bombs fell with a forward momentum and did not tumble. There were at least three or four, maybe six. Flames flickered with the explosions, spreading like lava across the hilltop, the earth quivering at our feet. Brief flames gave way to black smoke that remained dense for long seconds, finally thinning and ascending.

Cheers went up all around but I only stared in awe. Small flames flickered at the top of the hill.

The battle was brief and done. I thought about it a long time. With that kind of skill and fire power winning this war would be only a matter of time. But hindsight would prove the matter to be more complicated.

2.
COMING OF AGE

As the Twig Is Bent...

The decision to commit America to war has tormented presidents from Lincoln forward. George W. Bush was scorned for invading Iraq following 9/11, and Barack Obama characterized as feckless for redirecting that effort to rid Afghanistan of insurgents. It was a state not only unsettled for centuries but whose economy, dependent on the sale of heroin, offered little hope of sustaining victory on its own. In 1940, with much of the world already engaged against the scourge of Hitler and England hanging on by courageous fingernails in its greatest hour of need, Franklin D. Roosevelt chose not to go to war against the Germans for the flimsiest of reasons. Hardly more than a decade later, John F. Kennedy focused Americans on assisting the South Vietnamese to resist communism, an effort destined to unravel into home front tragedies, including bloody riots, wanton destruction of property, and the denigration of confused citizen soldiers.

But the following is not about politics, or casting blame. It is not even about a view of a bloody forest in Southeast Asia. It is a record of a small segment of an unpopular war experienced by a single doctor with his own eyes and ears. It is aimed at his grandchildren, in honor of the brave Americans with whom he served, in the hope that a Vietnam War, with all its distortions on front pages, television, and in theaters, will never be repeated.

The story begins in childhood.

···

"We interrupt this program to inform you that the president of the United States is dead," the man said.

I was six years old, huddled against a dusty old AM-radio, listening to Tom Mix, the "singing cowboy." He pitched breakfast cereal on the Mutual Broadcasting System. It was a few minutes before 6:00 p.m., Eastern Standard Time, April 12, 1945.

When I broke the news to my parents minutes later as I sat down to supper, I had the feeling I'd said something of significance for the first time in my life. I was on the road to being somebody.

The following night, in the wee hours of the morning, my sister and I were bundled into our 1936 Packard to meet the train carrying FDR home for the last time. My father was parking the car when we heard the first mournful strains of a train whistle in the distance. It clutched our hearts and put lumps in our throats.

In silence a crowd of a hundred or more moved along the old cobblestone side street at the rear of the station. The shadow of the ice-plant loomed behind us, a local landmark of the day, which, like the cobblestone paving, would become a casualty as the postwar economy heated up. With refrigerators in production, blocks of ice were no longer delivered house to house in wagons hitched to horses.

The towering locomotive, draped in red, white, and blue, lumbered toward us, coughing out white streams of steam which spread out on the platform at our feet, finally engulfing us in a magical cloud. The train, hardly more than four cars, reeked of coal and grease as double-jointed pistons powered it slowly past us.

My mom, choking back tears, whispered, "Two-fifteen." Announcing the time was her way of telling us we were never to forget the moment.

FDR's train rolled through our proud southern town without stopping. Salisbury's train station was among many between Warm Springs, Georgia and Hyde Park, New York. We stood in reverence, heads bowed, fighting back tears. I had heard President Roosevelt on the radio Saturday mornings. We had hung on his every word—not that we understood their implications—but because it was a voice we could trust.

Each car was draped in stars and stripes and every window shrouded in black. A conductor stood in a window of the last car. We saw no one else. My mom pointed out the hand-rail surrounding the platform at the rear of the car. It was draped in bunting, like it had been hardly a year ago when FDR campaigned around the country for the last time. I imagined him making speeches sprinkled with jokes from that very platform, focusing on it until the train gathered speed and rumbled out of sight, saluting the shivering crowd with a last long wail of its whistle. To a person we stood like stones until the sound faded to silence.

Like everybody else I felt close to Roosevelt. Few Americans did not respect him. It was an era of revering heroic leaders and the process through which they came to power and governed, inspiring us to be as American as we could be.

...

From D-Day on I had nestled with my grandfather beside his radio taking in the war news. On a tattered map he traced the route our boys took across France, explaining to me in detail what faced Ike, Patton, and Bradley, later General MacArthur. He encouraged me to collect old newspapers and tin cans in my little red wagon and deliver them to the pickup point at Lincolnton Road and Ellis Street on Friday mornings. He taught me to remove the paper wrappings from the cans, then flatten them. Rounding up metal for bombs and bullets became the neighborhood kids' part in the war effort. We also drew pictures of warplanes and bombs exploding, killing Japs and Germans.

Mom and my grandmother gave up nylons for years. Ration books were distributed, one per family, which governed almost everything we could buy. Through a point system the list of rationed items seemed endless: gasoline, fuel oil and Kerosene, automobiles, tires, farm equipment, bicycles, shoes, rubber footwear, even chicken-wire fencing and food, including sugar, canned goods, meats, fats, and cheese. We were all in the war together—everyone with a part—and none of us was certain we could lick the Germans and the Japs. We hung onto the fact that Roosevelt had told us not to be afraid.

•••

VE-Day followed FDR's death, and with Hitler dead and the Germans in hiding, our boys in Europe would be coming back to Salisbury, China Grove, Landis, Rockwell, and Mooresville and all around our state and nation. Within three months we would be caught up in the delirium over atomic bombs destroying Hiroshima and Nagasaki. Our boys in the Pacific would not have to fight and die in Japanese mud. Very soon all the American boys would be coming home.

•••

At age twelve, I was upset when President Truman fired MacArthur for wanting to take it to the Chinese, who were behind the Korean War. What did Truman know about fighting a war, anyway? I was less dependent on my grandfather by then, and had no grasp on how things really worked. But I still identified with our soldiers, and assumed everybody else did too. But what did I know, about anything?

For two years I planned to attend the U. S. Military Academy for college. I sent off to West Point for its catalogue so I could prepare for its entrance requirements. I even began pulling for the Army football team.

By high school, though, things began to change. I had been bitten by the football bug myself, and girls began to change the way I thought about almost everything.

In college I became a serious student, with medical school my goal. Signing up for ROTC seemed the right thing to do, if only for the few bucks it paid for drilling on Tuesday afternoons. Sergeant Jerry Crump was Davidson College's ROTC supply sergeant. I knew exactly who he was, even if my classmates didn't. His picture had been in the newspaper years ago. Crump, from Forest City, was a quiet, standoffish kind of guy, thought of as retarded by a few of my loud-mouth buddies. When North Koreans lobbed an armed hand-grenade into his bunker, Sergeant Crump covered it like it was a fumble on third down, absorbing the blast with his belly, saving the lives of four buddies. Somehow, he managed to stay alive that day, then survive the operations it took to put him back together. For his valor he was awarded the Congressional Medal of Honor. I knew I would never have that kind of courage, but in my heart I honored him for his.

Even my ROTC classmates didn't seem to remember World War II and Korea like I did. They showed little concern about the growing threat of communism. I even heard one parrot a popular hippy slogan of the day, saying he would rather be red than dead. That bothered me. How could any American actually say that? It dishonored all those who suffered and died at Valley Forge, at Gettysburg and Antietam, those guys who stormed the beaches at Normandy. I was forced to think about what those words actually meant. Sergeant Crump's heroism projected a certain romance in the telling, but laying one's own life on the line was much different. Could I really see myself dying for a cause? Deep down inside I didn't like the answer that kept coming up.

...

Medical school left little time for anything beyond study, examinations, laboratories, and learning to manage sick people. Everything else was a distant second. I owed two years' active duty for my ROTC training, but the government awarded me deferments all the way through med school, also as an intern and as a junior resident. Then the Army decided my time had come. I wasn't sure what doctors did in the Army, but I knew nobody expected me to fight, or expose myself to real danger. It wouldn't be a rational use of my ten years of education beyond high school. For Sergeant Crump, the Army had been a good fit—high school graduate, national hero, soft job for life—but I had a chance to be someone special. Duty? Honor? Country? What did that mean? What had I been thinking?

When I was called to serve I was twenty-eight years old, with a wife, two kids, and a promising career ahead of me. I would do my part, but I had no intention of being much of a soldier.

3.
FORT SAM HOUSTON, TEXAS

A Change of Plans

With orders for Fort Gordon, Georgia as my two-year duty station, I viewed the trip to the Medical Field Service School (MFSS) at Fort Sam Houston as a month of vacation. My family had never had one before. In mid-July my wife, a four-year-old, a five-year-old, and I struck out for New Orleans for a weekend, and then spent two nights in Houston before continuing on to San Antonio.

In fact, I anticipated my entire active-duty experience in the Army to be a vacation. With a monthly salary of over $700, four times what I'd made as an intern, I looked forward to a family meal out from time to time without feeling extravagant. We had lived on my wife's schoolteacher salary for years. Moving into a hotel in San Antonio, my entire family felt like we had won the lottery.

I had no idea what to expect at Fort Gordon, but it had to be better than life as an intern and first year surgical resident. Working twelve-hour days, spending every other night and every other weekend at the hospital had been a grueling experience. Seeing "sick call" daily was a boring prospect, but I was willing to give it a try. Advancing myself as a surgeon at

Fort Gordon was not in the forecast. At least I'd get to know my family again, maybe even catch a round of golf from time to time.

As one of a thousand new medical officers at Fort Sam, I had few expectations. Guys with no ROTC backgrounds would be learning how to wear the uniform, salute, and act like soldiers. One guy saw the MFSS as the Army's attempt to force feed doctors three days' information over a month's time.

Initially I was determined to give it my best effort. I'd never been paid to go to school before. Morning and afternoon classes, held in a huge auditorium, covered such subjects as the Army's Table of Organization and Equipment (TO&E), what the Code of Conduct had to say about not surrendering and being prepared to give up one's life, Geneva Convention rules for living in captivity, and the countless provisions of the Uniform Code of Military Justice. Pretty dry stuff, none of it pertaining to anything that might happen at Fort Gordon. After embarrassing myself by dozing off several times in the afternoons, I ended up playing golf most days after lunch.

...

I became increasingly aware of the countless clear-eyed, ruggedly handsome young men around me, mostly enlisted men and non-commissioned officers. They were trim and athletic, in pressed jungle fatigues and polished boots and brass. Their chests were decorated with rows of ribbons from their exploits in Vietnam. One gave a lecture after breakfast one day about the training and duties of combat medics, another on public health issues in Southeast Asia. They were knowledgeable, committed, enthusiastic. They were fine young men. Impressive. Enviable, in a way.

I couldn't get them out of my head. Were they born that way? They had to be the best of the best. Did Vietnam do that? Their pride was palpable.

Simultaneously I began to worry that Fort Gordon might dim the surgical skills I had earned. I'd been away from the tough hospital grind hardly a month, and already I sensed boredom. Could I really handle the boredom of sick call day after day? For six years I'd been in teaching hospitals, surrounded by young, forward-thinking guys, dreaming of the new techniques and operations we were on track to master. I was committed to a surgical career. What effect would two years at Fort Gordon have on that? I had thrived on challenges all my life. A professor at Duke had told me once: "Once you stop stepping up, you'll be stepping down. There is no in between. You'll lose sight of your goals in a heartbeat."

Wartime surgery had been the heart's blood of surgical progress for centuries, obviously from the Civil War through two World Wars. Vascular surgery came into being in Korea, leading to heart surgery a few years later. Surgeons in Vietnam would be on the ground floor of that kind of change.

Did I really want to take my first step down? Would be wasting two years at Fort Gordon?

...

When I explained to the Sergeant E-5 in the personnel office the next afternoon that I wanted my duty-assignment switched from Fort Gordon to Vietnam, he looked at me for a long time in silence. He was a big guy, with three rows of ribbons on the left side of his chest. He left the room for a few minutes, returning with an official form which he dated and initialed in my presence. He told me to appear at 0930 the following morning at the address he had scrawled on a separate piece of paper. "You'll need two signatures," he said.

The next morning, after a forty-five-minute wait, I came to my feet as a blond crew-cut officer, a psychiatrist, advanced across the waiting room toward me, waving off my salute. "Not necessary here," he said brusquely, then took the form I received in the personnel office. He was a major, in his forties, soft looking, with more chins than a Chinese phone book. His shoes and brass belt-buckle gleamed.

He glanced at the form, then at me. "So why is it you're so hell bent to get to Southeast Asia?"

My psychiatric assessment was underway. The Army was having enough trouble in Vietnam. They didn't need anymore kooks. Quickly I summarized my medical training and career goals, and my desire for wartime surgical experience.

"And you know what you're doing? You understand that Vietnam's not a laboratory for cowboy-types? Nam is nothing like Hollywood."

"Yes, sir."

The examination was over. The shrink with the flabby chins left the room to speak to another officer. Soon his colleague glared at me from a doorway. He was short, dark haired, and intense. He wore the silver oak leaf of lieutenant colonel on his collar.

One minute later I had my two signatures.

•••

Two nights later I presented my orders to Vietnam to my family at the supper table. My wife broke into tears, followed quickly by my daughter and son. Seeing their mother cry had an effect on all of us. With some trepidation I launched into an explanation I thought sounded reasonable.

I stammered that since President Johnson had called up more troops, raising the fighting strength in Vietnam to over a half-million men—we'd heard it on TV—that additional doctors were required to support the new troop level. Orders had been changed for a number of us. In my case the ROTC training probably had had something to do with it. When the tears increased, I explained I was going as a *doctor*, not to fight anybody. I would be perfectly safe, and they would be fine with my wife's folks in Spartanburg.

I ended up promising to see if there was a way out of it, but none of us had much supper that night.

•••

The following Saturday I was among a group with orders to Vietnam to appear for a dental examination. The dental officer spent ten minutes peering into my mouth and calling out numbers to an assistant. He was charting every filling, crown, and irregularity in my mouth. Not once did he ask me if I had a toothache. It finally dawned on me that his chart could be used to identify me if something happened. It was a chilling moment. I couldn't resist commenting about it.

"Oh, don't worry, Captain," he said with a smile. "This is just routine, the Army dotting i's and crossing t's. No medical officer has ever been killed in Vietnam."

"Really?"

"It's a fact."

I felt better.

...

At the midway point in the MFSS course, we were assembled to take the first of three written tests, all with of multiple-choice answers. It was on map reading. How to relate geographical landmarks and compass-determined azimuths to a relief map was a critical skill for infantry officers. Why it was important for a doctor I didn't quite understand, but by that point I had bought into whatever was asked of me. I had covered the same material as an ROTC student. In a way it was a fun exercise. After the test we were informed we would be putting our map reading skills to work at an upcoming four-day bivouac at Camp Bullis.

In the course of discussing some of the answers to test questions afterward, a loud-mouthed classmate seemed to take pleasure in belittling our interest in the test. From his speech I pegged him to be from New Jersey or New York.

"You guys are chumps," he said. "By flunking every test, I'll force the Army to cancel my orders to Vietnam.

Jaws dropped in silence.

"Don't be too sure of yourself, Einstein," someone said finally. "You can bet somebody's already tried that. Even the Army's not that dumb."

"But how can they send me to war if written evidence of my incompetence exists?" His deep-throated laugh was the only sound in the room. "Think about the legal repercussions."

I had no opinion about whether or not his plan would work, but I had to admire the guy's pluck. It would be cool if he made it. If I'd met him earlier, I could have eliminated his risk. He would have jumped at a chance to go to Fort Gordon. The government would have gone along. To Washington we were just warm bodies with medical degrees.

•••

They split us into groups of several hundred each to be rotated through a series of field exercises at Camp Bullis. Bullis was a 27,000-acre training reservation in nearby Bexar County. It resembled Fort Bragg in eastern North Carolina in that its terrain was sandy and wooded and hot as blazes in summertime. My turn came ten days before the end of the MFSS.

We were further divided into groups of four for a nighttime map navigation exercise. A few minutes before midnight they transported us in trucks to various locations around the reservation. Each group was issued a flashlight, a map, a compass, and a prescribed route to a destination point designated by eight-digit coordinates, presumably each at different sites along the same road. We were to be at the rendezvous point between 0300 and 0315 to be picked up. Anybody late had the option of working his way back to the barracks however he could—this was not recommended—or simply by stationing himself on any paved road after 0900 the following day.

The first order of business was to determine our location on the map by shooting azimuths to two identifiable landmarks against the horizon—we chose a telephone tower a mile or two away, and tallest of three hills nearby. After constructing azimuths through each landmark on the map, the point of intersection confirmed our location.

I was paired with two guys from New York and one from Oakland. The California guy admitted nothing, but neither New Yorker had ever been in the woods before. They reacted to every sound—from chirping crickets to a buddy's footfall. They had countless questions: about snakes, why didn't we have a weapon or a first aid kit, what would happen if we got lost, and did wolves inhabit this part of Texas? The deeper we got into the woods, the closer they crowded around me. I was no woodsman, but they recognized I had least had been in the woods before and was not uncomfortable there. Of course our roles would have been reversed had we been in an unfamiliar city, but tonight we were deep in the heart of Texas, with not even a town for miles and miles.

At 0230 we reached our rendezvous point. It was in the bend of a dirt road, easily confirmed on the map. Of course there were skeptics among us about whether or not we were in the correct place, but the argument ceased when I lay down to take a nap. I offered to surrender the map and the compass to anyone who wished to go someplace else. I didn't share with them my hunch that the truck driver would be at least twenty minutes late. I'd let them sweat a little.

•••

The highlight of our Camp Bullis experience came two nights later when we were to crawl forty yards or so beneath barbed wire and live machinegun fire. I was skeptical about the rounds being live, but I wasn't about to raise my head to find out. It rained cats and dogs that night so we got cold, wet, and very muddy. I showered twice when we got back to the barracks, once to rinse the mud from my boots and fatigues, then again to wash the sweat off my body.

•••

We graduated on a Saturday morning on the parade ground. Only Army graduations require standing throughout. It was overcast, and unseasonably cool. As a group I'm sure we looked a little better than we did at our first formation, four weeks earlier. I doubt anybody wore his garrison cap at a jaunty angle, and almost certainly there was nobody in red or green socks. Two guys had been called out of ranks during week-one for that transgression. If we didn't appear exactly military, at the least we were closer than before.

The commandant congratulated us on what he called an exemplary performance. He went on to make the dubious statement that he was certain we would all be outstanding medical officers, credits to ourselves, the units to which we would be assigned, and the United States Army. Just when he seemed to run out of nonsense to say, he surprised us.

"The Army is far more that a group of individuals," he continued. "It is first, last, and always a team. It is the greatest team on the face of the earth. But I would be remiss if I didn't recognize an outstanding performance by one of you a few weeks ago." He paused, and dug into his pocket for a name.

I couldn't make out the doctor's name. It sounded vaguely familiar, but I couldn't quite place it. But suddenly it was clear the commandant was referring to the character we had called "Einstein."

"His performance was sometimes uneven," he droned on, "particularly on the written tests you were asked to take. In fact, his test scores were so poor as to be of some concern since he was scheduled to be among you men moving out to Southeast Asia in a few weeks."

A few heads turned, searching for our cocky colleague from New Jersey.

"But I am proud to announce that this young medical officer redeemed himself as no one has in the history of the MFSS. He broke all previous records for performance at Camp Bullis. His ability to perform in the field will hold him in good stead in Vietnam. I am certain you take as much pride in him as the U.S. Army Medical Corp does."

Hey! Nobody was graded at Camp Bullis!

We broke into laughter. Even the commandant grinned as he dismissed us.

4.
LAI KHE

Forward Base Camp

September 19 we loaded onto an orange-and-white Braniff 707 and began following the sun across the Pacific. Our trip was interrupted by two refueling stops—in Honolulu and Manila—and eased along by over three hundred pages of James Michener's The Source, which had just come out in paperback. From time to time I gazed out my port side window at filmy sheets of clouds, then at the vague green of the ocean six miles below, trying to imagine what lay ahead. Landing a hospital assignment immediately was probably too much to expect so I was trying not to get my hopes up too high. In the end, though, I knew I would find a way.

As we passed the Island of Midway, a tiny dot from 30,000 feet, I realized my desire to go to Vietnam was not merely to boost my surgical career but to give me a shot at what might become the adventure of my lifetime. I had no illusions about being a warrior, but I understood that Vietnam was the only war I would ever see. How could I miss experiencing it?

Situations lay ahead I couldn't have imagined in a thousand years. First, within a few months I would participate in events so strange that I would never be able to discuss them without straining my personal credibility. Second, before I saw home again my life would be aimed in an entirely different direction, one I'd not considered before. I would also discover I'd been lied to at Fort Sam.

...

After what seemed like days we soared into darkness from the Philippines, the cabin suddenly silent as a tomb. Gone was the undercurrent of chatter and horseplay present for so long. Now no one bothered to read, or feel the slightest awareness of his seatmate. Only the monotonous roar of the engines was audible, maybe even a little magnified now, rushing us into who knew what. It was likely we all struggled with some variation of the same thought: with Vietnam a hundred or so minutes away, now straight ahead, who among us would thrive there and who would not?

...

Finally we were asked, in the crisp tone of every commercial airline pilot, to fasten our seatbelts, that we were about to begin our descent into the Tan Son Nhut Air Base (pronounced Tahn Sa Noot). It was a descent that felt more like a dive. To avoid random ground-fire from unsecured territories surrounding Saigon, our decent would not begin until we were virtually over the city. The steep descent brought all on board forward in our seats, gripping armrests, searching out the countless lights below. We were rolling toward the terminal in hardly minutes.

We passed a couple of machinegun bunkers as our bus entered what we were told was the 90th Replacement Station in Long Binh (pronounced Long Ben), said to be a few miles north of Tan Son Nhut. It would be home for three days and nights. We slept in wooden structures the walls of which were reinforced with sandbags stacked to a height of five or six feet. The upper half of the walls were open, only wire mesh separating us from the sights and sounds in the darkness. Concrete walkways kept us from having to wade through gullies of water and damp grass to the mess hall the next morning. We had had a considerable rain during the night. The day would be like the next four hundred: hot and steamy. My lightweight fatigues were soaked in sweat by mid-morning. Then, just when I thought I needed to change my clothes, it wasn't so bad anymore. My fatigues were no longer damp. In a few days I would learn to forget about the heat.

At night we were assured that the continual sounds of artillery were "outgoing" rounds, that "incoming" made an entirely different sound. Did they really have targets out there, or were they just firing at shadows? Or was it possible they were shooting simply to let Charlie know someone was thinking about him, someone with plenty of ammunition? I couldn't imagine what a night's artillery ordnance might cost. Were big guns pounding away simultaneously all over Vietnam? As far as I knew those guns were active all night long, sending the national debt to record levels. At last I drifted into continuous sleep.

An officer at the 44th Medical Brigade informed me I would likely be assigned to the 1st Infantry Division since it had eight slots for guys of my MOS (military occupation specialty) and only two were filled. With an MOS of 3150 I at least *qualified* for a hospital assignment, compared with the 3100s, who had only a single year of postgraduate training. A 3100 was basically a general medical officer (GMO), many of whom were destined to become battalion surgeons who slogged through jungles with the infantry. The codes and designations were all Greek to me. I couldn't imagine what a 3150 did in the infantry. The officer, though, was confident my chances were good of getting out of the infantry altogether after six months, and being reassigned to an evacuation hospital. I couldn't decide whether that was good news or bad news.

The next day we were taken to MACV headquarters (Military Assistance Command, Vietnam, pronounced Mac-VEE), then the following day to USARV headquarters (United States Army, Republic of Vietnam, pronounced USE-are-vee) in Long Binh. The buildings at USARV were multi-storied, seemingly new, of steel and concrete construction. Along with the vast number of troops, aircraft, land vehicles, and other assorted equipment, it seemed that Washington anticipated an American presence in Vietnam for a very long time.

Compared to most I was among the least knowledgeable about the politics of Vietnam. In six years as medical student, surgical intern, or junior-resident I'd had virtually zero time for newspapers and *Time* magazine. I didn't even keep up with the baseball scores. For two years I couldn't remember seeing a TV news program. Having barely twelve hours away from the hospital every two days had me falling asleep at the dinner table on my nights off. The vague arguments I'd overheard about Vietnam involved issues that didn't concern me. Now though, forty-eight hours after arrival, with time on my hands as the Army was cooking up an assignment for me, filling in the gaps of my knowledge didn't seem possible. Newspapers served up day-to-day facts and figures but very little background, and the only books available were paperback novels. Nobody had the slightest interest in discussing why any of us were in Vietnam. That, to me, was maddening. Finally I gave up thinking about it, and got back to Michener and *The Source.*

Looking back on it now, I don't recall any political discussion during my thirteen months in Vietnam. Not one. The men I was with weren't into "why," or "what if." It was the "how" that concerned us.

...

On September 24 I was taken to Di An (pronounced Zee Ahn), which was described to me as the "rear base camp" of the 1st Infantry Division. They had a saying: "If you gotta be one, be a Big Red One." I would wear an arm patch with a red numeral-one woven into a forest green background.

I met Lieutenant Colonel (LTC) Patrick Tisdale late in the afternoon. He was commander of the 1st Medical Battalion, the operational command of all medical units in the First Division, essentially four companies of eighty-plus men. He would be my boss for at least a few months, until I could wangle a transfer to a facility that might advance my surgical career. He was a man of swarthy good looks, medium height and build, about thirty-five years old as well as I could tell. After West Point he had gone to medical school, then specialized in pediatrics.

That got my attention. I worried about what kind of West Point graduate might choose pediatrics. Pediatricians' patients were children, but they had to reason with moms, whose expectations were sometimes impossible to understand. Even stranger would be a pediatrician who could stomach a military career. Pediatricians had to be sensitive, understanding people. Could an effective Army officer see himself with such characteristics? I wondered why a West Point graduate would bother going to medical school. I can't say any of my questions ever found answers.

Tisdale shook my hand warmly and told me he looked forward to having me in the 1st Infantry Division. He asked me perfunctory questions about my background, my family, and so forth, then glanced at what I recognized as my personnel file. It was a thin folder on the back of his desk.

Sensing an opportune moment, I launched into why I wanted to be assigned to a surgical hospital. When Tisdale said nothing, I droned on about my surgical training and my long term goals. I stopped short of mentioning what I had heard at the 44th Medical Brigade, still hoping he might truly make my day. I understood it was a long shot.

Finally he pushed himself back from his desk and in a cheerless voice said, "At this point let's don't get too far ahead of ourselves."

•••

The next morning Tisdale informed me I was being assigned to First Med's company B, which was located in

Division's "forward headquarters" at Lai Khe, out toward Cambodia. He said that's where the action was going to be, that a major operation was in the works.

For an instant I was intrigued. Maybe surgery could take a back seat to the boondocks for a while. I could almost envision myself running back and forth in the jungle. Excitement washed over me. I could almost feel my pulse rate pick up.

But the feeling did not last.

Tisdale explained that B company's mission was to operate a Korean War type "clearing station," a small forward "hospital" organized around an emergency room (ER) and a small ward for in-patients. He described what he called B-Med as a glorified first aid station where casualties were to be stabilized before being flown to the rear, to the 93rd Evac at Binh Hoa (pronounced Ben Wah) or the 24th Evac at Long Binh, hardly two miles apart. He assured me there would be ample opportunity to treat minor wounds, perform tracheotomies, and insert chest tubes for collapsed lungs, operations like that. It was not even close to my idea of real surgery, but I managed to keep my mouth shut, expecting I would get a chance to schmooze with surgeons at the 93rd or the 24th at some point, maybe wangle a surgical assignment that way.

He gave me a knowing look, then a patronizing smile.

"In time I promise to do whatever I can to see that you get the opportunity you're looking for," he said, "but right now there is a real need in the First Division."

I was not encouraged, but I did appreciate his attempt at being decent.

"Look, this is the Army. We're in a war," he snapped, his eyes now on fire. I blushed, suddenly afraid he saw me as a spoiled, states-side surgical resident. I looked at the floor, then out the window, determined to buck up.

"You have special skills," he continued. "At B-Med you will have important responsibilities, with good men under your command, including doctors and dentists. It's just the way things are."

Finally I got it. It *was* my damned ROTC training. It *was* part of my file. How had I thought that was not going to be a factor in whatever assignment I received?

...

The following day, a Saturday, Tisdale invited me and two other medical officers awaiting assignment to accompany him on a day trip to Saigon. There was an orphanage he wanted us to see. When was the invitation of a CO not a command? But I had nothing better to do. I was growing weary of Michener, and there was no news to write home about. Possibly Tisdale was only trying to brighten my day, help me to adjust to my disappointment.

Apparently the An Loc (meaning "happy place") Orphanage was one of Tisdale's missionary projects. It was located at 116 Nguyen dink Chieu, in a leafy semi-residential district where the mid-morning traffic was light. En route we observed Division policy to the letter, wearing steel pot helmets, flack jackets, and side-arms, .45 automatics. As we entered the orphanage, we left our weapons and gear to be guarded by our driver. Surely even the VC observed at least *some* limits, I told myself.

An Loc was operated by a saint. Vu Thi Ngai, a Vietnamese blue blood, was a plump, smiling woman of boundless energy. She could have been any age from late 30s to 60. Her English was flawless, and she communicated with her assistants in a gentle, lilting French. Tisdale had informed us that she had once worked in North Vietnam with Dr. Thomas Dooley, the renowned champion of the sick and homeless of Southeast Asia. I began to get the impression that my boss was at the very least an opportunist, possibly even a full blooded politician. What exactly was his angle?

Mme. Ngai was said to have built An Loc in the late 1950s with the equivalent of $600,000 of her own fortune. Her financial resources now virtually nothing, she kept the place solvent through her influence with friends and various creditors. The Tom Dooley Foundation had dried up, it's annual support no longer possible. An Loc's current debt was $70,000 and rising. Mme. Ngai still managed to raise much of the monthly $3,500 necessary to feed and clothe 360 children from Saigon merchants, even the U. S. government. So that was Tisdale's connection. We had brought bags of antibiotics, infant formula, and other medical supplies and assorted goodies. Through her association with President Thieu (elected only days earlier) and General Ky (Thieu's running mate), Mme. Ngai had conducted a TV campaign for An Loc during the election. One donor had pledged $50,000 but so far no cash had appeared.

Mme. Ngai had an affectionate word for each child, calling many by name. They returned her greetings and comments with their own brand of love and enthusiasm. One little tyke, about three, systematically ripped up the wrappings of the candy we had distributed, then, bursting with mischief, spread the paper remnants into every corner of the room. His actions drew a gentle ear twisting and a stern yet loving rebuke from Mme. Ngai.

We met two of her remaining assistants, both teenagers, both lavish in their affection for the children. Budget cuts had decimated the former staff. Later I would find that the wage of neither exceeded $1 per week.

Some of the kids were obviously mentally retarded, others with club feet and other orthopedic deformities. Many had the pot bellies and pale gums of the severely malnourished, castoffs from even poorer facilities. Each was cute and lovable in her own way. Like kids everywhere, they laughed, played, and cried with great exuberance. Every one of them craved candy and cookies, of which we were in good supply. For them, it was Christmas morning.

After seeing the three- and four-year-olds, we moved on to the newborn nursery. Three were obviously losing their battle with malnutrition and pneumonia, motionless in their bassinets except for the rapid rising and falling of their delicate chests. Not even the best food and antibiotics would save them. A lump gathered in my throat as I considered the unspeakable tragedies of their births. What horrible forces had separated them from their parents, what agony their mothers now faced if still alive? I found myself avoiding eye contact with the other visitors as my eyes brimmed with tears. Carefully I tried to swallow the lump away, desperately afraid of the embarrassment a choking sob would bring. Finally I exhaled, then dared a nervous breath.

Embarrassment? What was I thinking? Where was my humanity? Suddenly I longed to be alone, to surrender to the relief crying might bring. Speaking was unthinkable. What was there to say?

Tisdale had wisely moved to the far end of the room, where the infants were a little better off, able to clench their little fists and manage to cry weakly. He picked up one and clutched it to his throat, humming a little tune. "These kiddies have a chance," he informed us, "but antibiotics and food will not be enough. They never are. These kiddies must be held and loved, all day every day."

Eagerly I stepped forward with the others and gathered up the barest wisp of a child in my arms, then nestled it to my cheek, kissing it gently, breathing into its tiny ear, sensing its delicious scent. Whispering sweet nothings seemed to calm me. I understood exactly what Tisdale meant. Love rules everything. Without it there is nothing. Without human contact no child survives, with hunger and sickness upping the ante, particularly for the sickest and least nourished. The infant in my arms was desperate for her mother. At least the three- and four-year-olds had each other.

How was it possible for six workers to be nurse and mama for 360 kids, every one of them so terribly needy? But the impossible did not seem to deter Mme Ngai and her tiny team one bit. They seemed to draw sustenance from their work, caring for one child at a time, day in and day out. What a special calling.

Leaving that child, and the others, was difficult, indeed. I would never forget them. Clearly they gave me a better understanding of my CO, even myself.

•••

Tisdale announced he had a special treat for us at lunch. He took us to the Caravelle Hotel in a bustling downtown neighborhood to meet who he described as a special friend of the An Loc Orphanage. The Caravelle was the famous address and meeting place of news media covering the war. At the time it was a six or eight story structure, but forty-five years later it would be much larger, truly a luxury hotel. In 1967 it was said to have had bullet-proof windows, but I was more interested in its flush toilets and air-conditioning system.

Betty Moul, a beautiful young woman from Pittsburgh, was Tisdale's fiancée. Like Mme. Ngai, she had worked with Tom Dooley, and continued to maintain his clinics in Laos and Thailand after his untimely death six years earlier at thirty-four. She made her first trip to the An Loc Orphanage following Dooley's death, and fell in love with it immediately. As the communists would approach Saigon in April of 1975, Betty Moul Tisdale would be one of three leading the evacuation of 219 An Loc orphans to safety, which would later be the subject of a CBS television movie, starring Shirley Jones as Betty Tisdale.[1] After the fall of Saigon, the Tisdales

---

[1] *http://www.bettytisdale.com/dnn/Founder/tabid/62/Default.aspx*

welcomed Mme. Ngai and two of her assistants into their home in Columbus, Georgia, where Mme. Ngai would die three years later.

Tisdale beamed as Betty served us a lunch in her small suite on the sixth floor. When we left, she kissed each of us on the lips. It was a beautiful gesture, a fresh feminine taste of home. It would be months before we would see a woman with round eyes again. Betty Moul was special. Over four decades later I would not at all be surprised to find that the Tisdales had remained faithful to the An Loc Orphanage.

On the way back to Di An Tisdale explained that he was a widower, with a young family to raise. Wow! Did the Army really insist on sending him to Vietnam, with five boys at home, all below the age of twelve?

...

Lai Khe, a small plantation town, was a product of the vast rubber industry of French colonial times. Its airstrip had been cut through the center of a five hundred acre stand of rubber trees, adjacent to Route 13, a two-lane, heavily-rutted dirt road, the region's primary north-south thoroughfare. Saigon was thirty-two miles south, and the Cambodian border, forty miles north. Erosion during the rainy season required serious attention from the Army Corps of Engineers to keep it open. It was also a frequent target for terrorism and sabotage, necessitating heavily arming the day-time resupply convoys from Bien Hoa, near Saigon. They carried stores ranging from ammunition and gasoline to food and medical supplies.

Americans called Route 13 "Thunder Road," and for ample reason. The Viet Cong (VC) owned it at night.

The sprawling single story stucco and tile structure at the east end of the base camp, formerly administrative offices and research facility of the Michelin Rubber Company, had been commandeered by the 1st Infantry Division as its headquarters and one of its medical facilities. Division and 3rd Brigade staff occupied the center of the building and most of the right wing. The entire left wing was devoted to B-Med (operated by B company, 1st Medical Battalion). It consisted of large rooms with tile floors, some equipped with built-in counters and cabinets designed for rubber chemists. There was also ample room for storage. B-Med's dental unit was located in a small corner of the right wing.

On the opposite side of the base camp stood a luxurious two-storied stone-and-stucco château, also left by the French, which had been converted into a luxurious officers' club. It had a tall chimney and a peaked roof of tile. An elaborate bar lined the rear wall of each of two downstairs rooms. Majestic chandeliers hung from the ceilings. Mixed drinks sold for fifty cents, and beer for half that. But the good times were coming to an end. With the rainy season finally ending, offensive operations were gearing up on both sides. Within four months the First Division Officers Club would be razed to the ground.

By contrast, construction in the village inhabited by the locals consisted of discarded American beer cans flattened and set side-to-side and end-to-end and nailed to flimsy wooden studs. Such homes and businesses maintained strict architectural integrity in that each was built of like cans. For instance, a Budweiser hut stood next door to a Schlitz hut, and so on. Open produce and eatery establishments lined muddy streets with wide gutters into which shameless locals of both sexes urinated and defecated in broad daylight. From May to September, the "rainy season" or "southern monsoon," water stood in the gutters, an open invitation for teeming families of mosquitoes to breed dreaded malaria organisms, but for which there were few practical solutions. Standing water in the rainy season was impossible to eliminate. Fortunately, there is some evidence of natural immunity among the Vietnamese.

Sites for living quarters were staked out on either side of the damp but hard-packed, oval-shaped dirt road surrounding the heart of the base camp: the 3rd Brigade (the "Iron Brigade,") as it was called, commanded by Colonel Frank Blazey), including the 2nd of the 28th Infantry ("Black Lions," commanded by LTC Terry Allen), the 1st of the 16th Infantry (the "Rangers," commanded by LTC Cal Benedict), and the 2nd of the 2nd Infantry (mechanized).

A barber shop adjoined the post-exchange (PX), which was equipped much like a Wal-Mart. It was located at the southwest bend of the road. I jogged that road several times a week and can attest it was approximately one mile in length.

First Division commander, Major General (two stars) John Hay, lived in a narrow wooden building facing a concrete tennis court some three hundred meters west of B-Med. I wasn't aware if General Hay or his chief-of-staff (the full colonel sharing the building with him) considered the tennis court part of their personal compound, but I didn't hesitate to play a set or two at every opportunity. A regular opponent was a short, powerfully built chopper pilot, a former Olympic skier. Major Luce could really play, and pretty much had his way with me on a regular basis. Unfortunately the tennis court would be destroyed the same night the officers club was leveled.

The remainder of the B-Med complex was located immediately across "oval road" from the hospital. The small wooden headquarters building consisted of an orderly room (the primary administrative office) and a small office for me. Captain Green shared the orderly room with Sergeant Hernandez, B-Med's First Sergeant. Hernandez was a forty-year-old father of five children living in Arizona. My office was equipped with a steel desk, a telephone, a tactical map for which I had no need, and an electric fan, which was useless when I did need it. The B-Med generator was typically shut down at mid-afternoon.

The radio shack was two doors down, immediately west of the mess hall. It was a dugout fortified with concrete blocks and multiple layers of sand bags. It provided sufficient space for RTOs working in pairs, alternating round-the-clock. Destroying our radio shack would require special effort and special weapons.

The motor pool and the living quarters for enlisted men were located at the rear of the company area. Two wooden structures, similar to the enlisted men's quarters at the rear, each with a tin roof and a concrete floor, were side-by-side officers' hooches facing "oval road." Across oval road, and seventy yards away, were the Dust Off (medical evacuation) chopper pad and the B-Med "hospital." I shared a hooch with another doctor and up to four Dust Off chopper pilots. The

Dust Off guys came and went, but typically at least two spent several nights per week with us.

Dust Off pilots, who flew Bell UH-1 Huey helicopter ambulances, provided the primary lifeline to combatants in the Vietnam War. The brave Dust Off flight crews and reliable maintenance crews were consistent heroes to wounded American fighting men. Giving the wounded access to installations like B-Med and the several strategically placed evacuation hospitals preserved life and limb at a rate unparalleled in the history of warfare. They saved literally thousands of lives. The sound of those choppers ascending and descending to get the wounded to safety was a major morale factor for everyone. I would find that the helicopter-evacuation system would be the primary medical advance resulting from the Vietnam War.

Because of the risk of malaria, Army policy dictated that soldiers in base camps sleep inside mosquito netting, but most of us (medical officers, of all people) willingly took our chances with malaria, rather than having to struggle out of clinging mosquito netting to get to safety. Mortar and rocket attacks provided maximum terror for B-Med residents.

Immediately outside our hooch was a dug-out bunker for four or five, with room for two more in a pinch. It had walls of double rows of sand bags and layers of steel-supported sand bags overhead.

Medical officers took turns shaving each morning from a basin of cold water in front of an eight-inch mirror hanging from a tree just beyond the bunker. It was our only one! I never saw an electric shaver in Vietnam.

A latrine some two hundred feet to the rear consisted of a two-holer and a make-shift cold-water shower enclosed by waist-high wooden walls. Considering mid-day temperatures occasionally topping 100 degrees, I never heard a complaint about cold-water showers.

•••

In addition to stabilizing victims of major trauma with transfusions and occasional emergency surgical procedures before shipping them to the 93rd Evac at Bien Hoa or the 24th Evac at Long Binh, we managed lesser injuries ourselves—non life-threatening shrapnel wounds, for instance—generally admitting victims to our in-patient ward they if they appeared likely to be returned to duty within a few weeks. We had twenty-four beds in two rooms, supported by nursing personnel. Bed capacity could be expanded to thirty-six if necessary.

Normally B-Med beds were occupied by GIs with respiratory infections or flu-like illnesses which typically carried the potential of being a bizarre tropical disease. It was crucial that such patients be quarantined from healthy troops, however much it made our small facility a potential death trap. Somehow, though, cross-infections, if they occurred, turned out to be minimal and non-life-threatening.

Sick call was conducted each morning to care for any soldier not feeling well or clearly ill. Our top priority was always to maximize the fighting strength of the units we served. Conservative medical care was generally a plus in warfare, but we found that the First Division command appreciated medics and medical officers who did not hesitate to improvise in order to get the job done. B-Med was also charged with the responsibility of maintaining the public health in the base camp, including not only our own facilities but to do what we could in the village, where sometimes the problems were well beyond our capacity to control. Assuring potable water and sanitary kitchens in local eating establishments frequented by off duty personnel was something we could provide.

B-Med was equipped with rudimentary but efficient medical technology, including an x-ray machine, sterilization equipment, basic surgical instruments, and a backup generator for use in the event of a power failure. We also operated three two-and-one-half ton trucks (for resupply via convoys up and down Thunder Road), a half-dozen ambulances, at least three jeeps, and motor pool mechanics to service them.

B-Med vehicles were often loaned to other units for various non-medical resupply missions from Bien Hua. Vehicles were also swapped from unit to unit for the purpose of satisfying IG (Inspector General) inspections from time to time, particularly new vehicles. I doubt the inspectors were fooled by the ploy, but they probably did get a kick out of inspecting the same truck in our unit that they'd already seen in three or four infantry battalions! The Army really did believe in ingenuity and teamwork.

Medical companies were authorized up to four medical officers—young doctors whose post-graduate training was limited—plus two dental officers. We rarely had more than eighty men active at any given time.

Essentially half of B-Med's enlisted personnel served in medical roles—guys with field medic-nurse training plus laboratory and x-ray techs—making up the "Clearing Platoon," which in 1967 was led by Lieutenant Bob Cooper from Houston, Texas. Cooper was a straight up guy who said what he meant and meant what he said. The remainder served in food service, transportation, motor vehicle maintenance, and communication roles.

...

My first order of business on arrival was to meet and assess B-Med's executive officer (XO), Captain Spurgeon Green. Tisdale was specific when I left Di An that B-Med had experienced "personnel problems" in recent months, that my job was to eliminate them. I assumed he meant the weak link was the company commander, my predecessor, but there were also questions about Green. Apparently there had been complaints, though none were ever substantiated. The last thing Tisdale said to me before I left for Lai Khe was to meet Green, assess his ability, and to let Tisdale know if more personnel changes were necessary. He made it clear that he was weary of listening to an undercurrent of dissatisfaction with B-Med.

I liked Captain Green immediately. He was tall, well-spoken, and seemingly knowledgeable. He possessed very dark skin and was quite handsome, even dashing in appearance. When he announced he was from Natchitoches, Louisiana, though, I couldn't help wondering if it was a racially-charged area like other places in the Deep South at that time. But Green revealed no evidence of racial-scarring or the slightest resentment over having to serve under of a North Carolina white boy like me.

Sometimes he twisted whimsically and flashed spectacularly white teeth when he seemed to perceive being put on the spot, but he possessed an easygoing manner and obviously took pride in his appearance and actions. I had no idea how far I could trust him, but I sensed we would be fine together. Subsequent communications with LTC Tisdale were rare. With five kids and a celebrity fiancée he had six reasons to avoid trips to the Big Red One's forward base camp. I don't recall Green's name ever coming up again with Tisdale.

Green was trained as a Medical Service Corps (MSC) officer. He was knowledgeable about military policy and routines and how to get things done at the company level. He was well versed in public health matters and procedures, something I knew only a little about. He explained that he could manage the men for whom I was responsible, and was willing to do exactly that. That was his concept of his duty. The Army was set up to have doctor-commanders to serve in oversight roles, but I saw my job as being the best doctor I knew how to be. Green outlined specific non-medical matters I would have to manage myself, including company disciplinary actions. He was prepared to advise me as necessary about the Code of Military Justice, procedures such as summary court martial (Article 15) proceedings, for instance. In some cases men charged with certain offenses had the right to subject themselves to their CO's judgment and punishment. There were only two Article-15's in nine months, both for very minor offences.

"What about a change-of-command ceremony?" Green asked, flashing dazzling white teeth in the center of an all-out smile.

"What do you mean?"

"Do you want to have one?"

"Hell, I don't know. What does Division expect? I'd not thought to put that question to Tisdale.

He squirmed in his seat, and said carefully, "Things have been a little sticky at times between Division and B-Med. Without going into all that, it might be a good idea to let them know that new leadership is on board now. Show the brass the new face at B-Med."

Without going into "all that"? What did that mean? He may have had real criticism of my predecessor but didn't want to get caught up in actually saying it. That impressed me.

"Can these guys drill?" I said finally. "I mean form up and march?"

"Yes sir. We rarely do it, but I don't see why not. You mean the entire company?"

"Why not? Let the big boys see them all. Instill a little unit pride in them."

"I like it," he said. "What have you got in mind?"

When he pointed out where such ceremonies generally took place, I described a simple scenario. After I had officially received command, I would move the group out myself.

"You? You can do that?" He seemed surprised.

Of course, I wanted to scream. "Probably," I said finally.

"We'll see."

He seemed delighted. "Things are going to be different around here." His eyes flashed like his teeth.

•••

The change-of-command ceremony, the following morning, went off with only a single hitch. B-Med was literally on parade. The staffs of Division and Brigade were on hand, including a hard looking man with a black eagle stitched to his collar. I assumed he was Colonel Blazey, commander of the Iron Brigade. Our guys looked sharp, and moved like they drilled every day. Of course, I gave an incorrect command toward the end, but they handled it fine, executing it perfectly then wondering if I could come up with the required correction, which I managed to do.

As the ceremony ended, I thought I could make out Colonel Blazey grinning, his lips seeming to say to the young major beside him, "What was that all about?" I assumed he referred to my abrupt 180-degree change-of-direction snafu. They both laughed. Neither had seen a medical doctor move troops, but they probably noticed that we were striving to be a unit, that we were determined to succeed.

•••

September 27, my first night in Lai Khe without rain, millions of cicadas chirped in symphony, seeming to welcome the atmospheric change. Outgoing artillery continued to pound into the night, but I hardly noticed. It was the cicadas I heard. Maybe I was getting used to those guns, after all. I lay awake, listening, thinking. Ira Cohen, my medical officer roommate, was asleep, and there were no chopper pilot guests in the next room.

"Fuck you!" It was a high-pitched sound, like bird-speak. The words were so very distinct. "Fuck you," it came again. I held my breath, listening intently. I heard only the cicadas. I was well on the way to sleep when I heard it again. "Fuck you. Fuck you!" Twice in succession, rapid fire, insistent, even angry. It was a human voice: a man in falsetto. In incredibly good English, but not at all an American sound, it seemed to me.

I was out of the bed in a flash, wildly alert, my eyes straining into the darkness beyond the bunker outside. There was nothing. I glanced behind me, making sure my M-16 was in the corner, loaded and ready to go.

Yet I refused to jump to a crazy conclusion, only inching forward to the mesh screen, pressing my nose against it. I stared into the night a long time, trying to convince myself that what I thought I'd heard had never existed. If Charlie were out there, nearby, he wouldn't just walk away. Charlie didn't play games. Finally I returned to my cot and, somehow, managed to go to sleep.

•••

At breakfast Spurgeon Green set me straight. "It was a lizard," he said with gentle smile.

"No. You don't understand. It was a mocking sound, in perfect English. It said—"

"Fuck you," Callanan chimed in, finishing my sentence.

Grins faced me from around the table.

Weeks later I actually saw one. Green pointed it out, high in a tree. It was deep chestnut in color, huge, eight or ten inches long. Fuck-you-lizards were silent in daytime. I never heard one elsewhere it Vietnam, but they were everywhere in Lai Khe. Maybe the rubber trees predisposed their vocal cords to unusual flexibility.

...

Several days later a young infantry first lieutenant I'd just met took off in a bubble-type observation helicopter. It was a little after 1500 hours, a bright afternoon. I was alone at the time, walking from my quarters toward the hospital. I thought nothing of it as I watched the tiny aircraft lift off the chopper pad and head north, out over the swimming pool in the immediate distance. Enemy activities had been light for weeks, and I'd been tipped off that would continue until the coming of the dry season, which was only weeks away.

I watched the chopper sink below the treetops in the distance. Suddenly there was a great explosion beyond the tree line, with a great column of fire shooting vertically for what seemed like hundreds of feet, followed by black smoke that all but blocked out the northern sky. It seemed to last for hours. I was numb, and could not speak.

At dusk the young pilot's remains were brought in, and I was asked to confirm his death. I had seen him just days ago, and remembered him to be almost six feet tall and essentially 180 pounds. What was presented to me was densely black, essentially a solid chunk of ash, some three feet long. I did not touch it, only stared at it in disbelief. "You sure this is a body?" I asked the soldier who brought the lieutenant in.

"Yes, sir. We had to cut him out of the flight seat, what was left of it, anyway."

I couldn't keep from shivering.

...

We weren't even fighting yet. Historically the VC lay low in the wet season, for the most part anyway. The rains may provide respite from battle sometimes, but they brought problems of their own too. I had heard the story of a chopper crew dying while trying to answer a distress call on a rainy night just south of Lai Khe. Pilots had the final say about when conditions were too bad to consider extracting an injured soldier, but they rarely exercised their right to refuse to fly. They were fervent about their mission, valiant young men. They prided themselves about standing up to almost anything in order to save some GI's life.

The culprit had been a phenomenon pilots called "vertigo." Different from medical vertigo, "vertigo" is more or less a psychological phenomenon and occurs when a pilot cannot visualize the ground below or sense the plane of the horizon, generally in bad weather. Then he is forced to be dependent exclusively on his instruments, rarely a big deal, but for obscure reasons "vertigo" had a way of distracting a pilot from what his instruments indicated. When he couldn't see the earth or sense his horizontal alignment and refused to believe what his instruments were telling him, he was in a world of trouble, indeed. The reason so little was known about "vertigo" was that few pilots survived it when it occurred. The crash I was informed of occurred in late July, also in the rainy season, weeks before I had arrived in-country. Apparently the pilot flew directly into a lone little mountain a few miles south of Lai Khe. It was hardly a few hundred feet in height, and surrounded by miles and miles of flat land and rice paddies. I stared at in wonder every time I flew down to Di An or to one of the evac hospitals. I was told that five guys died that night, a single casualty and a flight crew of four, brave men all.

...

It rained like crazy a few nights later, continuing well past midnight. At 0200 I was in the ER treating a beautiful Vietnamese woman. She was in her mid-twenties, fully unconscious. Her pulse was fast and thready. Her family had presented an empty barbiturate bottle. She had tried to take her own life.

Her family was in the hallway outside, six or eight of them. The four adults were well-dressed and well-groomed. Both men seemed at least part-European. I was surprised to find Green with them. Later I would find he rarely made an appearance in the ER. He even seemed to know who these people were. He explained they were an important family, Vietnamese upper crust, he called them. They lived some distance from Lai Khe. I thought they were strangely calm, but he assured me they were more upset than I could imagine.

I instructed the medics to start IVs in both arms, then threaded a small tube through her nose into her stomach myself. IV fluids would dilute what barbiturate was in her blood stream then wash it out through her kidneys. I expected to irrigate undigested tablets from her stomach.

We recovered nearly a dozen tablets from her stomach so I assumed we had a fighting chance. We ran two liters of lactated Ringer's solution through her IVs, possibly doubling her blood volume. She was approximately five feet tall and something less than ninety pounds. If she had been older her heart might not have tolerated that much Ringer's, but if we weren't aggressive she could lose her chance.

Within twenty minutes her pulse had slowed a little, and her lungs continued to sound dry. I gave her another dose of diuretic and called for another bag of Ringer's. I felt we were in good shape. It would be a matter of waiting now.

When I told Green that the families of over-dose victims back home were almost never as calm as these folks, he explained that they were special people, leaders in their community. He also pointed out that they understood that some things were worse than death.

"What do you mean?"

"They're ashamed.

"Why?"

He explained that they had lost face. They were public people where they lived. Within hours all their friends and neighbors would know what had happened."

"Their daughter, or niece, had shamed them by trying to kill herself?"

I didn't quite understand.

"Not only that, but *why* she had wanted to kill herself." Green was convinced she was unmarried, and may be pregnant. It would have been bad enough if she had only lost her virginity. He pointed out that her family spoke French, almost certainly making them Roman Catholics. To them, suicide, being pregnant out of wedlock, even losing her virginity prior to marriage, were major sins. She could even be a prostitute. That would destroy her family's reputation. So many young girls were doing it. Prostitution was a major driver of the South Vietnamese economy. GIs had money to spend. Many girls were their families' primary bread-winners. A family with three or four young daughters could hope to be rich, but suicides approached epidemic proportion among Vietnamese daughters.

I was stunned. I had so much to learn.

But she had a chance to try to get her life turned around. By 0500 she was fully awake. By 0700 she and her family had disappeared.

···

The scuttlebutt was that with the passing of the rainy season, offensive activities would resume, possibly right away.

I couldn't quite get my arms around the idea. Our artillery had been pounding away every night for weeks, sometimes all night long. What had they been shooting at? Who would be on the offensive anyway? I'd been led to believe that even *finding* the VC could be a problem. The implication was that it would be *Charlie* who would mount the offensive, finally exposing himself to us. How exactly would that affect us in Lai Khe?

Early one afternoon late in the first week of October, I was summoned to the ER. There was something the medics thought I should see.

A Dust Off chopper had brought in a very dead American soldier of approximately my age. He had a bloody gash perfectly bisecting his nose and forehead. Blood had streamed into his eyes and mouth, and now soaked his fatigues. There were no other wounds.

"A machete?" I asked weakly.

"Yes, sir."

"But how?"

"We're guessing he was ministering to a GI, trying to save his life," one medic speculated. "Then his position was over run. I can't imagine it any other way."

Was he a medic? I didn't understand. Then I spotted the double black bars on his collar, and a black caduceus on the other one. *He was a medical officer like me.* His bloody, chalklike face and blood-soaked fatigues took on even greater significance for me.

This man might have been the first American doctor to die in Vietnam, but I sincerely doubted it. That dentist at Fort

Sam had lied to me. He did it without batting an eye. He had been prepared to tell anyone who asked that medical officers did not die in Vietnam. That was his job.

"Sorry, Doc," the medic said softly. "I thought you would want to know."

5.
A PARTY, A REVELATION, AND STUDYING HISTORY

Making Sense of Confusion

On October 1, I and two other medical officers from B-Med—one of them homeward bound within days—were guests in the home of a Vietnamese military officer. Nguyen Van Huy (pronounced Nooyan Van We) had been in the army since 1948, when it was the Vietnam National Defense Army under Vo Nguyen Giap, who was currently the four-star general in command of the Vietnam People's Army (of North Vietnam). Now a captain in the Army of the Republic of (South) Vietnam (ARVN)—which I understood to be the rank of colonel in the U. S. Army—he and his family lived inside the Lai Khe base camp as a liaison officer to the 1st Infantry Division. The headquarters of his unit, the Fifth ARVN Division, was in Ben Cat, a few miles south on Hwy 13. Green understood Huy to be a special South Vietnamese patriot, a highly decorated warrior.

Huy's home was within a few hundred yards of General Hay's quarters, on the opposite side of the road. It was a single-storied, flat-roofed stucco structure set a modest distance from the road. Grass was sparse, owing to the thick canopy of leaves overhead. The ceilings were high and the furnishings tasteful—several low, firm sofas and a number of colorful pieces of pottery in strategic places and Vietnamese art on the walls. A TV was playing a VHS movie in an adjacent room.

Huy was a wiry, fortyish man, approximately five-foot-four-inches in height. He moved from guest to guest like a politician, his smile waxing and waning but never leaving his face. His English was perfect, with a faint American accent. His wife, roughly the same age and height, was equally pleasant and engaging. Her hair was pulled back from the nape of her neck and wound into a bun. She wore a colorful outer dress with form-fitting sleeves and bodice over a white satin pant-suit. Below the waist her dress was divided into front and back ankle-length panels which flowed with her movements. When she noticed me admiring her outfit, she flushed and bowed. It was a far cry from the black and white satin pajamas women wore in the village.

Huy eased us toward the TV room where he introduced two of his five sons and their little sister, who was about four years old. Her parents beamed as she shook our hands, with a tiny "good evening," then all the children in unison, "welcome, GIs!" It was a memorable moment. No family, anywhere, could have been more attractive or more congenial.

During dinner we found that the children's oldest brother, age nineteen, was also an ARVN, but was presently studying English in Texas. Huy obviously had some influence with somebody, and going twelve thousand miles to learn a language sounded like the military was not his primary ambition.

We moved into the larger room for a round of Falstaff beer, which we drank straight from cans. Huy served hors d'oeuvres of tiny biscuits in the shape of pretzels. They were salty but tasty. I was surprised when our host, on learning that one of us was from Texas, quickly extended an index and little finger, issued a crisp "Hook 'em, horns!" It was the battle cry of fans at the University of Texas football games! After a good laugh we adjourned to the dining room, toward the rear of the house.

Mme. Huy served dinner, never taking a seat with us. The first course was a faintly salty but delicious onion soup, followed by a chicken dish. I was a little nervous about that since I'd heard at Fort Sam that the Vietnamese didn't disembowel foul before cooking it. It was actually quite good, though—boneless chicken rolled into a croquette and topped with a perfectly delicious brown sauce that reeked of the worst smell imaginable. Considering what might produce such a smell put beads of perspiration on my upper lip. Against my better judgment I asked how it was prepared.

With a wink Huy informed us that the sauce—he gave it a name, but I didn't ask him to spell it—was the best in all Vietnamese cuisine. He said it was prepared by layering fish and salt from the bottom of a large wooden box, three-inch thicknesses of whole fish alternating with one-inch layers of salt to a height of approximately four feet. After tacking the box closed, the mixture was stored at room temperature, eighty to ninety degrees or so, for six months! Then, after filtering out decayed elements, the supernatant was stored as this famous sauce. (I still wonder if he were pulling my leg.)

Huy flashed a grin when I dropped my chop sticks, then kept on eating, leaving me to ponder the biochemistry of rotting fish innards. My taste buds had bought into the taste, but my brain was close to shorting out. I had misunderstood at Fort Sam. It was *fish* they didn't disembowel!

Next came a pasta course, something like macaroni covered with shrimp, mushrooms, and tomato sauce. I could have made an entire meal of it. A large bowl of Cantonese rice followed, then a warm piece of cake that had the distinct taste of oranges.

With a flourish Huy announced it was time for serious discussion. He produced two bottles of Scotch whiskey, Johnnie Walker Black, no less, then went around the table, pouring two fingers of booze into a series of shot-glasses.

Who was this guy, a Vietnamese soldier surrounded by his family in the midst of our base camp? Not only living in uncommon luxury, but plying nobody-Americans like us with black market Scotch. I didn't like what I was thinking. An ARVN hero? Were they all corrupt?

Finally Huy held a glass of Johnnie Walker to eye-level and proposed a toast in Vietnamese, insisting we drink it bottoms up. "Only women sip whiskey, gentlemen."

I was not at all an experienced consumer of alcohol. Whiskey could be a route to disaster in med school. Although interrupted with questions from time to time, Huy spent the next hour summarizing his bio. The smile on his face faded to a bare memory.

At age nineteen Viet Cong had come into his home and executed his professor-father with a bullet between his eyes, then dragged his mother kicking and screaming into nearby jungle, leaving Huy to stare down the barrel of an AK-47 as he listened to his mom scream and struggle. She was found the following morning in a pool of blood, disrobed, her face swollen, hideously misshapen. Unequivocal identification was made from shredded clothing and a ring.

Of Huy's four brothers, only one remained. He described in detail the lives of the other three: a professor, a judge, and a medical doctor. All of them were murdered like their father.

Huy had spent weeks and months, then years adjusting, first learning to survive, then mastering the process of fashioning an unfathomable hatred into useful purpose. He had dedicated his life to revenge. The man who an hour ago had been so gentle and paternal was altogether different. His was committed to an ungodly mission: killing Viet Cong.

Along the way he had been wounded a dozen times, twice requiring almost a year to recover. He had received every decoration his country had to bestow, but true satisfaction still eluded him.

His face turned even grimmer, his voice somehow colder as he recalled his routine. "I take name, rank, serial number, important papers, then make notation in book." Then he extended his index finger to eye-level, cocking his thumb as one eye squeezed shut, the other sighting along his finger, finally pausing . . . one beat, two beats. . . "Then bang!" he uttered with savage finality. "They all die. No exceptions. Last thing they see is bullet."

Huy's story left us all speechless. What could anyone say? His memories had been twisted into nightmares. I was tempted to dismiss some of it as apocryphal, exaggeration at the very least. The business of execution-style killing smacked of blowing us smoke. For so long I had been taught to question everything. I valued the habit, but now I was desperate for understanding. Huy had not lived the sheltered life I had. The seriousness reflected in his face and body language was unforgettable, as was the gravity of his speech. I was much affected. His people were not only weary of war, they were hardened to it. I tried to imagine Vietnamese boys growing up. While boys back home were cutting their teeth on high school football, their Vietnamese cousins were schooled in the art of destroying their neighbors with deadly weapons. To insure their survival they were trained to be cold and ruthless.

After consuming my share of two fifths of whiskey, I was in no condition to question Huy further, or make anything like a cogent comment. It was all I could do to get back to B-Med.

The next morning I had a splitting headache, and zero interest in eating before well into the night, then diarrhea for days, leaving me suspicious of Vietnamese food for the rest of my life. At the very least, I would be wary of any Vietnamese sauce. I would never forget eating the liquor of rotten fish innards.

Huy's story resonated within me for days. I had no idea what my country was doing in Vietnam. Suddenly it was important to know. Continued ignorance for an entire year was no option. In the six years since college I had shut virtually everything but medicine from my mind. President Johnson, JFK before him, and Secretary McNamara had probably made the case for Americans in Vietnam in vivid detail, but I hadn't been paying attention. There were so many questions. Why were we in the middle of someone else's war? Polls back home indicated that most Americans supported the war even though they believed it was a mistake. Who were the Viet Cong, anyway? Where did they come from? How was Russia and China involved? I yearned for answers.

Within the week I came up with a well thumbed copy of Bernard Newman's 223-page *Background to Viet-Nam*. It seemed a godsend. It was in a box of discarded paperbacks behind the bar in B-Med's rustic, make-shift "officers' club." Someone else had been in my present predicament, possibly my predecessor as B-Med's CO. Our officers club was a simple wooden building of approximately ten-by-thirty feet. It had a single window. The only furnishings consisted of a long bar of unfinished pine, a card table, a refrigerator, and rustic seating for eight or ten. A pair of naked 100-watt light bulbs hung from the ceiling.

A blurb on the back of Newman's book attributed to *The New Yorker* promised it was authoritative and unbiased. That magazine was well known to me to be famously independent of the military and the government too, generally. I took comfort in that. I found later that Newman was an accomplished historian and author of over a hundred books on various subjects, including espionage and politics, even novels. His book was published in 1965 so I could be confident the information was reasonably up-to-date.

When Green saw me with Newman's book, he came up with two more books for me, copies of Bernard Fall's *The Two Viet-Nams: A Political and Military Analysis* and *Street Without Joy*. Their hard-back coverings had been warped by heat and humidity, and some pages stuck together.

In the coming weeks I read them all, but it was Newman's book that I focused on. From it I extracted a working idea of how the French had come to Vietnam and what happened after that. The bulk of the following is a summary of what seemed so important to me back then. Readers with an understanding of that history might choose to skip the next few pages.

...

Considering the prosperity World War I brought them, the Vietnamese of the 1920s had no reason to reject the French colonialism they had lived with since the 18th century, particularly from the 1880s when the French gained absolute control of Vietnam, Laos, and Cambodia. Even if the Vietnamese contemplated revolting, how could they have expected to bring it off against a mighty European power? The situation was different three decades later when the French were dead set on re-establishing its presence in Vietnam after Japan's defeat in World War II.

In September, 1940 imperialist Japan had invaded French Indochina as a means of preventing China from importing arms and fuel through the northern provinces of Vietnam. By 1945, despite the Japanese occupation, the Viet Minh, the local political arm, had achieved considerable power and influence. One might make the case that the Viet Minh was the product of pure nationalism since the majority of its rank and file were nationalists. But such a conclusion was possible only by ignoring that the Viet Minh's top leaders were hard core communists.

Twenty-seven-year-old Ho Chi Minh was in Paris studying Marx and Lenin in 1917. In 1920 he became a founder of the French Communist Party, moving on in three years to study revolutionary tactics in the Soviet Union. By 1924, unable to return to Vietnam without being arrested by French authorities as a subversive, he went to China instead, settling near the Vietnamese border. There he organized exiled Vietnamese into the Vietnam Revolutionary League, then the Indochina Communist Party, which would become the Viet Minh.

After the Japanese departed in 1945, the British, with only 1,400 Indian troops, were left to police the southern half of Vietnam. The Chinese troops responsible for the northern provinces were considerably less effective policemen since their primary interest lay in looting the spoils of victory.

The British withdrawal from southern Vietnam in late 1945 left a considerable vacuum, into which the Viet Minh promptly expanded. Their looting operation finally complete in the north, the Chinese were conceivably ripe for French bribes.

When the French fleet steamed into the Haiphong harbor, Ho Chi Minh, facing the decision to fight or negotiate, chose the latter. As a result the French government officially recognized Vietnam as a fully free state within the French Union, and Ho's new government agreed to receive the French troops as friends as they replaced the despised Chinese.

Within nine months, however, Ho Chi Minh's forces attacked a French settlement, massacring men, women, and children, thus launching the French-Viet Minh War. Eight years of near stale-mate fighting followed before the French were finally defeated at the siege of Dien Bien Phu.

The Geneva Convention of 1954 provided a ceasefire and that the country be divided into North and South Vietnam at the 17th parallel. The French understood their power and influence in Vietnam had come to an end. Their only option was to leave, and minimize their economic losses, a virtually impossible task. Their property was confiscated, and only the coal-owners in the north were remunerated (a million tons of coal over ten years).

The Geneva Accords also provided for the lawful transfer of Viet Minh in Saigon to North Vietnam and of anti-Communists from the north to South Vietnam. (More recent information indicates that up to five percent of the approximately 100,000 Viet Minh to be returned to North Vietnam were under specific orders to remain in South Vietnam to commit stealthy acts of terrorism and otherwise obstruct progress of the new government.) Such guerrillas became the seed of the Viet Cong, a term arising as a contraction of Viêt-Nam ông-san, or "Vietnamese communist" (also National Liberation Front). Conceivably some in the south were converted by this group, but it is more likely that larger numbers of Viet Minh returned from the north as VC in order to maximize Ho's investment in their training in guerrilla warfare skills and tactics.

The U. S. rejected post-WWII moves to reinstate any Western colonial rule, but its attitude changed when Chinese Communists drove American-backed Chinese Nationalists to the borders of Burma, Laos, and Vietnam. The U. S. was not about to support a communist attempt to control Southeast Asia. It never supported the French in its war with the Viet

Minh, but when Chiang Kai-shek's army was defeated, it labeled Ho Chi Minh a communist threat in the region.

After Geneva, the South Vietnamese were delirious with joy, anticipating finally a free Vietnam. But they were hopelessly divided, with multiple factions vying for power.

Ngo Dinh Diem was attractive, educated, and well connected politically. He was determined to organize South Vietnam into a free nation. As a long time Vietnamese Nationalist he was angry over his country's partitioning at Geneva, having resisted British and French pressure to side with them. Neither Diem nor the U. S. signed the Accords. Diem knew Ho Chi Minh and his pals quite well. He had personal reasons to hate Ho. When Ho offered Diem a position in the government of North Vietnam, he was flatly refused.

Ho was stunned by Diem's rejection. North Vietnam was rich in natural resources: coal, iron ore, phosphates and other fertilizers, plus small but vital quantities of uranium, tin, and tungsten. Communist nations had pledged continuing support. Between 1955 and 1961 the Chinese provided gifts and loans of 220 million £, with Russia donating another 120 million £. Other Communist nations contributed buses, medical supplies, fishing boats, arms, and technical advisors. North Vietnam possessed a French-constructed steel mill and a sugar refinery. It also produced paper, chemicals, tobacco, textiles, and plastic. Its government was stable. Ho had been elected president by 99.91% of the votes cast. Not even Stalin could boast such a percentage. South Vietnam, on the other hand, was an agrarian society and, with the exception of rubber, possessed of relatively few natural resources and virtually no industry. Ho anticipated overpowering South Vietnam in short order, then reunifying it with North Vietnam into an increasingly potent communist power.

Ho pressed Diem on the issue, demanding an explanation for his refusal.

"Why did you murder my brother?" Diem snapped. It was the final communication between them. Diem and Ho would be intense enemies for the rest of their lives.

The U. S. recognized that if Communist North Vietnam were to be contained, Diem needed considerable help. South Vietnam was in shambles, with no international support in sight. The British had never had an interest on Southeast Asia, and the French had wasted enough time, life, and resources there. Communications were chaotic, every road and railroad bridge in shambles. Diem and John F. Kennedy possessed similarities: Diem was Roman Catholic and Kennedy was the first Catholic president in the history of the United States. Both were staunchly anti-Communist.

It was a supremely uncertain time. Georgi Malenkov, Stalin's successor, continued to pursue the Soviet Union's goal of world domination. In East Germany, the Soviets already had a foothold in Europe. Communist China was determined to annex Taiwan at its earliest opportunity. America was the only power capable of neutralizing such dangers. Theorists anticipated that the fall of Vietnam at the hands of communists would lead, like falling dominoes, to the collapse of Cambodia, Laos, and Thailand. A fully communist Indochina would dangerously tilt the balance of world power. Decisions had to be made. Policy makers, in the absence of reliable crystal balls, were on the spot. Staying on the sideline seemed an unthinkable option. Supporting Diem as the first president of South Vietnam seemed the rational thing to do.

Dwight Eisenhower committed the first American troops to Vietnam, and following his election Kennedy gradually increased those numbers. As events played out, Diem became a huge disappointment for the U. S. Where Kennedy was considered a "good" Catholic, Diem turned out to be a "fanatical" Catholic. He even sought to wage holy war on Vietnam's majority Buddhist population. Diem became an embarrassment to the Kennedy administration, forcing it to seek ways of eliminating him. Increasing public abuses of Buddhists led to clerics' dousing themselves with gasoline and becoming flaming symbols in the streets. Photographs were circulated around the world, further embarrassing Kennedy. An American-supported coup saw to it that Diem soon had a bullet in his head. Three weeks latter, following Kennedy's assassination, American policy changed abruptly.

Washington's idea of disrupting the VC's efforts with napalm and further reducing their cover by spreading defoliants in jungles from helicopters were in no way effective. Collateral damage, including death to innocents and the destruction of crops, would not be tolerable to the American people. Kennedy's idea of having Americans serve only in an advisory capacity would end in 1964, less than a year after his death. Within three years a few thousand advisors in Vietnam would become more than a half-million American fighting men. By 1968 an increasing number in the U. S. would be weary of war and desperately searching for a way out.

6.
JUNGLE SCHOOL, SNAKES AND WHOREHOUSE MEDICINE

Jungle School was held weekly, Monday-through-Friday, for new troops in the First Division. Army Special Forces units had been sent to Panama (Jungle Warfare School at Fort Sherman) for eight intense weeks training, but The Big Red One's Jungle School was simply to update stateside training with Division routines and policies, plus a few tips to help the new GIs live longer, maybe even better.

B-Med's part in the process came after noon chow on Fridays. A medical officer—me, for three straight weeks—briefed a group of forty or fifty about how to keep themselves fit and healthy in the field. We also covered routines applicable if they found themselves sick or otherwise unable to perform.

The discussions were held in a mossy area beneath a dense canopy of trees. Shade, possibly by conjuring up memories of pleasant spring afternoons back home, created an illusion of protection from the heat, but it never lasted long. Lai Khe was not like anything back home.

Some topics were mandatory: "trench foot," for example, which had been a source of disability for infantrymen since

Valley Forge. Feet wet for long periods, then exposed to periodic falling temperatures at night—no lower than the sixties in South Vietnam—exposed troops to the risk of sores, blisters, decaying skin, and fungal infections which could impair duties on patrol. Soldiers had to be reminded to keep their feet dry, which simply required frequent changes of socks and allowing their boots to dry out at every opportunity. Since the Army's jungle boots were constructed of light, rapidly drying materials, I saw infected blisters from time to time, an ingrown toenail or two, but never a case of real trench foot. The Vietnam variety never resulted in frostbite which could lead to amputating toes or feet. I was instructed to discuss the issue, though!

Otherwise, we were given free reign to emphasize new topics as we saw fit. I dedicated twenty percent of the time to point out the dangers of malaria and other tropical diseases. Of course at that point I'd had little personal experience with tropical medicine beyond what I got from what books were on hand at B-Med. Plasmodium vivax malaria was the less virulent form and believed to be preventable by the mandatory weekly choloroquin-premaquin tablets. But the plasmodium falciparum variety was another animal altogether. In the coming months I would see two soldiers with fevers to 105 degrees, both unconscious from generalized convulsions. They were evacuated to Long Binh, but I doubt either survived.

About half the problems we saw at sick call related to venereal disease, mainly gonorrhea. GIs with "clap" or "the drips" were back feeling good about themselves and their social equipment within a week or two. They rarely missed time on duty. High doses of penicillin deep in the butt could do wonders for a nineteen-year-old's self-esteem. But GIs needed to get help before real problems set in, which required little preaching since they were particularly concerned about anything going wrong with their equipment.

We did preach condoms, and the importance of selecting uninfected partners.

Snakes posed a real problem for soldiers in Vietnam. Sometimes a snake-bite could take a 200-pound GI through convulsions and coma to death within twenty minutes or so. No GI died from clap.

Southeast Asian snakes could be huge. A king cobra, typically up to twelve feet in length, could sometimes be longer than eighteen feet. That's a lot of snake to be toting an arsenal of deadly poison too. A king cobra was said to be able to lift the upper-third of its body vertical to the ground when in the attack mode. A single bite from a king contained enough venom to kill twenty men, or an adult elephant. The common cobra was also endemic to South Vietnam. Typically a little smaller, it could be equally deadly. I had seen my first cobra only days earlier.

...

Captain Green, Sergeant Carr, and I were heading west on the oval road at dusk, Carr driving. From a distance of one hundred feet or so Carr slowed abruptly, then screamed, "Holy shit!"

At first glance it looked to be a narrow stake or a stump, black as midnight and sinister looking, squarely in the middle of the road. It stood waist-high, slowly twisting and swaying from side to side. As we drew closer, its flaring hood was obvious in the low light. Green lurched toward me from the back seat, his breath warm on my neck. "Cobra," he exclaimed, gripping my shoulders. "Go for it, Carr!"

Carr stamped the pedal to the floor, accelerating the Jeep's bumper into the deadly beast at what felt like fifty miles an hour. It was like running into a fire hydrant! With the windshield folded horizontal, I came close to being launched across the hood on contact.

Instantly all three of us were on the hard-packed clay, scrambling for a look at what was left of the snake. It lay motionless, but Green was not into taking chances. Without the slightest hesitation he blew a hole into the hood at the base of its head with his .45.

•••

"In South Vietnam," I found myself telling my Jungle School class, "the range of poisonous snakes is much wider than back in the states." The biological variation between the poisons of kraits, vipers, and cobras was great. Antivenin for rattlesnakes, copperheads, and water moccasins back home could be combined and marketed in a single vial as polyvalent antivenin, then distributed to emergency rooms around the country. A single injection provided effective treatment for 98 percent of poisonous snake-bites in America. Only the bites of coral snakes did not respond to the polyvalent antivenin. But in Asia there was no effective polyvalent antivenin for kraits, Asian vipers, or cobras. The antivenin had to be specific for the snake. Treating a snake-bite without identifying the snake amounted to pure guesswork.

"Bringing the snake into B-Med is as important as bringing the victim. Only by identifying the snake can we know how to treat your buddy." I often said that twice, letting the words sink in. I also specified that the snake should be dead. I didn't want to see any live snakes!

As I looked around at the class, I realized for the first time that everyone was wide awake and drinking in my every word. There were always questions, and never a flippant remark. A 19-year-old might take his chances with venereal disease, but never with a snake.

I purposely kept my snake-bite remarks to the end of the lecture since I knew redirecting their attention to other topics would be difficult. There was always a question about first aid techniques, were they the same as those in the Boy Scout Manual? for example. In the 1960s many southerners and westerners were familiar with that little soft-covered book. But I discouraged tourniquets, X-incisions centered on fang wounds, and the sucking and spitting of poisoned blood.

"Remember," I cautioned them, "your top priority is to find and kill the snake. Somebody else can take care of the victim, a medic or your battalion surgeon.

Usually at least one GI wanted to know if a tourniquet should be applied if the victim was in an isolated area, with no access to a medic. My typical response was that tourniquets could be as dangerous as the bite itself. To use a tourniquet or not should be left to a senior medic, one experienced in the precise method of its application. Under no circumstances should a tourniquet be applied so tight as to obliterate the arterial pulse at the wrist or ankle. I encouraged soldiers to keep a victim off his feet, certainly keep him from walking or running. The most important thing was to stay calm, and avoid doing anything likely to make matters worse.

Often questions about snakes went on interminably. "How can you tell if the snake is poisonous?" was another typical one.

"In this part of the world every snake is poisonous," I responded. "You've got to assume that, anyway."

I ended every session by reminding the GIs that thanks to helicopters and highly trained medics the chances of recovering from almost any wound were very good. Medical facilities were never more than a few minutes away, and the Army was setting records in medical care in Vietnam never seen before in history.

...

Within a few weeks a snake-bite victim was evacuated from the jungle to B-Med. At first glance I thought maybe my jungle school efforts had been worthwhile. The victim on the litter was quite calm, possibly from a morphine injection, with a pant-leg cut away revealing calf swelling surrounding a pair of fang marks.

A specialist-four produced a large plastic bag which he emptied on the floor with a thud. Every eye in the room focused on the snake. It was hardly four feet long, with black-rimmed tan medallions against a grayish background. It was as thick as a man's arm, tapering sharply at the tail. The snake's head was muscular and nasty-looking, distinctly triangular. Most important, the snake was still as a stone, obviously dead. A medic handed me the picture book, a thin collection of eight-by-ten glossy photographs of every poisonous snake in Southeast Asia. Slowly I flipped from one to the next, back-tracking once or twice. I read the physical specs and blurbs twice, then stopped. I could identify the snake.

It was a Russell's viper, the most poisonous snake in Vietnam, according to the Army's picture book anyway.

I advanced on the snake and rolled it over gently with a narrow arm-board for IVs, exposing its belly, then rolled it back again, giving me another look at the tan and gray.

I checked it with the book one more time—the brown medallions matched perfectly, and even though the background in the photo was not quite as gray as the snake in front of me, the match was as close as I could expect.

I turned to the medic with a box of thawing vials, and selected the one marked "viper antivenin." Checking the label a second time, I was startled by a collective gasp. Everyone was frantically focused on the snake.

It had righted itself and raised its head, now inches from the floor, its black tongue moving in and out. As I struggled to breathe, it contracted itself from its linear attitude into a series of zigzag angles and began to slither forward.

I took a step backward, fighting off panic, telling myself the snake was every bit as frightened as I was, reminding myself that most snakes are not aggressive, that the average snake, poisonous or not, is defensive in nature.

But still it came forward.

Suddenly an ear-splitting crack filled the room, the M-16's report a split second ahead of the bullet whining as it ricocheted off the tile, then echoing and reechoing.

The snake bounced at least a foot, and collapsed into a heap, its nasty-looking-head lifeless on the tile.

"That should do it, guys," I managed to say, far more calmly than I felt. "And nice shot, Sergeant." I grinned at the tall, bald-headed medic some fifteen feet away.

For what seemed like a long time no one said a word, giving me a moment to consider if there was another ER in the world where nurses packed heat.

"Where did the bullet end up?" I asked no one in particular. It seemed that somebody should be saying something.

"It's there, in the wall, wedged in the stucco," the big, burly shooter said in a calm baritone.

I could see nothing at all.

"About three feet from the floor."

I shivered. I was hardly two feet from the only line of fire he had.

"You sure didn't take a long time to figure out how safe that shot was going to be, Sergeant." I couldn't help commenting.

The big medic grinned, and the entire room broke out in laughter, even the pale GI on the litter, the one whose wound I had yet to treat.

Within a few minutes the antivenin was injected deeply into the GI's buttock. Soon he was aboard a Dust Off slick bound for Long Binh, where he would be observed for days. I sent a simple one-line note with him, along with the snake—its head now mangled beyond recognition—safely back in the plastic bag.

•••

In the future, Friday afternoon Jungle School medical instructors were required to insist that snakes accompanying snake-bite victims should be not only be dead, but in two pieces.

•••

I'd been at Lai Khe only a few days when I first accompanied Green into the village to inspect eating establishments frequented by off-duty GIs—their kitchens, latrines, water supply, etc. Since I was responsible for his actions, I needed to get a feel for the problems he faced and how he managed them. Toward noon we stopped for refreshments in what he called a "tea house." The waitresses were pleasant and solicitous, engaging Green with smiles and phrases of broken English. They were attractive, a few alarmingly so, but none of them were dressed garishly or wore excessive amounts make-up. Most were hardly more than children.

"Are these girls . . . uh . . . prostitutes?"

"Your guess is as good as mine," he said. "What do you think?" But his look indicated he knew far more than he was letting on. I wasn't surprised. All morning he had been treated like royalty at every establishment we entered. With the power to close down a café, he drew a lot of attention, all of it tasteful and professional, but still it made me wonder. Proprietors noticed the rank insignia on my collar, but to them I was only Green's guest, his assistant. It felt strange, and would take some getting used to. His demeanor with employers and employees was appropriate on the surface but still ... I couldn't imagine the trouble any kind of mischief might present, but I sensed I could count on Green. He was valuable to me in a dozen ways. I had no desire to deal with day-to-day public health issues myself. He had a knack for it. I couldn't have cared less if he was minimizing unscheduled inspections or allowing generous amounts of time to correct deficiencies before closing a business down. I had already seen Green treat enlisted men firmly but gently. It was his nature. Our mission was to maintain health standards that protected Americans, period. If Green could manage that, I was prepared to let him run with the ball any way he thought best.

I assumed all the prostitutes lived in the village, but I doubted that was where they conducted their business. Later I would find such facilities adjacent to the swimming pool in the mini-jungle just beyond the perimeter. The French left a pool of approximately ninety-by-forty feet, complete with a diving board and shower facilities. It was another place Green inspected. The surroundings amounted to true tropical splendor, with walls of bamboo and mangrove against stunning floral color. I could imagine returning years later to a hotel for hundreds of dollars a night. Only the appearance of a descending helicopter with a red cross on the sliding door reminded me I was still in a war zone. B-Med was hardly a mile away.

I went to the pool once or twice at late afternoon for a swim, another time at night, when I got the idea that the facility was mainly for enlisted men. I felt like I was at a high school prom, with heavily made up girls with flowers in their hair and boys in fresh fatigues and polished boots. The main difference from high school was that every single kid with a few dollars in his pocket was going to score.

The Army associated high VD rates with poor unit morale, reflecting a failure of command. Really? Wasn't the morale of men charged with fighting to the death dependent on balancing risk with lust? True or not, commanders with an eye toward promotion would see to it that VD rates were controlled!

In October B-Med was ordered to reinstate a previous policy of aggressively treating prostitutes as a means of minimizing the risk of gonorrhea infection throughout the Division. What kind of army thrived on limiting its personnel's sexual activities when off-duty?

The order made sense to me. Weekly examining every prostitute with access to GIs and treating those infected should manage the problem. It was also a humane way of treating the Vietnamese. Harboring untreated gonorrhea placed them at risk of localized pelvic inflammatory disease, which could lead to serious complications, including permanent sterility, even death. After being briefed on these methods, I reinstated them. I had no idea why they had been relaxed.

All girls with gonorrhea were treated until they were disease-free, usually after two weeks. Only then were they allowed to return to work. Their supervisor (the "madam"), who ruled them with an iron hand, received a list of those to be placed on sick leave. She was responsible for keeping designated girls out of work until they had notes form B-Med indicating they were gonorrhea-free. Each was required to wear her number in bold, block numerals on her clothing when working or when she was at B-Med for examination. Any girl failing to observe the routine would lose her job. Cooperation was one hundred percent. It was simply a matter of business.

We began performing pelvic examinations on all local prostitutes on Sunday mornings, usually extending well into the afternoon. Such duty quickly became tiresome indeed, leading me to turn the duty over to Green. Surely he could find some medics who were willing to play doctor with female genitalia. He could supervise them. Medical officers would be on hand to see any girl with specific pelvic symptoms.

Every Monday morning a list of disease-free prostitutes was posted on company bulletin boards throughout the Division. Vietnamese girls were identified by a numbering system which was far from complex. With over a hundred prostitutes in the village, even GIs prone to go daffy when exposed to feminine charms could manage numbers of up to three digits. Even then, though, we encouraged them to write the "clean" numbers down and keep them handy. GIs might lose an occasional letter from home, never their "numbers list."

The plan worked without a hitch. I didn't knock myself out looking over Green's shoulder, but no incidents came to my attention. Within a few weeks the VD rates reached record lows.

...

But all did not end well. In six weeks our Sunday GYN clinic was canceled by Division. One of the kids had written to his mom that she had no reason to worry about his contracting "a disease." Apparently he explained how our operation worked in detail. His mom promptly contacted her congressman, which led to a trans-Pacific phone call.

That soldier's mother wrecked what may have been B-Med's most effective public health program. Boys were boys, clap was clap, and it was certainly not the worst disease going around Vietnam. I only hoped that soldier's mother's efforts to inflict her moral standards on the 1st Infantry Division didn't result in some soldier dying a virgin.

In any case, VD rates began to skyrocket again.

7.
THE BATTLE OF ÔNG THANH

Bodies of Boys and Eyes of Men

I n early October Green informed me that Operation Shenandoah II was underway. He attended Brigade staff briefings each morning, and dutifully kept me up to date on the war. As usual, I had little idea what he was talking about. As he explained it, I assumed that Shenandoah II was the operation Tisdale had told me was coming. I had just settled into a routine of seeing sick call in the morning, playing tennis most afternoons, and writing letters home and reading paperbacks at night. It was an easy life, one I could get used to. I couldn't imagine what was about to happen.

Late in the morning of October 17 B-Med received an urgent request for litters. The 2/28 had made contact with Charlie somewhere north of us and was taking heavy casualties. We quickly rounded up two dozen and made them ready for pick-up at the chopper pad.

All hell must have broken loose out there. Whatever casualties I'd seen so far had come in twos and threes. I had treated some Black Lions at sick call—eighteen- and nineteen-year-old kids mostly, with minor ailments—but I didn't know any of the 2/28 personally. Their quarters in the base camp when they weren't in the field were hardly a stone's throw from B-Med. That was the extent of what I knew about the 2nd Battalion of the 28th Infantry Regiment. I might not know any of them, but I hated to think about my neighbors getting hammered.

Minutes later I was directed to assemble a "Go Team," and be prepared for deployment within ten minutes. Alpha company of 2/28 had been essentially destroyed, with the company commander and two platoon leaders taken out in the first few minutes of the fighting. Not knowing the status of the 2/28 medics or its battalion surgeon, we were preparing to take medical care to the Black Lions.

Without even asking for volunteers, five medics signed up to go, and they began to pack basic supplies into four large bags, including bandages, morphine, whole blood, IV fluids and other volume-expanders. I didn't consider asking volunteers from the other medical officers. That would be my job. Hell, Joe Callanan was headed back to the States in two months. Bad things had a way of happening to guys who were getting short in-country. Plus, he'd spent months in the bush before coming to B-Med.

I gathered up my steel-pot helmet, flack jacket, M-16 and half-dozen ammo-clips then sat down to scribble a few lines to my wife. If the rest of my life was going to amount to only a few more hours, I had to let her know how important she was to me.

A half-hour later the go-team was scratched, and I tore up the letter.

Casualties—wounded and dead—began pouring in around 1400. Until 1600 the ER was filled with men with wounds of varying severity. Medics were busy cutting off grimy, blood-soaked fatigues to expose chests, trunks, and extremities. To find one wound and miss a second could be disastrous. The wounded were in the bodies of boys, but they had the eyes of men. Most had very little to say, but others babbled nonsensically. A few were irrational, suggesting hysteria. Others could not speak. They only stared straight ahead.

Severe injuries were identified quickly. One guy had a gray look about him, and a blood pressure of eighty, pulse-rate 120. There was a small wound of entry in his upper abdomen, and no doubt the bullet was creating havoc in his liver or spleen, definitely his bowel, large or small intestine, maybe all of them. We got a couple of IVs started and hung two bags of blood and sent four more with him as medics carried him out toward the chopper we heard descending to the helicopter pad. That soldier had more than we could handle. Hopefully he could hang on until the Dust Off guys got him to the 93rd Evac.

Soon I was into an easy triage routine. Conscious GIs with unstable vital signs, like the gut-shot kid on his way to the 93rd, were evacuated immediately, as soon we'd hung bags of blood or plasma. Every Dust Off crew had a trained medic who was skilled at maintaining IVs in flight, administering morphine and other meds as necessary. The only unconscious kid with normal vitals we saw that afternoon went to the 24th Evac at Binh Hoa, two miles from the 93rd. The 24th had a neurosurgeon. We shipped the kid with IVs running with Lactated Ringers cut to a slow rate to minimize brain swelling.

The most worrisome guy had massive swelling in his neck. He needed surgery right away. There would be no passing him up the line. His trachea was deviated dangerously to the right, and he struggled to breathe. His face and hands were a frightening grayish blue, and his eyes bulged, giving him a desperate look. I swabbed his neck with antiseptic and slashed into it with a scalpel and began scooping out globs of black, clotted blood. With the mass gone, his breathing improved, his chest rising and falling again at a more natural pace. I could see relief in his eyes.

There was no fresh bleeding. I expected bright red hemorrhage from his left carotid artery. What could I have done about that? Neither I nor the other docs at B-Med were qualified to perform vascular surgery. Trying to expose the kid's carotid now could cause bleeding we couldn't control without ligating the artery. That could lead to a stroke, or worse. This was one sleeping dog I would let lie. Turning my attention to his trachea, I removed a ring of pale cartilage and slipped a hollow metal cannula inside. Suddenly air hissed back and forth through it. The tracheotomy would give him a fighting chance if the bleeding recurred during the twenty-minute trip to the 93rd. After securing the cannula to his neck, I still saw no sign of active bleeding from the carotid artery. I couldn't remember being so lucky.

The kid was awake without a whimper throughout the entire procedure. No local anesthesia, nothing. I told him what I was going to do and did it. I talked to him while I worked but doubt he made out a word of it. Now he couldn't speak because of the trach-cannula, but I told him he was going to a bigger hospital to get well. His eyes narrowed as he took that in, then a tear began to trickle. I would never forget that moment. I only hoped I hadn't lied to him. An old rule in surgery is that good luck does not last all day. He needed close observation, but somewhere near a vascular surgeon.

...

Late in the afternoon I went back to the temporary morgue we had set up in our main ward. It was a hideous scene: dozens of bodies lined the floor—cold, pale, American kids, in fatigues soaked with blood and sweat, some whose pallid faces were streaked with clotted blood. Soon I would be able to steel myself to such scenes, but this was my first one. For weeks I had been telling myself that war was about death. But, still . . .

One soldier caught my attention in particular. He was a tall guy, long and lean. His fatigues were damp but I saw no blood, no obvious wound. His face was the pale gray of death. I imagined him with dark, rugged good looks only hours ago. He was a major, and the olive name tape on his chest said H-o-l-l-e-d-e-r in black letters. It had a familiar ring to it, but I knew nobody named Holleder.

As I was leaving, a medic pointed out the body of LTC Allen, the Black Lions' CO. I knew the name but didn't recognize him. Terry Allen was a big name in Lai Khe, but I wasn't sure I'd ever seen him before. I turned away and kept going.

As I made my way down the rocky hill toward the company area, I found myself repeating the big guy's name. Holleder. Holleder. Who was Major Holleder?

When it came to me, I stopped in my tracks. Don Holleder had been a hero to me once, when I was sixteen. I was well over my plan to attend West Point by then, but I still pulled for Army against Navy at the end of the football season. Holleder had been an All-American end his junior season at West Point, and the following year Coach Blaik had converted him to quarterback even though his passing skills were limited. He had been a punishing ball-carrier. I had seen him lead the Black Knights of the Hudson over Navy in 1955. I'd played a little high school quarterback myself the night before. Saturday afternoon I settled in front of the TV with the current issue of *Sports Illustrated*. Holleder's picture was on the cover.

I turned and took a step toward the ER, then paused. Should I go back up there? I concluded to the contrary. Don Holleder was dead. The best way to show my respect was to not gawk at his remains.

•••

Fifty-eight American boys died on October 17, the largest number of First Division deaths in a single day since spring. The official count of the wounded was sixty-one. The final count—119 dead or wounded—amounted to a seventy percent casualty rate, worse than anything in the Civil War, when men charged into fire shoulder to shoulder.

At B-Med we felt we had done all we could, but we would always wonder. There was little chatter in the mess hall that night, many of us struggling with a single question: what had it been like in the jungle out there?

I was awakened at 0300 by a telephone. It was a sergeant from the hospital. He announced that the death certificates were ready for my signature. Was he kidding? Did he really expect me to get out of bed to take care of paperwork? I mumbled something about putting them on my desk, that I'd take care of them first thing in morning. Then I hung up.

Minutes later I was awakened again. A sergeant and two enlisted men were at my bedside. The sergeant respectfully explained that the dead were about to be loaded into a C-47 already at the air strip. Their bodies could not leave until the deaths had been officially certified. I was holding up the first leg of their final trip home.

Of course the Army insisted that all ten copies be signed. After I'd scrawled my name 580 times, my right hand felt like I'd just worked a crowd like a politician running for office. But it was not the aching hand that kept me awake awhile.

•••

The date October 17 remained fixed in my memory for the next forty-five years. The ambush of the 2/28 was the bloodiest battle fought during my time with the Big Red One. What had actually happened that morning and early afternoon? Black Lions just didn't get whipped like that. Little was said about it in the base camp, only that it had been bad out there.

...

In 2007, on a warm May night, I attended a baseball game in Atlanta. The Braves were playing the Mets. I was visiting my daughter Carroll, who was a sports writer for the *Atlanta Journal-Constitution*. She had introduced me to a colleague, Patty Rasmussen, who wrote for for *Chop Talk*, the Atlanta Braves magazine. They had come down from the press box during the seventh inning stretch.

Carroll had alerted me that I had something in common with Patty's father: we both had served with the 1st Infantry Division in Vietnam.

Patty was brimming over as she told me about her dad, who was a hero to her, their family, and probably many others. He had written a book about Vietnam, and she was curious if any of his experiences might resonate with my own. When she told me he was in Lai Khe in 1967, I instantly knew I would do anything to get a copy of that book.

"The 2nd Battalion of the 28th Infantry—the 'Black Lions,' as they were called—were in a huge battle that October."

"I know," I said, "it happened on October 17." I went on to tell her what I knew about that afternoon.

She gave me a weird look, as though she couldn't believe this was happening.

I listened with excitement as she told me her dad's book was about what happened that day. We had known each other hardly minutes, and here she was, providing a link to details I had yearned for most of my life.

But, a book? What happened that morning in 1967 near Lai Khe was not the Normandy Invasion or the Battle of the

Bulge. As important as that day had been to us at B-Med and the Black Lions and the people who cared about them, I could hardly believe it would interest others. Everybody I knew was still trying to forget Vietnam had ever happened.

And to be directed to authoritative details about what happened October 17, 1967 by Patty and Carroll was almost too much. Neither had been born by then.

···

Patty's father was Brigadier General James E. Shelton, who had been the operations officer (S3) for the 2/28. I contacted him the next day by e-mail, and he sent me a personalized copy of his book. He had been reassigned just days prior to October 17, and promoted to G-3, Division's operating officer, an important job. He had been haunted by the deaths of friends and fellow warriors that morning. He struggled with guilt that he had not been at Ông Thanh himself. He was convinced he could have done something that would have changed the outcome that day, something that might have kept his buddies alive. It became an obsession with him that ultimately led to months of poring over official records and discussing them with surviving Black Lion contemporaries, sharing his views and speculations with them about exactly what had happened, based on the facts he'd learned. Buoyed by the enthusiasm and input of his 2/28 friends, he wrote a book about it all.

Though born of obsession and guilt, his book was also a work of admiration and love. He dedicated it to Specialist Fourth Class Ray Neal Gribble, who, though desperately struggling to survive in that steaming jungle, made the conscious decision to risk his own life in an attempt to save his buddies. Shelton aptly described Ray Gribble's act as fulfilling the purpose of his existence by inspiring those around him to serve the better interests of mankind. This twenty-four-year-old, thus enhancing the nobility of mankind, assured immortality for his name.

···

In *The Beast Was Out There*, Jim Shelton pointed out that the Black Lions entered the jungle from their NDP on the morning of October 8.[2] For nine days they would "beat the bush" from dawn to dark in stifling heat and humidity, every minute apprehensive about what might happen next. The beast in Vietnam came in various forms, all deadly, typically coming with little warning. The physical and mental fatigue those men endured was intense, and relentless. Within a week many had shed fifteen and twenty pounds. C-rations were plentiful and nutritious, even tasty at first, but soon they became so monotonous that many lost interest in eating anything.

For nine days the Viet Cong eluded them. But finally the beast was sighted a few minutes past 1000 hours on the 17th. The fighting took place just south of a stream named Ông Thanh, a few miles west of Highway 13. The operation consisted of two rifle companies supported by a weapons

---

[2] James E. Shelton, *The Beast Was Out There, from the Cantigny Military Series,* (Chicago:First Division Foundation, 2002, 15-35, 118-155.

platoon. It was led by LTC Terry Allen, Jr., son of a legendary World War II general.

Alpha company led the column out of the NDP at 0802, with Delta company following. Within forty-five minutes their movement slowed as security patrols were deployed in clover-leaf fashion in the interest of caution. Eyes so focused ahead on the bush for days now strained to see the slightest movement. Hearts pounded. At 0956 the head of the column crossed a well-traveled trail littered with fresh sandal prints and newly cut trees. Shelton quotes Army historian Lieutenant Colonel George L. MacGarrigle in his book *Taking the Offensive* in reporting that the jungle was only moderate that morning, with no complete canopy, that foot movement was unobstructed but that ground visibility was limited beyond fifteen or twenty meters.[3] Suddenly Alpha company's 1st platoon sighted VC on the trail and scrambled to form a hasty ambush.

But as quickly as it had appeared, the enemy was no longer visible, leaving first platoon in an eerie silence. Finally the platoon leader heard movement high in the trees—first a vague rattling of metal then the unmistakable sounds of clicking rifle bolts. Sergeant Willie Johnson of Alpha Company's second platoon was on the radio to his company commander, saying, "The trees are moving, and I think someone's in them."[4]

With the first volleys of sniper fire, the battle was on, sending a forward observer ahead to direct artillery fire. Instantly

---

[3] *George L. MacGarrigle, Combat Operations: Taking the Offensive. October 1966 to October 1967 (Washington, D.C.: U. S. Army Center of Military History, 1998), 335.*

[4] *David Maraniss, They Marched Into Sunlight (New York: Simon & Schuster, 2003) 259.*

came the deafening sounds of hostile fire raining from the trees. Captain Jim George, Alpha company's CO, was struck in the face by shrapnel from a claymore mine, the concussion rupturing his ear drums. The wound immediately beneath his left eye led to swelling which quickly extended to his lower eyelid, compromising his vision. Two platoon leaders already dead, George had no choice but to order Alpha company's first sergeant, to assume command.

...

Shelton told me about another book on the Battle of Ông Thanh by best-selling author David Maraniss, who has written books about personalities ranging from Vince Lombardy (1999) to Bill Clinton (1996) and Barak Obama (2012). Maraniss interviewed survivors from both sides of the action at Ông Thanh . Shelton was highly complimentary of the book, leading me to feel I could trust it, particularly the Vietnam chapters.

In *They Marched Into Sunlight*, Maraniss movingly describes the devastation and carnage of the ambush at Ông Thanh, plus the many heroic acts. His narrative flashes back and forth between events unfolding that October, from the Black Lions at Ông Thanh to the University of Wisconsin in Madison where students were rioting against the Vietnam War, and to the White House where Lyndon Johnson agonized over his shrinking military options against pressures threatening to smother his presidency from every corner.

Maraniss describes Second Lieutenant Pinky Durham, Delta company's artillery forward observer as being stationed in the command group, near LTC Terry Allen, 2/28's commander.[5] The enemy was skilled at identifying the command group as the battle commenced, making it their primary target. RTO Jim Gilliam reported witnessing a rocket grenade exploding nearby, knocking Durham off his feet.

Radios squawked in the background. Someone at the artillery firebase requested a cease fire for the purpose of calling in an air strike.

Durham screamed into his radio, "No! Bring it in. I know what I need."

First Lieutenant Welsh, Delta company's commander, heard the radio-exchange from his location farther back in the column and supported Durham's request. He knew his forward observer had a good view of the enemy.

Suddenly Durham was up and running to an even better position. There he adjusted the artillery fire to the left (east since the patrol was heading south). It would give the Black Lions an opportunity to collect their wounded. As he started to move back toward Delta company, he was hit again. Sergeant Calvin Moore at the firebase told Maraniss that radio transmission from Durham was getting weaker and weaker, with longer and longer pauses.

An airborne observer above also sought to direct fire. He had the downed Durham in view, cheering him on over his radio, addressing him by his call sign, "Please, ninety-three, old boy, just tell us right or left. I know where you are."

Durham called the fire closer and closer to him. He was within meters of Charlie. At some point a forward observer

---

[5] *Maraniss 210-211.*

must call off artillery fire when he was closely engaged with the enemy. But Durham rejected such thinking. He was committed to bringing fire right into his lap if necessary. "I can't see it, but it sounds good. Bring it closer," he told Sergeant Moore.

Delta's first sergeant, Brad Barrow, "Top" to his comrades, had been hit by a rocket propelled grenade and was down behind a tree hardly meters away. When he came to, he saw Durham struggling to raise himself to an elbow. "Top!" he screamed finally, pointing out two enemy soldiers racing at Barrow. It was his last word and his final act.

With Durham falling on his face, Barrow wheeled and squeezed off two rounds, killing both enemy soldiers. At that moment he understood that Pinky Durham had saved his life.

Much later, the family of Second Lieutenant Harold Bascom "Pinky" Durham, of Tifton, Georgia, would accept the Congressional Medal of Honor in his behalf. The fresh-faced, dimpled, blue-eyed kid with the golden grin was far more than a favorite of Delta company, he was an absolutely fearless warrior, a true American hero.

...

From eye-witness accounts, Maraniss reports that Durham's CO, First Lieutenant Clark Welsh, was preparing Delta company for the second wave of the enemy's attack.[6] Already a possessor of the Silver Star, he was about to prove that no soldier was superior to him in determination and courage.

---

[6] *Maraniss 260-283.*

Welsh had taken over Delta company several months earlier, and as his letters home confirmed, his goal was to make his outfit the best infantry company in Vietnam. He was equipped for that purpose as few others were. He even spoke Vietnamese. But he had known for months that he would have to work fast if he were going to succeed. Except under unusual circumstances company commanders carried the rank of captain. Welsh was given Delta company because he was the most qualified available man for the job, whatever his rank. The Black Lions were short of captains at the moment, but that would change. As soon as the vacant captain-slots were filled, the battalion commander would have no choice but to give Delta company to the next captain to arrive.

From early in the fight Welsh had worked with Durham to place artillery fire. Now with Delta company's strength down to a perilous level, the enemy's attack was about to accelerate.

Mananiss's eye-witnesses told him that Welsh was suddenly up and "shooting like a madman," briefly appearing to take on the entire VC regiment by himself. He took out an RPG gunner with his .45, then turned and shot a sniper out of a tree. The dead man's body didn't fall, but bucketfuls of his blood poured to the ground. But any frenetic fighter in the open runs great risk, as illustrated by the following sentences by Mananiss:

> . . . The first bullet pierced his [Welsh's] back and cut between two ribs, causing a sucking chest wound. If he leaned over, he could not breathe. If he stood straight he could breathe. So he stood

during the battle, his uniform drenched in blood. Men were moaning all around him. He estimated that fifty percent of his company was down by then, dead or wounded. He made his way through the clutter of fallen soldiers . . .

Welsh pressed on to the rear, toward Delta platoon. Seeing Terry Allen down, he sent a medic to help. "Doc," Joe Lovato, began crawling on his belly with his heavy bag of medical supplies. Within seconds he was dead.

. . . Upright and hurting Welsh kept moving. He found Lieutenant Luberda near the rear. *We're moving back on a 360*, he said. *If nothing else, don't let them get around to the north of us.* It was a few minutes after noon now, the battle almost two hours old. Welsh found shelter behind another ant hill. There was a ten-yard clearing that he wanted to cross. Halfway to the other side, he was hit, this time in the arm. Machinegun fire ripped through him with such power a biceps flew out and fell to the ground, a piece of muscle wriggling like a hooked fish. He looked down and thought, *what the hell is that?* He assumed a biceps muscle would be red, but it was blue. . .

In minutes Delta company's commander, first sergeant, artillery forward observer, senior medics, two platoon leaders, and all three platoon sergeants were either wounded or dead. Thus the absence of experienced command left the Black Lions to depend on instinct and luck for survival.

Later that day Lieutenant Welsh was on the operating table at the 93rd Evac in Bien Hoa. Two more operations followed. He had a pair of machine gun bullets in his left arm, rendering it useless, plus serious shrapnel wounds in his back, hands, and face. For his heroism he was awarded the Distinguished Service Cross, our nation's second highest military award. After weeks at the 93rd, he was evacuated to Japan for the long road of rehabilitation necessary to bring him back to health and humanity.

...

Normally functioning as part of the Third Brigade, in the opening weeks of October the 2/28 was assigned to the First Brigade, under the command of Colonel Buck Newman. According to Maraniss, with LTC Terry Allen dead, at 1315 Newman made the decision to take over command of the 2/28 himself.[7] He planned to have Major Don Holleder, his operations officer (S-3), airborne in a helicopter to help run things from above. What was left of the battalion was still in the jungle, communicating by radio that they had wounded with them, that they feared the enemy would soon attempt to overrun their position.

The celebrity of the former West Point All-American made him a sought-after staff officer throughout the First Division. With his legendary leadership skills and indomitable will, many expected him to wear three stars one day. But that afternoon he could not see himself watching from a press

---

[7] *Maraniss 286-295.*

box. He was determined to be in that fight himself. He bombarded Colonel Newman with reasons why he should be on the ground. Maraniss describes Holleder "pulsating with an adrenaline rush, like an untamed mustang, pawing the turf, urging Newman to let him run." Holleder kept saying over and over "We've got to get in there and help. They're in trouble and need help." He had never seen circumstances he could not overcome.

Finally Newman relented, and assigned Holleder to lead the recon team that would go in first. Holleder hastily organized a team and started through the high grass of the draw, relentlessly picking up speed, splashing water right and left, losing his balance at times, then regaining it gracefully, racing at the trees ahead. As Holleder neared the dense jungle he was far in advance of his men, gripping his .45, his knees churning as they had when he had once shredded linebackers and defensive backs on the gridiron.

It was a race to his death. Suddenly hit by an AK-47 round to his chest and one to his thigh, he went down, and died after a few short gasps.

As gifted and admired as Holleder had been, he was never the smartest man in the Army. Like Terry Allen, he had finished in the bottom ten percent of his West Point class. He knew next to nothing about caution. As willing and as equipped as he was to lead men to victory, he had never found it necessary to look before he leaped. As Maraniss emphasized, fellow officers who knew Holleder best saw him as intensely head-strong, one who, when falling behind in a debate, was more likely to threaten to whip someone's ass than to re-assess his position. Undoubtedly Colonel Newman got a taste of this as Holleder plead his case minutes prior to his death.

***

The final casualty counts hardly reflected victory for the Americans, as Division staff claimed. Maraniss reports that Captain John A. Cash, a particularly qualified and thorough Army historian called to investigate the details of what happened at the battle of Ông Thanh, was confident that the 103 VC dead, as initially claimed, was false, calling it having been "concocted, sloppily, if not intentionally, though as sort of battlefield confidence scheme."[8]

***

Nineteen-year-old Specialist Fourth Class Schultz of Queens, New York, an Ông Thanh survivor, reported eye-witness details of the ambush to gathered news media:[9] "It was an ambush. They were just on all sides of us. I never heard such fire in my life." But after being briefed by General Hay and 2/28 officers, General William C. Westmoreland, commander of U. S. forces in Vietnam, described the battle as an "engagement" of opposing forces. He was adamant that an "ambush" had not occurred. At the news conference General Hay supported Westmoreland's statement. Maraniss found no one among the numerous survivors he interviewed

---

[8] *Maraniss 411–414.*

[9] *Shelton xxiv.*

who saw the battle as anything but an ambush. Westmoreland and Hay alluded to the idea that the requisite practice of deploying advance patrols in a clover-leaf configuration made ambushing a First Division operation impossible. The fact that this tactic was clearly carried out makes Westmoreland's and Hay's sticking so firmly to their story almost comical. Maraniss estimates the enemy outnumbered Alpha and Delta companies that afternoon by almost eight to one.[10]

Maraniss uncovered Army intelligence reports indicating that prior to the battle's onset Viet Cong regulars were known to be amassed in large numbers in the area. Clearly mistakes had been made. Hay placed the blame squarely on the shoulders of then-deceased LTC Terry Allen. Had the action been an "engagement" as Hay claimed, any commander anticipating contact with a force of the size predicted by intelligence would have been expected to employ heavy B-52 bombing of the area prior to sending a patrol of two undersized rifle companies into the area, at least first clearing out the jungle with napalm or initiating a massive artillery attack.

Even more worrisome is Maraniss's discovery of "records at the Military History Institute in Carlisle, Pennsylvania indicating that Major General John J. Hay, in General Orders Number 174 issued on February 24, 1968, was awarded the Silver Star" for his actions on October 17, 1967.[11] The accompanying citation speaks of Hay's having "distinguished himself by gallantry in action (by radio) . . . taking charge of the situation" (from a helicopter) . . . adjusting fire on the insurgents. . . and

---

[10] *Maraniss 411.*

[11] *Maraniss 484–485.*

directing organization and redeploying troops on the ground. . . cool and calm approach . . . his courage under fire, aggressive leadership, and professional leadership were responsible for the complete rout of the numerically superior Viet Cong force."

Black Lion survivors of Ông Thanh provided no support at all for this citation to General Hay. None of them was aware of his presence on October 17. It had been common knowledge that Hay had been in Saigon that afternoon, at least until the brunt of the battle had been fought. Documents supporting the citation were reported to be missing.

Terry Allen never mentioned it, but he had been under considerable personal stress in the months leading up to Ông Thanh. For him duty came first. He had received a letter from his wife expressing disillusionment with him, the military, and the war. Few were aware that his emergency leave in June was to attempt to resolve serious problems with his wife. Their marriage was caving in. Only years later, after the death of Allen's mother, did Jean Ponder Allen express grief over her husband's death. She informed Maraniss that she had thought that "anybody who was in the war was a bad guy."

8.
LAZARUS

"Did I not tell you that if you believed,
you would see the glory of God?"
John 11:40

I n the first days after October 17, doctors and medics
working sick call at B-Med heard complaints of
insomnia, irritability, and undue fatigue—all symptoms
of battle fatigue. Although they weren't limited to guys in
the 2/28, I couldn't help wondering if they might have been
related to the news of what had happened to the Black Lions.
Rumors and speculations went on for weeks. Battle fatigue
generally subsided with a few days' rest, but sometimes it
didn't. One afternoon I watched a medic lead a soldier to
a chopper scheduled to take him to the rear for psychiatric
care. I knew I couldn't help him from the minute I first spoke
with him. Rest, reassurance, and mild sedation would not
solve his problem. In his mind he had lost his way. With tears
streaming down his face, towering over our medic—he had
to be six-four or six-five—the soldier inched along with baby
steps. Desperately he latched onto the medic's hand, like a
child with his father.

One soldier's intractable headaches and poor appetite
went on for days, letting me know I would soon have to
give him up too. He seemed to have a problem that was way

beyond me. The more he talked, the more uncomfortable I became.

"You want *what?*" The word sounded like "fished." I sensed I knew what he was talking about, but I wasn't sure. Pushing him would run the risk of embarrassing him, but I insisted he spell it out.

"I want to be *fixed*," he said, his frustration moving toward irritation.

"Fixed? I don't understand?" Shivers began to work up my spine.

With his clear, astonishingly blue eyes fixed on me, he whined, "You know . . ." Then he passed his hand from one nipple to the other, then cupped his groin.

"You want . . . uh . . . sex change surgery?"

"Yes, sir," he said calmly, with apparent relief.

What could I say? What could I do?

···

Toward the end of their twelve-month tours, as their DEROS (Dee-Rows, date eligible for return from overseas) neared, it was not uncommon for soldiers to develop the most imaginative symptoms to keep them from going back to the bush. Every soldier counted off those final days, most with only a few left, some up to three months or so. I was amazed how many, if asked, came up with the precise number. Too many of their buddies had "got it" within days of their DEROS. Living under the specter of Charlie and the jungle made even the best of them sense their luck could hold out only so long.

Being objective with them—doing my duty—became tougher and tougher, particularly with guys I'd seen before, when their fears were manageable.

Self-described "grunts," draftees, faced a special kind of agony. They saw themselves at the mercy of junior officers under stress imposed by career officers above them, "lifers" to grunts. Grunts distrusted officers who saw their advancement dependent on battlefield glory. For draftees the term GI, or "government issued," amounted to how they felt about themselves. They were not objects to be discarded. Standing up to danger was not central to them. When ordered to perform a dangerous act—to disarm a claymore mine or expose himself to direct fire to achieve an objective, for instance—a draftee faced real risk of being maimed or killed versus the certainty of a general court martial and all that came with it: the lasting shame, prison time, dishonorable discharge. Recognizing their predicament was crucial to understanding them at sick call.

Their distrust of officers was never voiced to me directly, but soldiers rarely held anything back from the medics, their peers, who passed on such scenarios to me. I came to respect the plights of soldiers trapped in such circumstances. Whether through peer pressure, solidarity with their buddies, or desperation for self-respect, most of them did their duty in spite of the potential consequences. There were ways out for them, but if I ever treated a self-inflicted gunshot wound, I failed to recognize it as such.

In the coming months B-Med medics would face rocket attacks and mortar fire inside the base camp, and several times the threat of a breach of the perimeter. But they were never called on to go face-to-face with Charlie in the bush. They were thoughtful men—many with one or more years of college under their belts—and they had great respect for the foot soldiers they saw at sick call. They came to recognize and understand the fear they saw in others.

•••

For a man to convince himself he is bullet-proof has to be an uphill battle. No doubt few succeed. I saw a guy once, on October 17, I thought might well be bullet-proof.

At mid-afternoon a litter bearer, a specialist-four, carrying the dead from a Dust Off chopper to the temporary morgue we had set up in an empty ward, thought he saw a body move as he helped transfer it to the floor. Of course, that was impossible. The bodies had already been pronounced dead by a medic, or somebody, and afterward had been loaded onto the chopper at least ten minutes prior to arrival at B-Med. The movement the spec-4 saw had to be the result of gravity repositioning the soldier's leg as he was transferred from the litter.

But the wide-eyed soldier lingered when his partner turned to leave. For almost a minute he stared at the corpse, his heart no doubt hammering his chest wall when he convinced himself he saw movement again. It was the same leg. All but jumping out of his skin, he screamed, "Hey! This guy's not dead!" He said it over and over.

His partner, also a spec-4, ran to the ER where I was finishing up a wound debridement. Seeing his excitement,

I left a medic to dress the wound I'd treated, then followed the spec-4.

I was met by a gray and grimy kid sprawled on his back. His eyes were sunken, half-open, glazed, and his fatigues were soaked in sweat and stiff with clotted blood. I ripped open his shirt and saw a small wound of entry in the right upper quadrant of his belly. He was clearly not breathing. His skin was cold, and there was no carotid pulse.

"Are you certain this is the one?" I asked him.

"Yes sir," he said firmly, still gaping at the motionless soldier. "He moved. I swear he did. His left leg." He stared at me with what seemed real expectation, as though he really thought I could do something. It was ridiculous.

I had been CO at B-Med for hardly weeks, and we were in the midst of the most stressful day we had experienced together. We had never confronted mass casualties before, even attempt to resuscitate anybody from cardiac arrest. Here was a chance to practice the routine. I had no idea how skilled our guys were in the techniques of cardio-pulmonary resuscitation. Their stateside training had covered it, but I suspected few had actually participated in the real thing. This guy had just fallen into our laps. Why not?

Plus, what if word got around that I'd blown off a medic for imagining things? Nobody in our company would ever be up to going to the limit for me when we faced a guy who was hanging by a thread. It was important to set an aggressive tone at B-Med.

"Okay," I snapped, "get him to the ER, on the double!" What did we have to lose?

...

I found the soldier's neck so stiff I could hardly move it. *Rigor mortis* didn't set in until hours after death! I forced his jaw ajar and wedged the blade of a laryngoscope inside his mouth, gently prying his teeth apart. But slipping it in farther would be impossible. His jaw muscles had clamped down, and they were really strong. But there was no way to back out now. If we say we're performing a drill, we perform a drill. Stopping was no option. It would create confusion.

Medics bent over the body from both sides of the table, working to place IV catheters. The entire room was abuzz. I had never intubated a corpse before. Was it even possible?

I laid the laryngoscope aside, then re-gripped the cold, damp skin behind the soldier's jaw with both hands, then yanked it upward with all the strength I could muster, tilting his head backward simultaneously. His neck was tight, but so far, so good. But I needed my right hand free. Could I maintain this position with only my left hand? Somehow I managed to do it, but I knew I couldn't hold the neck in that in position long. I slipped the tip of the laryngoscope into the soldier's mouth, then advanced it deeper, easing the tip upward a little as I searched for his epiglottis.

I was aware of a sudden *cr-r-a-ack*. I felt it as much as I heard it. The laryngoscope had broken one or more of his front teeth. *Dammit*, I wanted to scream. It was really bad form. But, hey, this guy didn't need his teeth. He was dead.

When the cartilaginous epiglottis popped into view, I pinched it upward with the blade and advanced a little deeper. In a few seconds I got a glimpse of the vocal cords. They were obscured by shiny bubbles of mucous and saliva. Somebody handed me a suction tip, and I heard the machine rustle up to speed nearby. My left hand was killing me. It was all I could do to overcome rubbery muscles clamping his mouth shut My hand, numb with fatigue, began to lose control of the laryngoscope. Stretching inert flesh with one hand was hard work.

With a couple of swipes of the suction tip, suddenly I had a clear view of the vocal cords. I took the curving endotracheal tube handed to me and slipped its tip between the cords and into the trachea. Then I withdrew the laryngoscope, shaking out my cramping left hand, then gripped the endo-tube with my right hand and blew a series of quick breaths into the lungs, watching the chest rise and fall.

The rest went relatively easily. Better than expected, actually. The medics were sharp, better trained than I thought they would be. They seemed to anticipate every step of the process. I would never have gotten that tube in place if I had had to explain anything to the guys helping me. I promised myself I would never attempt to intubate a cadaver again.

A medic handed me an Ambu-bag already connected to a line of pure oxygen. I saw the green tank out of the corner of my eye. I connected the bag to the endo-tube and quickly squeezed a series of oxygen-enriched breaths into the soldier's lungs, beginning to sense that my left hand really might come back to life.

As if on cue Callanan happened into the room and injected a vial of epinephrine directly into the soldier's heart, then began to rhythmically depress his sternum against his heart with powerful strokes of his wrists and palms. Quickly we fell into a rhythm, Callanan "massaging" the heart a few beats then pausing for me to inflate the soldier's lungs with fresh oxygen. After a few minutes we switched.

Medics had two IVs in place within minutes, and several fifty-milliliter vials of sodium bicarbonate had already been drawn into syringes. Two hundred milliliters were pushed into the blood stream quickly while large bags of saline were hung on the IV stand. Other medics milled about in silence, some with bags of blood and Dextran, another rolling up a back-up oxygen tank.

After Callanan and I had alternated a few times, we relinquished the massaging and breathing duties to senior medics, and I began to consider how much longer to continue before deeming the drill a success. I was satisfied the medics were up to speed with the routine. They worked quite well together. Somebody had taught them well. We could keep this up for a while with IV fluids and oxygen, but blood was precious. Wasting blood on a dead man was dumb.

I had to balance stopping the drill with the expectations of some of the men, particularly the kid who saw the guy move. He expected the corpse to be up and talking to us any minute now.

Suddenly the medic at the head of the table exclaimed, "He took a breath!"

Cheers went up around the room, but I only shook my head. Executing a drill well was one thing, resuscitating a dead man was quite another. As a group we must remain rational.

"There! There's another one," another medic said.

"See his chest move?" said the medic at the head of the table. "I'm not bagging him at all!"

It was true. But how could it possibly be so? I began to feel a little dizzy.

I went to the soldier's groin in search of a femoral pulse. It was there! It was weak and thready, but it was real. I had to be dreaming.

For forty-five minutes we transfused the soldier with four bags of blood, a bag of saline, and a bag of Ringer's. A third IV had been started in a foot, and someone had inserted a Foley catheter into his bladder. His blood pressure hovered just over eighty, and his pulse rate was steady at a hundred.

It was unbelievable.

And there was more. The soldier's eye lashes flickered a few times, and he opened his eyes. They stayed open for only seconds, but this soldier was alive!

This time I was part of the cheer.

What started as a drill was ending as a miracle! It wasn't exactly a miracle, of course, but there was plenty I did not understand. I had some thinking to do.

Soon we loaded the soldier into a Dust Off chopper with the endo-tube in place and oxygen flowing. A fresh owygen tank was loaded on the deck beneath him. His hemoglobin was barely seven so we gave the Dust Off medic four more bags of blood to be transfused in flight. With an abdominal surgeon standing by at the 93rd or the 24th , and a little luck, this soldier just might have a fighting chance.

...

The next morning a medic informed me a Brigadier General had wandered into the ER the night before to see what all cheering was about.

"What did you tell him?"

"I told him everything that happened."

"Which was?"

"That we raised a GI from the dead, sir."

"Oh, no, no, no. That didn't happen at all. If you say that, people will think you're crazy."

"Then what did happen, sir?"

"We were very lucky to have a guy who refused to die. He was never dead. I promise you that. People do not rise from the dead. We were just too dumb to understand he was alive. We should have been giving him the full court press much sooner. All he needed was blood and a fast helicopter."

"Sir, you stick with your story, and I'll stick to mine."

...

Since he was thought to be dead when admitted to B-Med, he never made our wounded list. After emergent treatment, he was evacuated right away. Later in the afternoon the bodies stored temporarily in the B-Med morgue were transferred to the Graves Registration area set up nearby, where official identifications were made and filed. As a consequence, he wasn't listed there either. We weren't so hot as record-keepers.

The next day someone referred to him as Sergeant Lazarus, and the name stuck.

Judging Sergeant Lazarus dead that afternoon amounted to a preventable misdiagnosis, of course. Somehow we had made a crucial error. First, I had been anything but patient as I searched for his carotid pulse. Possibly he had had one. Second, I had listened to his chest only a few seconds. I was so sure the guy was dead that I rushed ahead with the idea of turning him into a practice tool. That was unprofessional. Finally, I should have taken the time to place my hand on his belly to determine the slightest movement of his diaphragm. It was a far more sensitive test. The bottom line was my examination had been cavalier, even reckless. I had allowed myself to be carried away by snowballing events. I had fallen for the overall stiffness. Some doctor I was, thinking I was looking at *rigor mortis* in a live GI!

•••

On October 21st I went to Long Binh to see if Lazarus was still alive. At least I would get his name. The doctor I aspired to be did not accept the validity of miracles. After going through charts in several surgical wards, I found him at the 24th Evac. He was admitted at shortly past 1800.

A nurse went out of her way to help me. I suspected she was not used to doctors showing up from infantry clearing stations to see patients they had treated. I told her I wanted to speak to him, but that I would examine his chart first.

The operative report indicated he had undergone a laparotomy on the evening of admission, and bleeding was confirmed from his liver and spleen.

Progress reports indicated he was still quite sick but was making a satisfactory recovery. A dentist had seen him about the chipped tooth, but no dental treatment was planned.

I watched him from across the room. He was more slender than I remembered him, and a naso-gastric tube remained in place as did a single IV. His face was obscured by a large soft oxygen mask. He was sleeping, probably from the morphine the nurse said she had given him earlier.

I did not wait for him to wake up, and I knew I would not return. I had no intention of speaking to his surgeon. I had to see if he was still alive, and that was confirmed. I wouldn't have been surprised if he had died in flight on the evening of October 17. Did I want to tell him I was one of the people who had saved his life? I'm not sure how I would have gone about saying that. I realized that thinking we had saved his life was a subconscious reason I'd come in the first place. I was ashamed of my vanity. I had to be looking squarely at the patient to realize that.

I left. The nurse looked at me in alarm from across the room. I gave her a waving salute and kept going. There was nothing more to say.

Looking back now, I made another mistake by not saying at least something to the specialist-four who saw the soldier move in the morgue. Without him the guy *would* have died.

He seemed to expect things to turn out well, had faith in it. He had faith when I didn't. I wish I had talked to him about that.

•••

Something happened that afternoon that was another reason I wished I'd put Sergeant Lazarus behind me a week ago and never saw him at the 24th. I had just had chow in the mess hall.

I should have seen it coming. Randy Radigan was a Dust Off chopper pilot who bunked at B-Med from time to time. The twenty-one-year-old lieutenant from South Dakota possessed the same can-do attitude and good looks as Tom Cruise did two decades later in the classic flying film, *Top Gun*. One evening I overheard him and his crew-chief relive shared experiences of some months earlier. Radigan, in-country less than a month, had hit the ground running in his search for trouble.

As they told it, the engine of their helicopter had been taken out by ground fire, leaving Radigan to feather its rotor into autorotation, converting the aircraft into a nine thousand-pound parachute, thus saving the million-dollar chopper and the lives of his crew of four, two of whom bore the stinging shame of having pissed in their pants. And that was the good news. Then they faced a platoon of VC deployed around a rice paddy. Over the next twenty minutes or so, between the four of them, they sent nineteen VC to meet their maker, and Randy had won himself a silver star. And similar tight-spot episodes followed. He seemed destined to prove himself one lucky dude, and some of his crew scrambled to seek safer assignments.

This particular afternoon, with me in the cabin behind the flight deck, Randy's chopper lifted off the pad at Bien Hoa, ascending east, then north to follow Highway 13 back to Lai Khe.

Suddenly the roar of the UH-1 Huey engine seemed to cough and sputter, then into a very empty sound, sending my world twisting and spinning and the clouds shifting and rolling as the ground raced up with alarming speed.

We'd been hit! A lucky AK-47 shot had knocked out our engine. But, how? Bien Hoa was a secure area, and it was in broad daylight!

Then, as quickly as it had happened, the cabin was upright and steady again, the helicopter resuming its ascent.

I had vomited all over my boots and pants and into every corner of the cabin.

Radigan, flying the chopper, turned in his seat and yelled at me, "Hey, Doc, get a grip, will ya! Don't mess up my helicopter!"

I managed a smile, then a weak reply, "I thought we were going to die."

Both pilots laughed. For the remainder of the flight they turned at intervals to poke fun at me. I was fifteen minutes getting back to normal.

I didn't find out what had happened until we were on the ground. As Randy explained it, the overhead rotor provides the helicopter's lift, simultaneously resulting in torque that must be balanced by the rotor in the tail, the chopper's rudder.

When the smaller rotor's foot pedals aren't engaged, the chopper flies without a rudder, sending the cabin spinning wildly in the opposite direction from the overhead rotor. This sends the aircraft immediately plummeting! Actually the copilot had the controls at the time of take-off, planning to turn the flight over to Randy at a certain altitude. Randy simply missed a beat engaging his foot pedals, sending my lunch in every direction.

After considerable denial, Radigan admitted that he had been concerned too, sending his copilot into peals of laughter describing Radigan's momentary but very real sweaty gray face. Even cool hand Luke had moments of being human.

9.
MEMORABLE PATIENTS: A COMMANDER, A GRANDPA, AND TWO SORRY BASTARDS

Early in the afternoon of November 2nd I received an order to assemble a "go-team" to take to the Loc Ninh area, near the Cambodian border, where intense fighting had just broken out. My thoughts turned immediately to October 17 and the aborted go-team experience that day. Since then I'd thought a good bit about setting up a mobile emergency room in or near a battlefield, and it looked like that day had come. I assembled the five medic-volunteers of October 17 and reviewed with them the list of the equipment and supplies we would need, then headed for my hooch to dash off a quick note to my family.

From three thousand feet the surroundings of Loc Ninh appeared much like Lai Khe: lots of rubber trees. Except for a thinning wisp of white smoke drifting beyond a stand of trees there was no sign of fighting. We flew north and turned back and began to descend near what I assumed to be the southern edge of Cambodia, back-tracking a mile or two. Finally the pilot made a wide sweeping turn back north and dropped to the treetops, finally announcing his intention to go in fast, and get out even faster. He emphasized he would be on the ground just long enough for us to hit the deck. We were to release our gear at ten feet or so from the ground, then get out the instant we touched the landing zone. "I repeat," he said, "we will not be on the LZ longer than five seconds. You guys get the hell out!"

I understood that helicopters were major prizes for the VC, that on the ground they were most vulnerable, however disguised their approach by flying low and fast over the cover of trees. Finally we churned up a cloud of reddish brown dust and dirt as we set down, and I saw a stream of red smoke at the tree line in the distance. We hit the ground running, coughing and sputtering through the dust as we made for cover some thirty yards away.

Several unarmed GIs waved at us from deeper in the trees. One guy wasn't even wearing a shirt. They seemed to be expecting us but reported no casualties or anything about a fire fight. I felt silly gripping my M-16 so tightly, and finally flipped the safety back on. We had answered another false alarm. As my pulse rate gradually returned to normal, emotions poured through me that ranged from confusion to relief. Disappointment was not among them.

•••

On November 4 I got a phone call from Al Maroscher a little after evening chow. It was about "the old man." Apparently Colonel Blazey was sick.

A few minutes later I found Blazey at Brigade Headquarters hunched over a radio, talking to a battalion commander at an NDP. His voice was weary but still all military. He was a man struggling, pale and sweaty, leaning forward on elbows bracing him from collapsing into the radio set. He hardly resembled the stern-faced ramrod-straight soldier I'd met a few weeks ago, then a young-looking forty-three. Now he seemed fifty-five. Bird-colonels

Major Albert G. Maroscher, a highly decorated 1st Infantry Division warrior and a good friend, gave his life for his country in April, 1968. (Photo courtesy of www.ohioheros.org)

in the infantry are not permitted to look like "death warmed over," but Blazey was getting close.

When the colonel finished his communication, Maroscher, his S1, Brigade's personnel officer, motioned us to an adjoining room. Blazey didn't say a word, just shuffled toward the doorway, giving me a sheepish look, embarrassed by his incapacity. Soldiers like Frank Blazey saw illness as weakness for others to endure, never himself. He was above that kind of luxury. I could imagine him skewering Maroscher later for summoning me.

His lung sounds were unremarkable, but his heart rate was elevated and his temperature was 104. He was clearly sick, and soon to be in bed, whether he liked it or not. Convincing him of that would be a battle.

"Okay, Doc, you're right," he said at the outset. "I don't feel so good at the moment, but I've got a job to do so that's the end of that."

Some part of me wanted to scream, don't feed me that crap. Instead I took a deep breath and said, "You're really sick, Colonel. You've got to back off now and adjust. You're vulnerable in a way you don't recognize. You're in no condition to even talk about your job, or making decisions right now. Chances are, though, in a few hours you'll be better—we'll work out a plan to get you back up to speed then. We'll do it together." After all, he was a special man, responsible for thousands of men. I needed his input. I had treated General Hay weeks earlier for a viral sore throat—possibly more a reaction to stress than a virus—but this was different, not at all a self-limited illness. "Right now you've got to get some rest so we can figure out what's happening with your body. Pushing too hard now risks screwing up more than your health."

The look on his face changed, signifying something like relief, a little anyway. "Okay, Doc. What do you want me to do?"

That comforted me. Round one was over. I'd come out the doctor, and he, the patient. We both had a chance.

If we had been at the 93rd Evac, I would have ordered immediate blood cultures—while his fever was peaking—but B-Med was equipped with neither an incubator nor culture media. I considered sending him to the 93rd but rejected the idea. That would be overreacting, at least at this point. That could stir up things with Brigade unnecessarily. I settled for a white blood count and a urinalysis.

After I gave him some aspirin, Maroscher took him to B-Med's lab at the other end of the building. While he was getting some blood drawn, Maroscherl and I had a minute for small talk.

"Your XO told me yesterday you were at Loc Ninh a few of days ago."

"Green. Captain Green."

"I see him at morning staff meetings."

"Oh, yes. I see. Yeah, I spent a night up there. Tisdale, my boss in Di An, ordered a B-Med detail up there to back up a battalion surgeon they thought might be overwhelmed."

"And?"

"It was a false alarm. I spent the night in Quan Loi, and returned the next morning. Nobody at Loc Ninh could figure out why we were there, including me. Still can't."

"The 1st of the 18th was in a big fight about that time. You just missed it."

"Really? Nobody told me anything. Were there heavy casualties?"

"Not for us. The VC got hammered, though. Twenty-four dead on the 29th, and eighty-three the next day. They found another hundred bodies or so when the VC withdrew on November 1. They say things are still hot up there. The 1/18 is kicking ass. Your CO probably based his decision on delayed reports. Two NVA regiments converged on the Loc Ninh airstrip at daybreak. Engaging amassed VC doesn't happen every day. He was preparing for things going the other way."

Within days rumors around the base camp had the enemy's killed-in-action at Loc Ninh at over six hundred against fourteen Americans dead and sixteen ARVNs. VC regulars rarely took on a dug-in force en mass. That was unusual, pitting their weakness against American strength. Nobody was sure what it meant.

···

I'd had dinner at Colonel Blazey's villa several times, the first, three weeks earlier. One of his staff had extended the invitation through Green.

The colonel's villa wasn't as grand as the officers' club, some two hundred yards away, but it was the same kind of two-story structure, stucco and tile. The living area and the dining room adjoined, adjacent to the kitchen. Before supper the colonel and his guests—there were two besides me, in addition to his staff officers—milled about with drinks or sat in comfortable chairs in the living room. Unspoken protocol limited the drinking to a single beer or a glass of wine, then maybe another with dinner. I recognized Majors Maroscher and (Ed) Trobaugh, Blazey's S3, or operations officer, but had no idea who the others were. I was the only captain there. Everyone called me "Doc," which made me feel special.

Maroscher made it clear when he introduced himself that his name was Al, that he expected to be called that. It stoked an immediate relationship, a budding friendship. He was tall and lean, his fair complexion tending to give him red cheeks much of the time. Every time I saw him he seemed to have just shaved. His bearing reeked of West Point, even though he was a graduate of Ohio State. He was open and engaging, a straight-to-the-point guy, with no time to beat around the bush.

On the colonel's signal we moved into the dining area and took seats at a table covered with linen. We ate from real china, with freshly laundered cloth napkins in our laps. The fare of the day was steak—real steak, over an inch thick. I hadn't seen such steak in a while. No one was asked to specify how he wanted it cooked, but mine was a perfect medium-rare. The salads were of fresh lettuce—cool and crisp, not a single leaf daring to wilt—and there was butter and sour cream for the baked potatoes. I couldn't imagine a better meal in a New York restaurant. Blazey had resources we didn't have at B-Med.

The colonel joked with Maroscher and Troubaugh and two other majors, all older than me—ranging from early- to mid-thirties—but he was especially solicitous toward two guests whose names I didn't catch, and would never see again, one a major, the other a lieutenant colonel. Later he turned his special charm on me, asking where I was from, about my family, where they currently lived, and so on. He went out of his way to make me feel part of the group.

Eventually the conversation turned to football, what kind of season Army was having and what they could expect from Navy in a few weeks. Maroscher and Blazey's guest lieutenant colonel were intent on speaking quietly about the Ohio State Buckeyes. Trobaugh steered the topic from football to recent Brigade activities which went straight over my head. He was engaging, energetic, and seemingly smart, with a great deal to say. I listened in silence, trying to understand.

I ran into Maroscher a few days later in the hallway between B-Med and Brigade Headquarters. He gave me some background on Blazey. After West Point he had had a brilliant combat record in Korea, then had some key jobs in Washington before Vietnam heated up. Al said he was everything he appeared to be, a man on the rise, almost sure to make general before going home.

...

B-Med's top lab technician was a slim young sergeant/E-5 in his early twenties. I was tempted to do Blazey's malaria smear myself, but rejected the idea. I knew what to look for, but to identify parasites in an officer like Blazey's red blood cells was work for sombody who did it every day. I watched as the sergeant studied the slide beneath the microscope. After a few minutes he looked up and assured me the test was negative.

"You understand whose blood this is, don't you?" I reminded him. Applying a little pressure never hurt anybody.

"Sir, I don't care if this is General Westmoreland's blood, he does not have malaria."

I liked his attitude, and the cool way he looked at me. Of course I couldn't resist looking at the slide myself, but when I finally looked up the sergeant had left.

The urinalysis was negative too, as were the white count and differential. I figured Blazey had some kind of a viral illness, maybe something as simple as flu. That would have been the leading diagnostic bet if we were back home, which we weren't. I had some studying to do.

B-Med's library consisted of three volumes, four counting the picture book of snakes: textbooks of medicine, pediatrics, and tropical diseases. Even with photographs the book of tropical diseases was hardly three hundred pages long. By midnight I had devoured it, not feeling much better when I was done.

...

I examined Colonel Blazey again a little past midnight. His temperature was down and he was feeling better, but he knew he was sick and was prepared to act like a patient.

"How did you know I'd feel better than I did a few hours ago?" he asked.

"A fever as high as yours was doesn't last long. It's the way the body works. It will return tomorrow, though."

"Did the aspirin take away the fever?"

"Maybe it helped."

Actually the colonel was becoming more cooperative than I expected. His lungs remained clear, and his neck was entirely supple. When I examined him earlier I hadn't considered the possibility of early meningitis. He still denied headaches.

He had the beginnings of a very fine rash on his chest, but otherwise his examination was unchanged. I might have missed the rash earlier, and the book on tropical illnesses had influenced a closer look. There was no evidence of a tick bite or anything like that.

The rash and the fever were consistent with scrub typhus— a Rickettsial infection—even if he had no headache. It was at least a starting point. I hesitated to start him on tetracycline because if he got worse and had to be sent to an evac hospital, being on antibiotics might interfere with the offending organism being detected by culture. On the other hand, any chance to get on top of a disease like typhus early could not be ignored. The book mentioned cases involving heart muscle, and even the brain.

I put him on tetracycline after all, five hundred milligrams every six hours. The recommended dose was two hundred fifty milligrams, but I was eager to get ahead of the disease. I'd make my mistakes on the side of over-treating him. There was simply too much at stake. I had one of our medics stay with the colonel overnight in his villa, with instructions to call me at the first sign of trouble.

We discussed sending him to the 93rd Evac first thing the next morning, something he did not want to do. He was adamant about not leaving Lai Khe unless it was absolutely necessary. That seemed reasonable so we decided to see how he would be in twenty-four hours. Joe Callanan had had a couple of years of internal medicine residency, and could have been a real help. But he was on R & R in Hong Kong for five days, and LTC Buswell, the Division Surgeon, was out of pocket too. Buswell was an orthopedist by training, but I would give anything to have any kind of a doctor looking over my shoulder. The only other option was Ira Cohen, our new medical officer. Cohen was fresh out of his internship and was having enough trouble simply adjusting to being in Vietnam.

The following morning Blazey looked and felt better. "Looks like your medicine is working, Doc," he said. Of course

I wasn't going to be that lucky. No fix would be that quick. If Blazey had typhus, the chills and fever would return in the afternoon.

I would find out later that he had tried to listen to the Army vs. Air Force game by short wave radio, but he couldn't stay awake. He was happy to hear later that Army had won, 10-7.

•••

Later in the morning I was called away from sick call to the ER. Medics huddled around an unconscious soldier in the uniform of the Army of North Vietnam. He was ashen and sweaty, with no detectable blood pressure. Immediately I went to his groin in search of a femoral pulse.

But there was a curious bulging in his pants pocket. It was very hard, blocking me from the soft tissues surrounding his femoral artery. It seemed to fill the entire pocket. Carefully I worked it back and forth but had trouble gripping it. Eventually I got it in my fingers and slipped it out. It was a metal cylinder that looked like a short, narrow beer can. It was brown.

"Grenade! Grenade!" a medic screamed, sending everyone scrambling in different directions, one guy knocking me off balance as he dove to the base of the wall behind me.

"Hang on to it, Captain!" A deep voice boomed from behind me. "DO NOT DROP IT OR PUT IT DOWN!"

I shivered as I stared at the deadly object in my hand.

My grip had trapped the firing lever against the length of the body of the grenade. Its spring mechanism was at the top. Charlie knew he was going to die, and was determined to take someone with him: me! He had removed the safety pin securing the firing lever against the grenade, then wedged the armed grenade into his pocket, the narrow lever facing outward. Had it faced inward, against his thigh, it would have sprung away from the body of the grenade the instant I removed it from his pocket, thus igniting the detonator. I would have been dead in seconds!

The realization left me breathless, and suddenly weak. I was desperate to be rid of it, to be miles away from it. But what could I do?

"CAREFUL, DOC." The voice was closer now, steady and confident. "Hold it still. Do NOT move your fingers! Easy, now."

He appeared beside me, just the two of us with the dying VC in the center of the ER, everyone else was flat against the floor or in the hallway outside. He was short and blond, a new guy, someone I'd never seen before. He was a spec-4. There were hardly 120 pounds of him, surprising for such a big voice. Almost leisurely he stripped adhesive from a roll of tape, then wrapped it round and round the butt of the grenade, securing the firing lever to it. He was done in seconds, like it was something he did every day. Then he took the disarmed grenade from me and moved away like he had just disengaged a tennis ball from the jaws of a golden retriever. In seconds he was out of the room.

I was numb, hardly moving for what seemed like a long time, aware of hushed stares from around the room. In time I focused on the little bastard on the litter. He was breathing, but barely. He was a brave man, one who believed in his cause and was doing only what he was trained to do. He was from another world, one I had no interest in trying to understand.

Neither the oath of Hippocrates nor my Christian values dissuaded me from what I did next. Without another thought I turned and left the room. I needed some fresh air. He could die on his on.

As I made my way down the hallway I heard a muffled explosion outside. Reaching the doorway I saw a waft of smoke rising against the tree line beyond the helicopter pad. Forty yards closer was the little man with the big voice. He was making his way toward me, adhesive tape crumpled in this hand. As he drew near, I returned his salute, then hurried to him to shake his hand. I thanked him but realized how inadequate my words were. I will never forget that little soldier with the big voice standing with me in the middle of the ER, talking me through my crisis, with everyone else diving for safety. I wouldn't forget that VC either.

...

Colonel Blazey had a chill at mid-afternoon, and an hour later his temperature was 102 and probably rising. Soon he was as sick as he'd been the night before. We gave him more aspirin, even a vial of Solu-Medrol intravenously. His fever would lyse in a few hours, but I was uneasy. I didn't think he was in any real danger, yet, but I longed for some means of confirming my diagnosis. I also wished I knew how long it took tetracycline to turn the course of the disease around. Our book on tropical diseases did not address that issue. I didn't expect his fever to be resolved in two days, but I was growing uncomfortable waiting.

Al Maroscher and Major Trobaugh met me as I came out of the B-Med mess hall a little after 1800. Trobaugh, particularly, was grim. They wanted to know what Colonel Blazey's diagnosis was and when was he going to be better. I explained that the presumptive diagnosis was typhus, and that I expected him to improve on the tetracycline he was taking. It could take days, even a week or longer. That didn't come close to reassuring them. They wanted certainty—facts, not flimsy hunches and ideas. Hells bells! I wanted somebody to reassure me, too!

"Why don't we send him to the 93rd Evac?" Maroscher suggested.

"That's fine with me. I'm sure they have an internist there who knows a lot more about tropical medicine than I do. My only reservation is that the colonel wants to stay here for now."

Neither said a word, but from their looks I suspected they were trying to decide whether or not to question me about Blazey's *competence* to have an opinion about his medical treatment, specifically whether or not he should be evacuated to the rear. I sensed they were *really* interested in his competence to make decisions about giving orders affecting thousands of men. I imagined that *competence* was a difficult word for officers to use when speaking of their CO, particularly in front of witnesses. And Trobaugh seemed to have an opinion about *my* competence.

"Of course the colonel is unable to make decisions when he's having a chill or a high fever," I volunteered, "but most of the time he is entirely lucid. It's like making decisions when you're tired. We're all vulnerable then, but we can manage to do what we need to do."

Traubaugh looked at me as if I'd made the most ridiculous statement possible. "But what about running the 3rd Brigade?" he cut in. "Can he do that?"

"Through you guys. I assume he thinks that's workable." I realized I had not been addressing either of them as "major" or "sir" and that I was no longer simply a dinner guest. I was beginning to feel miffed about being called on the carpet about a medical issue. I doubted they were better qualified for their jobs than I was for mine. I managed to keep that thought to myself, though.

"You do understand that at some point you're responsible for evacuating Colonel Blazey to more specialized care, don't you?" Traubaugh was a tough guy, one with an astonishing presence. His gaze burned into me.

"Yes, sir," I snapped. "I am well aware of my duty."

Most medical officers in the Army receive their basic medical training at a civilian institution, where the doctor-patient relationship ruled supreme. As long as patients were mentally competent, they were consulted before treatment was initiated or changed. Doctors answerable only to the Army might do things differently, but I couldn't function that way, not so long as I could communicate with someone as intelligent as Colonel Blazey. But Traubaugh was correct: medical judgment involved a fine line.

"What happens next, Doc?" Al asked.

"We've got some more blood in the lab right now. I should

have the results within the hour. If they're okay, the plan will be to re-evaluate him in the morning."

...

The next day Buswell returned. I took him to see Blazey immediately. He had already heard about the colonel's illness. I doubted he knew much more about tropical diseases than I did, but I was nearing the end of my rope. The surgeon in me limited my patience. Dealing with surgical problems amounted to understanding the nature of the risks and alternatives, then if and when to perform whatever operation. Such decisions typically were made sooner rather than later. Waiting to see what happened after surgery—the possible evolution of a complication: an infection or postsurgical bleeding, for instance—required watchful waiting, but only after one's best effort in the operating room. Replaying a well executed operation in your mind took some of the sting out of the waiting. Making a diagnosis in internal medicine, on the other hand, amounted to waiting days to judge the effect of treatment in progress. It required an entirely different mindset. Buswell was a surgeon too but maybe he would see something I had overlooked. His view was a straw I wanted to grasp.

He asked the colonel a few questions, then listened to his chest and looked into his throat and ears. He seemed awkward as he went about it. I was even more surprised when he folded up his stethoscope and announced to Blazey that he had dengue fever.

I almost laughed. I'd read about dengue for two nights running, and knew it was unlikely at best. Buswell was guessing, grand-standing for a superior officer. It dawned on me that, at best, he was one of those guys who were occasionally wrong but never in doubt.

"What does that mean?" Blazey wanted to know.

"If you have dengue, it means we're on the right course," I said gently. I had no idea how Buswell would have answered that question, but I was in no mood to chance finding out. He only looked at Blazey and smiled.

I had planned to ask his opinion about whether or I should evacuate the colonel to the 93rd, even let him know about being confronted by Maroscher and Traubaugh. But in the end I changed my mind. Buswell would have opted for the personal safety of transferring Blazey out of Lai Khe. For him it would be a military decision, not a medical one. It also took some heat off all of us. I understood that could be the correct course, but it took Blazey's opinion out of the process. Buswell had no feel for Blazey as a man. I, on the other hand, had at least some kind of a relationship with him, and was determined to keep personal politics out of medical decisions in his behalf. I had no idea about what Medical Corps policy dictated in such situations, but tonight I had to put Blazey first, not because of my perception of his duty, but because of my assessment of his capacity.

The following morning I laid all my cards on the table with Colonel Blazey. I told him I thought he had typhus and that he was on appropriate treatment. I admitted I had never seen a case of typhus before and had no feel for how long it took tetracycline to work its magic. I told him there was likely someone at the 93rd with more experience with tropical diseases than I had.

"What about dengue fever?"

"If you've got dengue, the chances are excellent you'll get better without any treatment at all. It's a self-limited disease. Drinking plenty of fluids and getting a lot of sleep will do the trick. Aspirin helps with the fever."

"And how long does that take?"

"Not sure. A week, maybe longer."

"Am I in any kind of danger?"

"Not today, not at the moment. If you get worse, it could mean you have something besides typhus. I wish I thought you had dengue."

That night his temperature was 101.5, clearly improved after two full days of tetracycline. I began to feel a little better, but the following evening it was 102, not greatly different but I did not like the trend. Colonel Blazey didn't like it either.

"If I've got something besides typhus," he said the next day. "What could it be?"

"Colonel, it could be one of a number of diseases, all reasonably rare so far as I know. I don't have any basis to lean toward anything else at the moment."

"What could they do at the 93rd Evac that is different from what you're doing here?"

"I'm not sure, possibly nothing."

"Do you think they might have some sort of test that could help?"

"Maybe. I'm confident they have the capacity to culture bacteria, a technique to identify them. I've never worked in an evac hospital." I paused. "I've been trying to get assigned to one since the day I arrived in-country."

His eyes twinkled. "Do you think I should go to the 93rd?"

"I think it's an option. If I thought it was absolutely necessary I'd have told you days ago. The fact is you're making some progress, but you're also still sick. You're in no shape to fly over battlefields in a chopper, making observations and giving orders, but you do have the capacity to manage your staff. Only *you* know if that's adequate for getting the job done."

I had no idea what options he had to relinquish his command temporarily, whether one of his staff could pinch hit for him awhile, or if another colonel would be reassigned by Division. I assumed the latter option could pose potential jeopardy for Blazey personally. His assignment was important to him, and I assumed he did not want to risk losing it if he might be healthy again in a week or two. I suspected he was having such thoughts. Even though he was somewhat improved, he was in the fourth day of his illness. His strength had ebbed, increasing his anxiety and frustration.

"So you think that's a decision for me?"

"Yes, sir. I do."

The following morning Colonel Blazey evacuated himself to the 93rd. I would not see him again for weeks.

...

Aware of my interest in surgery, and the limitations of quality surgical equipment at B-Med, one of our more honesty-challenged non-commissioned officers took it upon himself to scrounge up some really nice instruments for me. He either traded something of value for them or he stole them. He wouldn't say which. Top quality stuff, like fine-tipped Halstead hemostats and a pair of Satinsky clamps that seemed brand new. They were beautiful. There was also a heavy-duty self-retaining thoracic retractor. I grinned as I inspected it. We'd never need something like that. Lung surgery at B-Med was out of the question. Cleaning up shrapnel wounds didn't require fancy tools, but I had high hopes of being able to use them at some point. On November 21st I got my chance.

An old Vietnamese gentleman, in his early sixties I guessed, hobbled into B-Med on a short, stubby walking stick. The woman accompanying him was a patient of one of the other medical officers. He had sent her in from our Ben Cat clinic for an x-ray and some lab work. The old man looked after the woman's kids, two little girls, while she was in the lab. I couldn't help watching him, how he walked and how careful he was when taking the younger child from her mother's arms. He had to be their grandfather.

He was tall for a Vietnamese, and he shuffled along with a decided stoop as if standing upright caused him pain. But he didn't have the look of a spinal deformity. The forward angle was not right for that. Even more remarkable was the huge mass in his groin. He seemed to have a soft ball in his pants, maybe two. I summoned Sergeant Chuong, and ended up convincing the guy to let me examine him.

He had a moderate-sized hernia in his groin, but the main problem was a huge hydrocele which increased the size of his scrotum four or five times. It was the largest one I'd ever seen. I couldn't understand how he could walk at all. His daughter told me later the problem had been present for years. With Chuong interpreting, the old man talked about it, but with reluctance. For him it was a source of intense shame. I gathered that his hernia caused him pain from time to time, but he was mainly concerned with the hydrocele. Of course it was the hernia that could cause him serious problems one day. For years it had posed a risk of bowel obstruction, and one day that would happen. It definitely needed to be repaired. I knew I could manage that, and since the hydrocoele was all fluid, relieving him of that hideous bag between his legs should be easy.

As Sergeant Chuong explained to the old codger what I proposed, and listed the risks I dictated to him, with and without surgery, the man's eyes lit up and he began bobbing up and down, bowing to me. After a brief discussion with his daughter, he agreed to let me do the operation. I had some thinking to do, but I was sure we could make it happen. Thanks to the new Halstead clamps, I knew our equipment was adequate. My only reservation was about exactly where the operation could be done. The Army was bound to have a regulation against that kind of non-emergency surgery on a Vietnamese civilian in a facility like B-Med so I decided not to ask. I could do the surgery in the middle of the night in my own hooch if necessary. If the brass found out about it later and the shit hit the fan, I would just deal with it. I'd think of something.

As word spread throughout B-Med, I even gave the old man a name: Biff Gump. The anti-war movie, "Forrest Gump," wouldn't come out for almost three decades.

We did do the operation in my hooch, where it was less likely to draw attention. The medic who assisted me helped me construct an operating table by tying two card tables together, hardly ten feet from where I slept. Surgery was in the middle of the afternoon. I commandeered a goose-neck lamp from the orderly room, and it proved to be perfectly adequate. After giving Biff Gump a generous slug of Demerol and some secobarbital, I injected Lidocaine subcutaneously in strategic places in his groin and began what was to be a one-hour and forty-five-minute operation under "local and vocal" anesthesia. Mr. Gump was comfortable throughout, dozing off from time to time, and, since I knew no Vietnamese, there was very little "vocal" to it.

The makeshift circumstances threw me off a little at the beginning, but by the time the hernia was repaired, I was feeling like a surgeon again. Draining the hydrocoele was fairly simple, but reducing the size of the old man's massive scrotum took some thought. I made a long incision down one side of his scrotum, then trimmed away large amounts of excess skin then put the scrotum back together. I'm sure any plastic surgeon watching me would have said I was making something easy into something difficult, but the end result seemed fine to me.

One of the medics took some photographs before and after surgery, but I never got to see them. He shipped the film to Hong Kong for processing, and it was likely we had our hands in so many more pressing matters later that we forgot about Biff Gump. As we applied a dressing, he was still sleeping like a baby.

I wore a smug grin and walked with an extra spring in my step for days. Finally I was doing real surgery! Operating on Biff Gump was the biggest thrill of my first three months in Vietnam. I had not forgotten how to do the kind of work I would be doing some day back in the world.

Mr. Gump was up and back and forth to the bathroom within an hour or so and seemed to enjoy a light supper that evening. We kept him in a little used section of our rear ward, essentially a private room, for five days, and I saw him again in a week, then a final time after five or six weeks.

Every time he saw me, he bowed and shook my hand over and over, almost to the point of making himself seem a buffoon. I considered asking him to stop, but I didn't. Some of the medics kidded me about Biff Gump for weeks, calling him the card-table miracle!

The last time I saw him he seemed truly a happy man, fully transformed from years of shame and misery. He was able to stand to his full height, almost anyway, and even walk that way. He no longer needed his walking stick.

...

On the night of November 23rd we were hit hard with mortar fire, and a rifle company took off in hot pursuit. By morning a VC with a serious injury was brought in. His lower leg had been destroyed by a Claymore mine. His mangled foot and leg dangled by hardly more than a bridge of skin and soft tissue from immediately below his knee. The intelligence guys had already determined that he either had nothing for them or couldn't be convinced to give up what he knew.

His main problem was shock. He was still conscious but had a systolic blood pressure of thirty or so and a heart rate of around 130.

Through Chuong I explained to him that he needed blood in the worst sort of way, that we would give him some if he agreed to give our intelligence people whatever he knew about his unit's operation. I pointed out we would be doing him a big favor, since transfusing American blood into the enemy like him didn't make much sense. I told him he would be dead in twenty minutes without blood, that I couldn't have cared less. It was his choice.

"Đuôc đong ý! Đuôc đong ý!" (Okay! Okay!)!" He said it over and over.

I summoned the intelligence guys and gave the vermin three bags of blood.

As he began to feel better, he was more oriented toward what happened to his leg than anything else. He refused to even look at our intelligence guys. They rolled their eyes at me, reminding me that deals like I had proposed never worked out, that the VC knew we took care of them in the end, no matter what.

"Think so?" I said. "You guys might want to hang around another few minutes, while I trim these jagged bones down enough to make him a functional stump." The bones below his knee were fully exposed, splintered and jagged, and the soft tissues were beginning to ooze again. I snapped hemostats on a couple of bleeders as I spoke. His blood pressure was around ninety.

A medic opened a different surgical tray, and I picked up a gigli saw and demonstrated to one of the intelligence men how it worked while Chuong explained to the VC what was about to happen.

"Suddenly the VC was screaming unintelligibly. Sergeant Chuong informed me that he wanted to know if we were going to put him to sleep.

"That, unfortunately, is a service we don't provide for guys like you, Buster," I said as I began to gently separate bloody tissue surrounding a salvageable segment of his tibia.

The VC's eyes bulged as I clamped another bleeding vessel. When I picked up the giggly saw, he began screaming again.

"This must be done, my friend," I said. "We can't close your wound without removing some bone." I waited as Chuong translated, then said, "Or would you prefer dying instead? The only problem about letting your sorry ass die is that it will waste good American blood."

Taking my cue, Chuong explained to him we would use anesthesia only if he agreed to talk to our intelligence men.

"Open up your notebooks, boys, and start asking questions," I said as my patient indicated a sudden attitude change.

I have no idea how good the intelligence was that he provided, but he chattered on for fifteen minutes or so, answering questions quickly without pausing to reflect.

Then we loaded him up with morphine and Lidocaine and fashioned him a stump.

In today's world someone would accuse me of committing a war crime. Of course this is not the case. What I did was bluff the performance of a life-saving operation as it had been performed sometimes for over a hundred years, with whiskey taking the edge off screams and gritting teeth. This guy slept through his operation like a baby, thanks to a huge slug of morphine.

10.
CÔ BAY'S STORY

Of South Vietnamese Patriotism

C ô Bay was like the girl next door, now grown up and transformed into the body and mind of a Vietnamese woman of twenty-three, her skin clear and unblemished as the rest of her, body and soul. Aging among Vietnamese of the 1960s was first detected in their eyes, and the transition from young to old could happen overnight, in those lucky enough to live very long. Cô Bay's eyes were a deep

From left: Spec-4 Novak, Cô Bay, and Sergeant Choung. Bay, a beloved civilian nurse and midwife to local women, and Choung, on loan to B-Med from the Army of South Vietnam as an interpreter, risked their lives daily after establishing common cause with American soldiers.

brown, almost black, reflecting both youthful playfulness and yearning for stolen innocence, spelling out the vulnerability of her haunted existence. It begged the paradox: was the Cô Bay I came to know the result of her courage or her hatred?

She was the antithesis of other Vietnamese of her sex I would meet. Young women likely to speak openly to Americans too often were forced by necessity to sell something of themselves for survival. However understanding of their circumstances, Cô Bay refused to excuse their behavior. In their presence she only averted her eyes, neither speaking to them nor of them elsewhere. She admitted the shame they inspired in her, but she did not permit herself to look down on them. Cô Bay was nothing if not humble. Her beauty was unimaginable, with a face undefiled by make-up or her body clothed gaudily, only the tasteful jumper and ubiquitous trousers that reeked of purity, ethnic and otherwise.

Green alerted me that she was to come to meet me within days of my arrival. As midwife to the village of Lai Khe, Ben Cat, and environs, she made it her business to be known to the CO at B-Med. I sat in my office for an hour one afternoon awaiting her only to be informed that she had arrived but did not make it past the orderly room.

"She just left?" I asked.

Green cocked his head, then nodded, a smile of understanding spreading over his face.

"But why?"

He explained that was simply Cô Bay. She was not exactly shy, nor paralyzed by fear, but she had good reason to be careful. He speculated that she had spotted someone in the street outside, or had a chilling premonition. She avoided openly fraternizing with Americans. Taking advantage of B-Med's resources only made sense, but even that could be overdone. When not at what was formerly the French hospital, which she essentially ran, Cô Bay moved around like a ghost, showing up when least expected, then disappearing without warning. Of course she was emotionally insecure, but who wouldn't be considering the life she likely lived? She was very private, rarely giving voice to her disappointments and losses, and Green assumed there had been many.

"She's afraid of us?"

"No," he said. "It's the VC she fears." Green explained that Division Intelligence had her on every hit list the VC might have. Her American contacts placed a bull's eye on her back. The mystery was how she'd survived so long. Intelligence chalked it up to unerring instincts and a special brand of cunning.

I exhaled a long, low whistle.

"She's a piece of work all right. Very religious too."

"Catholic?"

"Maybe, from her exposure to the French. I'm betting she's still got some Buddhist in her too."

Green didn't have any ideas about why she exposed herself to harm day in and day out, but he speculated it went beyond a sense of duty to the local women and children. He saw her as an unarmed ninety-five-pound agent of death to the VC. Somehow, she would see them destroyed.

I couldn't even imagine that as I rolled around in my head the other snippets I'd heard about Cô Bay. Perhaps the service she supplied to the locals—as nurse and midwife—was the basis for her security. Her importance in the community placed her beyond the clutches of VC operatives.

"Maybe," Green said, considering the possibility. "But the VC still wants her dead. The S-2 is certain about that. One day . . . when there is someone to take her place as a nurse/midwife, and we are no longer here . . . they will kill her."

•••

Some days later, Cô Bay returned, unannounced. Sergeant Hernandez summoned me from the hospital.

She sat across the desk from me, as happy and relaxed as a school girl. She was not at all prim or prudish, as Green described her once, or guarded in any way. On the contrary, she was deliciously open, almost playful. She beamed at me, fixing me calmly, peeping at me through a bright smile. She had teeth, beautiful teeth. What teeth the older women in the village possessed were terrible—black from the betel nut they chewed.* But only the whores had fine teeth, virtually all of them teen-agers. Cô Bay was neither prostitute nor teen-ager.

"Dai uý (captain)," as she called me, her eyes reeking of intelligence and charm, her cheeks creasing into tiny dimples, "you must come when I call for you." Her English was near perfect. Green had told me her French was even better.

She explained that one day circumstances would arise that she could not handle. Whoever had trained her taught her to think that way, that one day a real doctor must be on hand to help her, perhaps even operate to save the mother or her baby. Potential problems included breech presentations, or bleeding in the birth canal, or a fetus of excessive head size. Any of such circumstances carried the potential for an obstetrical nightmare. Breech presentations, for instance—where the infant's buttocks, a foot, or a knee, appeared first in the birth canal rather that its head— required either manually turning the infant down-side-up in the uterus, allowing its passage head-first through the birth canal, or attempting special maneuvers if that were not possible. Either way, the infant's life was at risk of death from lack of oxygen if the umbilical cord was compressed during delivery from the mother's pelvis. Too often a Caesarian section was required to save such an infant.

Cô Bay's teachers had warned her correctly, and undoubtedly she had experienced such frightening circumstances herself. However skillful she might be, I shuddered to consider those outcomes. I never asked about them, and she never volunteered details.

But, *me*? How could *I* help *her*? My experience in obstetrics was nothing compared to hers. Two years' training in surgery beyond medical school made me adequate to stabilize war wounds, shipping those I couldn't fully manage to an evacuation hospital. I may have been the only surgeon for miles, but I knew next to nothing about obstetrics. I had delivered hardly a dozen babies in my life, each uncomplicated and under perfect conditions, beneath the watchful eyes of experts. There was little chance I would be of much assistance in the settings she worried about.

"Sure, Cô Bay, of course I'll make myself available to you, but I'm sure you know more about delivering babies than I do." She had supervised hundreds of deliveries, possibly thousands. Immediately I began to dread hearing from her again. I might be able to manage a Caesarian section if I had to, but I'd never done one before. The only C-section I'd ever seen had shocked me. Veins draining a pregnant uterus expanded to many times their normal size over the course of nine months. Some approached the size of my thumb. To nick the wall of such a vessel could result in unthinkable disaster. The walls of veins were tenuous. Handling them could make matters worse.

"Ah, no, no." As a smile graced her face, she launched into a mock tirade. "You bác sĩ (doctor), all (you doctors are) same-same. Americans! Incredible!" She stamped her foot as she screwed her face into a demanding look. "You know how! I call you, you come? Okay? Then everything (will be) okay. Right?"

Right. There was no convincing her otherwise.

Before she left me that afternoon she thanked me for my presence in her country. She praised the American effort to rid her country of its invasion by Ho Chi Minh's henchmen. She hardly believed me when I told her our mission in Vietnam was not approved by all Americans. "That can't be," she replied with great vigor. "America (is the) greatest country in the world. Always take up for (the) little people. I know that (to be) true."

She was serious. She intended no irony. That was not her way. Cô Bay had more confidence in America than I did.

•••

One of our doctors went to the French hospital on the outskirts of Lai Khe for an hour or two every Monday, Wednesday, and Friday, usually late morning, after sick call had been completed at B-Med. I had read Dr. Tom Dooley's first book about committing his life to fighting diseases of the poor of Vietnam and Laos when I was in high school. I was impressed, and even considered a life like that for myself, before I witnessed the miracles possible with surgery in the U. S. I was less enthusiastic about the Army's idea of using modern medical care as a means of wooing local civilians' allegiance to what Americans were trying to do in their homeland. Something about it seemed phony. To truly take care of their sick required a Dooley-like commitment, almost a generation earlier. I didn't think the Army had that kind of project in mind and was reluctant to buy into using medical care as a tool of psychological warfare. But treating the desperately ill of perfectly treatable disease one by one carried an allure that no doctor could resist. One didn't have to be a religious fanatic to identify with Dooley's work. At the "French hospital" we saw patients through their illnesses, having them return for follow-up examinations until they were out of danger. Joe Callanan and Ira Cohen were also enthusiastic about this kind of medicine, and they were actually more a presence at the French hospital than I was.

They enjoyed the pace and the attitudes of Cô Bay and her assistants, all trained in the French tradition. Several of her colleagues were graduates of the nearby elementary school. The clinic was housed in a spacious brown stucco building, similar to the one at B-Med but much smaller. The elementary school was a similar structure. I assumed Cô Bay was a competent mid-wife—there were never any statistics to monitor, and whatever obstetrical complications she had, she kept to herself. Not once did she call on me or my colleagues to help out with an obstetrics problem.

It was clear to everyone that she was a very good practical nurse, always industrious and hard-working, constantly down-playing her skills as seeming backward to us. But that was rarely the case. She was also a jewel in her administrative activities, uniformly firm and professional when dealing with her assistants.

I was impressed by Cô Bay's management of her pre-natal patients. I noticed several pregnant women coming and going. Whatever French doctor had trained her knew what he was doing. She was always humble and solicitous toward me, but with her obstetrics patients she was firm, all business, sympathetic only when entirely appropriate. In some ways she seemed a different person, then. Occasionally I could hear expressions of displeasure with her patients through the walls. She never volunteered any of her obstetrical methods or routines, but she rarely dodged a question. Routinely she followed her pre-natal patients' blood pressures and dispensed French anti-hypertensive medications from time to time. There was no lab to determine whether or not they were anemic, but she routinely dispensed iron tablets and vitamins, always under French labels, supplementing her patients' diets of primarily rice. She rarely saw a post-partum patient more than once or twice. After a Vietnamese baby was born, its mom was more or less on her own, or so it seemed. It seemed a cultural thing.

•••

I did have to go into the village once in the middle of the night when I anticipated more terrifying circumstances than a woman struggling to birth an infant whose head was too large to exit her pelvis. Cô Bay had called on me to see a pair of sick children. She had examined them earlier in the evening, and became very afraid. They were said to have rashes over their faces, trunks, and bellies. The young staff sergeant who passed Cô Bay's message on to me had used the word, "smallpox." He seemed to understand the implications of the term so I understood that rumors were beginning to make the rounds through the base camp.

Smallpox! I couldn't imagine a worse disaster. If two kids were already affected, others would follow quickly. It would spread through the village like wild fire, then around the country. All the GIs had been vaccinated so they weren't at risk, but how many of the locals had been vaccinated? Within days we could be facing an international disaster.

I had never seen a case of smallpox, and had no idea how to make the diagnosis! What American doctor had any direct knowledge of smallpox? And what I learned about pediatrics in med school was years ago.

But I was lucky. We *did* have a copy of Nelson's *Pediatrics* in our four-volume library at the hospital. With a huge lump in my throat and shaking hands, I poured over the double-columned page of very fine print. Smallpox lesions were described as distinguishable from chicken pox lesions by having the same level of development. Chicken pox lesions were of different ages in the same patient, either immature or fully formed. A med school lecture was coming back to me, now.

Despite my hasty refresher course, I was nervous as I entered the tiny, unlit shanty house, but at least I had a plan. It was a two room structure with sleeping quarters for an entire family—including three children, ranging in age from four to seven. All three were huddled in the same bed. The room was hardly ten-by-ten feet, with a dirt floor. There were no windows, and it was very hot and stuffy.

As if I knew exactly what I was doing, I made the diagnosis of two classic cases of chicken pox! It was a slam dunk. There could be unexpected consequences, of course, but we did not face an epidemic of smallpox!

In thirty minutes I was back in my bunk and sound asleep.

...

Convincing Cô Bay to join Green, Callanan, and me for noon chow at the B-Med mess hall one day took some doing. Coming to my office, and seeing us at the French hospital was one thing, socializing with us was quite another. And it wasn't solely about her fraternizing with Americans, which the VC saw as enemy invaders. She was sensitive about her friends and neighbors seeing her befriending American soldiers, who were famous for fueling local prostitution. That was clearly questionable behavior. Cô Bay was quite vain about her sexual honor. She longed for a marriage like our mothers had and took great care to protect herself from malicious rumors.

She was careful to position herself away from windows facing the front of the mess hall, and her eyes were alert to anyone coming in the front door. The chow crowd had thinned out, and few GIs remained.

She told us about her family, how things had been in Ben Cat when she was eleven and twelve. Her father had been a favorite of the French in the late 1940s. He was a scholar, devouring books in three languages, keeping volumes of journals of his own. His wisdom was legendary for miles. For as long as she could remember he had been the village chief, or mayor. Her mother was a nurse who had been trained by French doctors and nurses. She delivered babies and practiced a French-Vietnamese brand of family medicine, particularly ministering to the women and children. Two aunts made up the faculty of the local grammar school. Both were honored throughout the village. As a boy, one of Cô Bay's uncles had exhibited a knack with tools, and ended up with a business repairing and rebuilding motorbikes in and around Ben Cat. As a teen-ager he had hung around the French Army's motor pool, watching and listening. Later the French had sent him to Paris to learn the secrets and workings of small engines, then hired him as an assistant mechanic. With motorbikes and motor-scooters still plentiful up and down Highway 13 after the French had left, his business continued to thrive.

The communists had come in the middle of the morning.

It was in the dry season, and the sun was particularly hot. Cô Bay had just turned twelve. It chilled me to hear her pronounce the word, "communist." It stood out from other words in any sentence, each syllable crisp and memorable. She never smiled as she spat it out. And "Ho Chi Minh" was a name she gave special attention, three words exploding rapid fire off her lips. She saw Ho as the ultimate traitor to her people.

The Viet Minh contingent was armed but seemed friendly enough, even engaging as they explained their ideas and plans for the village, and for all of South Vietnam. Cô Bay's family and the other village leaders had no choice but to cooperate. Their visitors' rifles and side arms were very real.

At mid-afternoon Cô Bay's father assembled the inhabitants of the village in front of the stucco building where we normally held our MedCap clinics and began to explain to his neighbors who the visitors were, and what their mission was. Cô Bay and her family and neighbors assembled in their finest, including young children, even the infants.

Then, one by one, the Viet Minh delegation lined up and shot every village leader and anyone else of prominence—first her father, then her mother, then her uncles and aunts, finally the rest of them, anyone likely to wield influence in Ben Cat. The carnage was complete in hardly minutes. Now the Viet Minh could control Ben Cat from afar for a generation.

Limp, broken bodies sprawled in the middle of the road, their blood pouring into slick patches on the dusty surface. Then the communists stood each corpse up and bound them to stakes in the village square. There the bodies would stiffen in the hot sun for two weeks, slowly decomposing. No one was allowed to leave the village, or disturb the bodies on display in any way. Cô Bay recalled the terrible stench, how the birds went first for the eyes. No one present would ever forget it. She told it bluntly, without a tear, without the slightest display of emotion. Only her eyes and voice did not betray the hate she felt.

As difficult as losing their relatives and talented neighbors must have been for others in Ben Cat, for Cô Bay it had been even worse. Soon she would reach a marriageable age. Her parents, possibly an uncle or an aunt in their absence, would have seen to her betrothal. Now there was no one. With her family wiped out, marriage became an infinitely more complicated matter. Her heart was bound to the philosophy and religion of her ancestors. She had an idea how it could work out though, but she was never willing to share that with us, however much she longed for it to happen.

...

That afternoon the reading I had done to discover the history of Southeast Asia became less important to me. I had done that in hopes of fostering a belief that my presence was worthwhile, that I wasn't wasting my time in Vietnam. Now, thanks to Cô Bay I had living proof that my presence in Vietnam was meaningful. No one would ever be able to convince me otherwise. The kind of evil she described could metastasize anywhere. Those young men back home who were sneaking off to Canada to avoid serving in Vietnam were simply uninformed, or had agendas I would never understand.

To me, our generation should be committed to making the world a better place. Was it the responsibility of Americans to rid the entire world of evil? I didn't know about that. Apparently some of our politicians thought so, and saw to it that over a half-million of us were in Vietnam in the interest of that end. Disastrous decision? Maybe. Reasonable decision, not prosecuted correctly or far enough? Again, maybe. But Cô Bay's story made me proud I was on hand to help. From that day forward my presence in Vietnam would never be a source of shame or confusion.

...

For Cô Bay, America seemed to be her best and last hope for survival and happiness. That understanding alone negated the accusations that Americans were participating in an immoral war. If she'd known the details of the public discussions back home, she would have second thoughts about America.

...

Later, as the spring wore on in 1968, I was concerned that I'd not seen Cô Bay for weeks. I couldn't help worrying for her safety. Soon I would be reassigned to the Central Highlands, where I continued to worry. To me she really was like the girl next door. I still worry about her, hoping that somehow she managed to survive. She was a special human being.

*Betel-nut (actually the areca-nut) chewing is an Asian custom commonly practiced for social reasons, not unlike westerners gathering for coffee or tea. It is also believed to have medicinal value in illnesses ranging from headaches to skin infections, or as a link to supernatural forces intertwined with the rites of animistic worship, believed to produce magical powers. It is also used symbolically in ceremonies celebrating the rites of passage, and as an aphrodisiac for both sexes. (Dawn F. Rooney: "Betel Chewing in Southeast Asia," a paper prepared for the Centre National de la Rocherche Scientifique (CNRS) in Lyon, France, August 1995.)

11.
18ᵀᴴ SURG:
A PORTABLE HOSPITAL

On October 16 LTC Buswell informed me that the 18th Surgical Hospital, in Pleiku, was being transitioned into a fully inflatable, mobile surgical hospital and would be flown into our area in December. Heavy fighting was anticipated, related to our relative proximity to enemy sanctuaries beyond the Cambodian border.

I couldn't imagine what a hospital of balloons would be like, but I didn't see it as particularly good news for me. I assumed it would dry up what surgery we did, relegating B-Med to conducting sick call, and little else. Somehow I had to wangle myself onto the 18th Surg staff, maybe as an assistant surgeon. Treating battlefield wounds had been my reason for coming to Vietnam. My surgical background and training as a surgeon had been limited, but I knew I could prove myself if I got a chance. Buswell anticipated my thinking and assured me I would probably have an opportunity to participate in some way at the 18th Surg. Its arrival was five or six weeks away. By then he expected B-Med to have its full complement of four medical officers, freeing me up to be away from time to time. For weeks Cohen, Callanan, and I had been the only doctors.

In mid-November Colonel Blazey introduced me to LTC Kakoe, the commanding officer of the 18th Surg. He was head of an advance party making arrangements for the new installation. He was an engaging man, who essentially promised me I would be welcome to assist his staff whenever I was available. I was elated. The possibilities were suddenly endless. Immediately I could see myself being appointed to the regular staff.

···

What were mobile hospitals all about anyway? At the end of World War II, Army surgical consultants, including world-famous Houston heart surgeon Michael E. DeBakey, developed the concept of mobile ORs and support elements as a means of improving survival from serious wounds by bringing surgeons to the battlefield. The resulting MASH (Mobile Army Surgical Hospital) units, though not always fully mobile, achieved that goal in the Korean War, not only in overall mortality among casualties treated promptly but particularly with extremity wounds. Early operations to restore blood supply resulted in vastly reduced amputation rates in Korea.[12] The Korean War provided an important laboratory for surgeons putting into practice the new methods of arterial repair. The lessons learned resulted in widespread peripheral vascular surgery in peacetime. Soon even heart surgery became available.

Richard Hooker's 1968 book, *MASH: A Novel About Three Army Officers,* led to the 1970 movie, "MASH," which Larry Gilbart developed into the wildly successful television series

---

[12] *http:www.medicalinspection.net/the-mobile-army-surgical-hospital-the-korean-war-the-war-that-defined-the-mash.html*

"M*A*S*H," staring Alan Alda, which ran for eleven years after 1972, then the airing of re-runs for decades.[13] Though based on the success of MASH units in Korea, "M*A*S*H" was different in a number of ways.

VC guerilla warfare was dramatically different from WW II and the Korean War. The new realities resulted in new philosophies of combat medical support. "Battlefronts" in Vietnam were not readily evident. Fighting could break out almost anywhere with little warning. Military medical planners were not in agreement about how to handle such circumstances. Many favored rapid helicopter evacuation of the wounded to stationary hospitals like the 93rd and 24th Evacs, then evacuation of recovering soldiers to hospitals in Japan, while others considered the resurrection of the mobile hospital concept.

The first mobile medical facility in Vietnam was the 45th Surgical Hospital, which was assembled in Tay Ninh in November, 1966.[14] It was a MUST unit (Medical-Unit, Self-contained, Transportable). Disaster followed within two months, with the 45th being struck twice by mortar fire, sustaining massive casualties, including the death of the hospital commander. The VC had no qualms about destroying buildings and vehicles with red crosses painted on them. The medical planners went back to the drawing board. They ultimately decided that the semi-permanent idea must be scrapped in favor of increased mobility and armor-reinforced structures, hence the 18th Surg, with its multiple inflatable buildings.

---

[13] http://www.tvland.com/shows/mash/.

[14] http://the45thsurg.freeservers.com/History.html.

The 18th Surgical Hospital was air lifted to the northeast perimeter of Lai Khe on December 1, 1967. Giant Chinook helicopters gently set down the heavy elements suspended beneath them. I was like a boy watching a traveling circus coming to town by railway. It was a massive operation. Holes of various sizes and shapes were excavated, some eight or ten feet deep, others smaller and connected by a network of shallow trenches. My first guess was that they were an elaborate system of defensive dugouts. Defending a hospital on the perimeter of the base camp could be problematic for elements of the First Division. But these excavations were more complex than bunkers. I imagined one system of trenches to be part of some kind of plumbing infrastructure. LTC Buswell said the entire hospital would be air conditioned. I questioned an enlisted man I assumed to be part of an engineer detail, but if he understood the trench system he was a long way from being able to put it into words. He did point out two generators being set up, and explained their proximity to the sites of ORs.

At noon on December 2, giant, pale, rubberized tent-like structures were spread out flat on the ground. When I returned hours later, the tents had been inflated into buildings with arching roofs. They resembled giant igloos. I tried to figure out which were ORs and recovery rooms and which were wards and staff living quarters, but with little success. I observed the placement of sheets of armor inside the inflated walls of several buildings. No armor was installed in the ceilings. Within another forty-eight hours the 18th Surg was to be fully operational, hardly a few minutes' trip by jeep or ambulance from B-med.

Again I was impressed by the Army's effort to spare no cost or trouble to provide top quality medical care for our troops. Only weeks ago I had grumbled under my breath about not having a certain exotic antibiotic as I examined a GI with a wound infection. Chloromycetin (chloramphenicol) was the newest wonder drug of the day back home. It would be ideal for this soldier whose infection was feared to be resistant to the penicillin and streptomycin we had given him. The medic at my side questioned me about the new drug, mainly how to spell it. Actually I didn't expect the latest in medicine in a war zone. We were doing fine with a decades-old x-ray tube and other outdated equipment and medicines. I was shocked twenty-four hours later when a box of vials of Chloromycetin arrived. The medic had passed my remark up his chain of command, and Spurgeon Green had made it happen. Possibly he got it from the 93rd or the 24th Evac, but I chose to believe it had been flown out from Oakland following a trans-Pacific telephone call.

...

On December 4 I ran into LTC Katoe again and was delighted he remembered our previous conversation. He assured me I would be contacted soon by one of his medical officers. Little did I know then that I would be contacting 18th Surg personnel myself.

Ten days previously I had treated a young GI with a fractured rib on the left side of his chest. I thought about sending him to the 93rd for observation, but since his chest x-ray indicated the associated lung remained inflated, I decided to keep him in our surgical ward. He had some mild pain when taking deep breaths, but in general he was comfortable on very little pain medicine. I was confident he could be returned to duty within a few weeks. After a week he developed a low-grade fever and his urinalysis confirmed the presence of a urinary infection. It seemed to be a minor set-back, but actually it was a godsend. It kept me from discharging him too soon. Since a kidney was located immediately beneath the fractured rib, I again considered evacuating him to Long Binh. Complications of a bruised kidney could become a real problem overnight. I ended up rejecting the idea, and started him on antibiotics, planning to keep him if his fever could be controlled.

On December 5, during late-afternoon rounds, I found him strikingly pale with a blood pressure of only eighty. He said had eaten hardly anything for breakfast and had felt bad since then. His belly was slightly swollen and tender, and his spleen was huge, several times the normal size. His blood count revealed a very low hemoglobin, confirming that the rib fracture had nicked his spleen and that blood had been oozing inside the spleen for ten days. Focused on his urinary infection, I didn't recall examining his belly for several days. He was in shock and needed immediate surgery to save his life. I sent word to the 18th Surg that we were on the way.

At the 18th Surg he was given two bags of blood in addition to the two we had already given him. I waited nervously while two medical officers examined him, now ashen and very quiet. He seemed more sleepy than alarmed. One doctor was red-headed and freckle-faced and the other, I assumed to be an anesthesiologist, was tall and thin. They wasted no time, but they methodically examined the kid from stem to stern, repeating everything I'd done an hour ago. I couldn't help glancing at my watch.

It had been five months since I'd been in an air-conditioned OR. Since my body had become accustomed to temperatures ranging from the high seventies to over a hundred, it seemed even cold. The lighting was hi-tech and all instruments were brand new, even the disposable paper scrub gowns and fancy operating tables. I was in a real OR for the first time since coming to Vietnam.

Performing a splenectomy in such desperate circumstances was beyond my level of training. At Duke I had only scrubbed on a couple, but never as first assistant. The surgeon—the guy with red hair, in his early thirties—nodded curtly when I asked if I could assist him. He didn't even bother to look at me.

Deftly he opened the abdomen through a mid-line incision, hardly pausing as we entered the peritoneal cavity. He dipped into the pool of blood and began working one hand over the surface of the perfectly huge spleen, which was black, tense with old blood, his fingers advancing blindly toward its hilum. In seconds he muttered, "Got it." The nurse popped a second suction tip into his other hand and he began to help me clear away the blood still obscuring his vision deep in the narrow exposure. Finally he readjusted the overhead light to examine the splenic artery and vein he had trapped between his thumb and index finger. With no words between us, we doubly ligated and transected both vessels.

The spleen approached the size of a soccer ball as the surgeon placed it into the stainless steel basin presented by the circulating nurse, a guy of about twenty. We had been operating hardly six or seven minutes, but our major goal had been accomplished. Only then did the surgeon address me.

"Now—exactly how did all this happen?" he asked, as he began to search for signs of injury to other abdominal organs.

I was apologetic as I summarized pertinent details of the past ten days. "I wish I had sent him to the 93rd Evac the day I first saw him. I nearly cost him his life."

In silence the surgeon stripped the small intestine methodically, advancing ten-inch segment by ten-inch segment through his index and long fingers held parallel to each other. Midway through the jejunum he said, "Don't beat yourself up, Doctor. Older and wiser guys than you have missed a subcapsular splenic dissection. They're impossible to spot in the early stages. Trust me, you could have done a lot worse." Then he explored the colon hand over hand all the way to the upper segment of the rectum. After inspecting the liver and pancreas he announced, "I believe we're done. This guy's going to be fine."

He ripped off his gloves and allowed me to close the wound, reminding me to suture only the fascia, leaving skin and subcutaneous layer open, standard procedure in Vietnam to minimize the risk of infection. The superficial layers would be closed in Japan after five days.

Without another word, he left the room. I was inspired. I had been in the presence of a master surgeon. He had wasted neither word nor movement. He was slick. I made it my business not to mar his operation as I closed the abdomen and dressed the wound.

As a guy rolled the patient off to the recovery room—the 18th Surg had an all male nursing staff—I heard the sounds of chopper rotors descending.

...

After a coke and some saltine crackers, I was invited by the red-headed surgeon to help out with another case he would be starting soon. The Dust Off chopper had brought multiple casualties. There was no predicting where this would end. I was on the way to insinuating myself onto the staff of the 18th Surg. B-Med had turned out to be more challenging and satisfying than I had imagined it would be, but I yearned to work in a full-fledged hospital.

In the middle of the next case, a neck exploration for bleeding, we heard the unmistakable sounds of mortar rounds exploding outside. Repeatedly fragments crashed against the fortified wall behind the anesthetist but to no untoward effect. I glanced at the ceiling, knowing it was the OR's only vulnerability. Nobody said a word. The operation moved forward as though we were surrounded by nothing but peace.

The attack was short, but a series of additional in-coming rounds came hardly twenty minutes later, but no more fragments struck our walls. It was strange. Charlie's standard procedure was to fire a few rounds then move on to safety. But I made myself refuse to think about what was going on out there.

After the neck exploration—only venous bleeding had been encountered, both carotid arteries intact—I scrubbed in on a complex abdominal exploration. Fragments had disrupted bowel in several places, and there was also bleeding from the right lobe of the liver. It went on for hours. The primary surgeon was even more laconic than the red-headed guy. He had the circulating nurse mop sweat from his brow repeatedly.

It was well past midnight when I asked a nurse to call B-Med for Sergeant Carr to pick me up. I was starving. Except for the saltines, I'd eaten nothing since noon chow. I was beginning to feel some fatigue too, but I was a very happy, and even more hopeful of latching on at the 18th Surg.

...

I anticipated the blast of warm night air as I stepped outside the air-conditioned OR, but not the intense darkness. I couldn't see the hand in front of my face. Of course there were no lights. Not after the mortar attacks. Clouds dominated the sky, with no sign of the moon.

Rather than wait a few minutes for my eyes to adjust, I started walking like I had some idea where I was going. Finally I hesitated and tried to reconstruct my path of entry hours ago.

Suddenly I stepped off terra firma and fell, straight down, tumbling, landing on my back and a shoulder with an aching thud. Quickly I scrambled to my feet and stumbled into a damp wall, the smell of fresh earth engulfing me. I turned in panic and bumped into another wall. I was at the bottom of a very deep hole.

My eyes now fully adjusted, I looked up and could make out a crease between the clouds, even a single star. I chanced a few steps in another direction, slowly gaining a sense of the dimensions of the trap I was in. It was rectangular shaped. My mind finally engaging, I remembered the excavations I'd seen days ago. For all I knew this was the first day the 18th Surg had been operational. At least one OR building had full power and running water, and a recovery room, but construction was not yet complete. What had I fallen into, anyway? A giant latrine? A garbage pit? I was less confused, but claustrophobia began to set in. I was desperate to get out of the hole.

Pulling myself to the ledge was no option. The hole was too deep, perhaps eight feet. I estimated it was ten feet long and three feet wide.

I backed into one wall, thinking I might be able to wedge myself between the walls and walk up the one in front of me. It didn't work. The hole was too wide.

There was no way to get out without help.

For a while I only listened, hoping. There was nothing, only the hum of a generator in the distance against the natural calls and retorts of the night, nothing resembling anything human. I had to consider calling for help. The guys in the OR wouldn't be able to hear me, but surely somebody would. But it was over an hour past midnight. Maybe there would be traffic between the OR and the recovery room building some fifty feet away.

We were on the perimeter, for Pete's sake! *Charlie* could be lurking! It was unlikely but possible. The VC with mortar tubes could have been miles away when they fired at us hours ago. Almost certainly they moved away when their ammo was expended. But what if they'd come closer, and were nearby?

"Help," I called out with some hesitation. I repeated it several times, each time a little louder. But I was self conscious about screaming. Sounding desperate would put me in the middle of a comical scene. I had no wish to be part of a joke, but my desperation was mounting with each passing minute. I called out a few more times, then stopped, fully understanding I would not be rescued anytime soon.

As I sat down to think, a GI with a New Jersey accent spoke to me from the ledge. He had a rifle and a steel pot helmet, which he wasn't wearing. "What are you doing down there, pal?" he said, with the hint of a snicker.

"I'm not exactly happy, if that's what you mean, soldier," I snapped, beginning to feel heat gather in my face.

I never understood exactly who it was who got me out. Maybe he was a sentry. Guards were put out at night at B-Med, but we were infantry. Had Brigade sent out a detail to protect the 18th Surg? I was determined to ask no questions, and he had the grace not to interrogate me further. No doubt there would have been some serious ribbing had he not suspected me of being an officer. My rescuer dropped his helmet and lowered the stock of this M-16 to me. Then he and a buddy pulled me out. In the dark I could make out neither guy's name tape or insignia of rank.

"Are you okay?" the second GI asked.

"I'm fine." I fall into garbage pits every night, I considered saying.

"We can get one of the docs to check you out, or take an x-ray."

"Thanks. Not necessary." I could have sworn the guy with the rifle was grinning.

...

It was almost 0200 when Carr got me back to B-Med. I was starving. Carr agreed to wake up the mess sergeant, but it was clear he had reservations about it. Where was this coming from? Hell, all I wanted was a hamburger, or a ham sandwich. I could fix it myself. That, plus maybe a dish of ice cream.

The mess sergeant was one of the oldest man at B-Med, at least forty. He was big and wide and had thinning hair. He had rarely said a word in my presence, but Green said he was very efficient, running a tight ship in the kitchen.

"You sure you're up to this, Captain?" he asked, his eyes twinkling.

What was he talking about? I was really hungry. "I'm sorry, Sergeant, about waking you up in the middle of the night just for a sandwich. If we had an all-night McDonald's around here, it wouldn't be necessary."

He didn't acknowledge my attempt at humor, but began cursing under his breath as he fiddled with the padlock. That surprised me. Was he really pissed, and had the temerity to let me know it? Finally, though, it became clear he was simply having trouble with the key. "Gotta do something about this fricking lock," he grumbled without looking up.

Finally he shoved the screen door open and felt along the inside wall for a light switch. I was in no way prepared for what happened next.

As the mess hall lit up in dazzling brightness, the sights and sounds of heavy dark images seemed to fall from the rafters, flying in every direction, thudding to countertops and tables, then bouncing up and down and scattering in confusion. There were dozens of them—huge, gray, fierce creatures, each brimming with frenetic energy. A chair tipped backward across the room and clattered to the floor.

Then there was silence. Where did they go? Every cabinet, refrigerator, and table was uncluttered and pristine, exactly as it had been left following the evening clean-up. The silence was broken by the sound of a single salt-shaker rolling across a table in the middle of the room, finally tumbling to the floor.

"We share this place with the rats," the mess sergeant quipped with a straight face. "At night they seem to own the place."

I was no longer hungry.

12.
A TAR HEEL TANK

December 21st started as a quiet day and stayed that way for a long time. At mid-afternoon Major Luce and I got out for a set of tennis. I was down a few games when, at a few minutes past 1500, the ground shook, followed by a thundering sound. Luce was serving from the north end of the court, and was first to see the huge black cloud rising above the trees in the southeast, maybe a mile away. Another explosion followed, then another and another.

We were under attack! But how could it be? In broad daylight? We had way too much fire power for the VC to dare attack our base camp in daytime.

We hit the road running, heading east, Luce for the chopper pad and me for B-Med. Halfway, we were met by Sergeant Carr in a B-Med jeep. He informed us the explosions were coming from the ammunition dump off Thunder Road, at the south end of the base camp. Other vehicles were headed that way.

"Charlie?" I asked him. "Inside the perimeter?"

"Don't know, sir. There are casualties, though. They need a doctor out on the highway. A GI is in a bunker down the road, at the point of attack. They say he's in a bad way. No way to get an ambulance down there."

At the hooch I threw on fatigues and boots, scooped up a flack jacket and steel helmet, and raced back to the jeep.

All traffic on Highway 13 was stopped at some thousand meters from the smoke still rising against the clear blue sky. MPs at the barricade recognized our jeep and waved us through. After two hundred meters or so we were stopped by Major Williams, Brigade's S-4, the logistics officer. I'd met him at Colonel Blazey's villa. His jeep idled at the side of the road, the radio squeaking and squawking. He threw up his hands for us to stop.

"Hold on, Doc. You don't want to go down there."

I said nothing, only stared at the smoke in the distance. It began to drift northward. There was a lull in the explosions, but suddenly the rat-tat-tat of automatic weapons fire broke out.

"Flying shrapnel and live rounds," Major Williams explained. "They're everywhere."

"But what's going on?" I asked.

"The ammunition resupply pad is on fire. Thousands of artillery rounds, small arms ammo too. Lots of heat. Chain reaction. Shrapnel's everywhere. There's nothing you can do. Damn little anybody can do."

"VC?"

"Don't know. No combatants sighted. Not yet, anyway."

"Sabotage?"

'That's a good bet, Doc."

Another jeep pulled up from the south. An MP, a first lieutenant, got out and saluted, then addressed me. "A GI's holed up in a bunker down there," he said. "They say he's hurt bad."

"But isn't a medical officer already down there?" Major Williams interrupted him. "A medic too?"

For the first time I could make out flickers of flames in the grass to the left of the road some hundred meters down. A gentle breeze gave them new life, stirring up diffuse white smoke, now swirling and working its way toward us.

The lieutenant explained to Major Williams that the doctor he'd mentioned was a battalion surgeon. He and a medic were farther down, well beyond the smoke. They were from the 1/16. The GI he had referred to was in a bunker much closer, no more than five or six hundred meters away, in the second of a series of three bunkers to the right of the road. He sounded quite sure of it.

"Roger." Major Williams said, squinting into the sun.

I sent Carr back to B-Med with instructions to let the others know where I was, that I would be back as soon as I'd checked out the guy in the bunker. Callanan would be coming soon if he weren't already there. Then I hopped in the MP's jeep and away we went.

For fifty meters only two, maybe three urgent, whispering sounds crossed in front of us, well down the road, then shrapnel raining into the trees to our right. It dawned on me that flying shrapnel would be heard but not seen unless impacting something. I concluded that the shrapnel I heard had already passed by, that the fragments I had to worry about I would neither see nor hear.

Sh-o-o! Sh-o-o! Sh-o-o!

The number of whispering sounds picked up, a few seeming closer. In an open jeep we were exposed. Bouncing along at a high rate of speed, we were headed in the wrong direction, straight toward the conflagration with virtually no protection.

The MP swerved behind a disabled vehicle and skidded to a stop. It was deuce-and-a-half truck, now abandoned. It straddled the road at an odd angle. We scrambled out of the jeep to take cover behind it. I took a knee behind a rear wheel, the lieutenant to my left. Suddenly a piece of shrapnel shattered the windshield ahead, sending glass crashing into the truck bed. Fine shards ricocheted off my helmet. I moved behind the lieutenant and peeped down the middle of the road. He tugged at my arm, pulling me back.

"Hey, Doc. You don't need to see that. There's nothing you can do."

When I saw the body I almost threw up. A little girl, nine or ten, was wedged beneath the left front wheel. Dead. Her black hair was disheveled and filthy with fine red dirt. There was no sign of blood, but her abdomen and pelvis were trapped beneath the huge wheel. I took a step forward, then thought better of it. I had seen all I needed to see.

I looked away, gasping for air, waiting for the nausea to pass. She had panicked and ran into the path of the truck.

"Look, Doc, we gotta get back. I thought the worst of this was over, but it's getting worse."

"What about the guy in the bunker?'

"He may be like that kid by now. I got the call twenty minutes ago. A PFC was on the horn, hysterical. Who knows what's really down there? What are you gonna do, anyway? You don't even have a first aid kit."

I wasn't excited about moving forward either, but what if . . . "How far away are we?"

"Five hundred meters, maybe less. The bunkers are about seventy, eighty meters apart, on the right side. They were just constructed in the spring. Don't go, sir. It's not worth it."

I did not reply.

"You can't go, Doc," he said firmly. "All we can do now is wait. When this shit clears up some, I'm going back to the control point, and you're coming with me."

He meant it as an order, and in a way it was legal. I outranked him, but he was a military policeman. I was in *his* backyard.

"Sir," he began, seeming to have reconsidered his order, "going down this road any farther, at this minute, in an open jeep, is worse than dumb. It's absolutely crazy. Trust me on this. Please."

At that moment a low rumbling approached from the rear, seeming to shake the earth. It was a tank, an M-48 Patton, heading south toward the flames and smoke. It was literally tons of armor. From its radio antenna, extending eight or ten feet from behind the turret, flew a familiar tri-paneled flag—red, white, and blue, trimmed in gold. It flapped in the breeze. I blinked. Was I seeing things? Could this be an omen? It was the flag of North Carolina, my home state. The guy driving that tank was from home. He was my ticket to getting to where I needed to go. He stopped and backed into some debris to the left of the road, then jerked forward again at a different angle. He was hardly twenty feet away but beginning to pick up speed.

If I didn't go now I never would, and I would never forgive myself. All that armor, beneath that flag. It could not be ignored. Without another thought I was up and running. I would follow that Tar Heel to the gates of hell and back.

I eased in behind it and fell into a relaxed pace, edging up as close to the hull as I dared, trusting it to shield me from danger.

Almost immediately doubts crept into my thoughts. What was I doing? What if the tank picks up speed, leaving me uncovered? And how far is it going? What will I do if it turns around, and heads north again? What if it stops suddenly? The driver had no idea I was following him.

But the decision had been made, and I was determined to make it work. At the tank's present speed I knew I could last to the bunkers—I could make out the first one in the distance. If that Tar Heel driver decided to speed up, I would hang with him. I had to.

Sh-o-o! Sh-o-o!

The whispering whistles and shrieks came one or two every twenty meters, then nothing for significant stretches. Most soared over my head, and none of them seemed to strike the tank.

After what I guessed to be a hundred meters, all remained well. I was still jogging easily and felt no fatigue. How fast could a tank go, anyway? Just when the whistling overhead seemed to dissipate, a large fragment clanged off the front of the tank.

I eased away from behind the turret for a better view, positioning myself just inside the churning right track. In the excitement I had lost track of the three bunkers. The one looming ahead was some thirty yards away. Had I missed one? I saw only one in the distance. This had to be the one.

"So long, Captain Carolina," I muttered under my breath. "Thanks for the lift." I peeled off and sprinted for the bunker.

I sensed panic with the discovery that both openings, one facing the road and the other north, were too narrow for me to wiggle through. They were wide enough, just not tall enough. There would be a larger entrance on the far side, at least some kind of opening. I raced for it, skidding in the sand as I turned back south, and dove head-first through the window. My momentum carried me across the ledge of sandbags, sending me tumbling to the floor, some three feet below. Falling willy-nilly, I hit the floor head first, my steel-pot helmet clattering off the wall of sand bags ahead of me. Soon I was in the outstretched arms of two middle-aged Vietnamese women. Scrambling to my feet, I heard a thunderous thud into the earth immediately beyond the window.

It was a plate of gray steel hardly a foot beyond the sandbag I'd dived across. It was precisely on my path of entry. Fully ten-inches across, it seemed to give off heat. I stared at it and shuddered. Suddenly I could barely breathe, and my mouth was dry as bone.

If I'd been a step slower, I would be toast. My name was all over that slab of steel. It was as big as my helmet and would have knocked it off. There was no way my flack jacket could have stopped that kind of fragment.

And I was in the wrong bunker!

Five Vietnamese civilians surrounded me with wide eyes, all but one, women. There was no injured GI. Through a window I could see another bunker in the distance. That was where I needed to be.

But I was fresh out of nerve. That ten-inch fragment had made an impression on me. The MP-lieutenant had been correct. I'd met my quota for mistakes for the day and would stay in this bunker until dark if necessary. I dropped to the earthen floor, suddenly weary. I struggled with my thoughts for a while, long enough for the locals to adjust to my rude interruption.

The relief of safety lasted only so long. What was I doing here? The women began to loosen up a little, and start to speculate about me, and the papasohn seemed to be thinking about taking a nap. And here I was, hiding out with them.

Suddenly I was outside again, sprinting to the bunker in the distance. I had no conscious thoughts, and was unaware of further shrieks and whistles around me. I just ran like I'd never run before. It was liberating. I ran and ran.

I remember the approaching bunker, and rolling in the side entrance. There were people inside, GIs, many of them. I remember nothing else. It's crazy: the memory of those four Vietnamese women and the old man remain vivid to me even now. I can't explain it. I remember losing my helmet and bumping my head on the floor of the bunker, but I didn't hit it *that* hard. Or did I? I don't know. Maybe I was just overwhelmed emotionally—something akin to psychogenic shock? It's possible. What happened from the moment I reached that second bunker and later, possibly up to an hour, I had absolutely no recall. There were eye-witnesses that afternoon, as evidenced by the Appendices at the end of this book. Appendix B didn't reach me until three months later. What it describes remains confusing, approaching incredible.

LTC Tisdale read it at the little awards ceremony he set up in Di An. The overall flavor rings true to some extent, but the details seem to have involved somebody else. I simply have no recall of a lot of it. I was out of sorts for the few days after the event, and had a little trouble concentrating. It is possible I *did* have a mild concussion. Who knows?

...

Later, with the sun sinking to the treetops, I was picked up by Major Jones, executive officer of the 1/16. I'd been walking north on Thunder Road. He drove me along the edge of the ammunition dump as he inspected the state of the fire. Grass was scorched along the road and the smells of burned wood and spent nitrates were in the air. Wisps of white smoke drifted harmlessly. Gone were the sounds of exploding ammunition. Several tanks moved back and forth extinguishing what remnants of fire remained. Their tracks only rolled up more smoke. All flames had been snuffed out.

We passed a hooch that was essentially destroyed by blast concussion. One end of the roof had been blown away, the front door was gone, and window screens were twisted and torn. Other buildings nearby had fared better, some with no evidence of destruction whatever.

We passed the Tar Heel tank as we moved north. A guy in a baseball cap sat in the open turret. He waved as we passed. I watched him closely but have no memory of what he looked like, only that he didn't even seem even slightly Southern to me. It was confusing, disorienting.

We stopped several times as Major Jones spoke to various lieutenants and non-coms, then he took me all the way back to B-Med.

•••

LTC Buswell was waiting for me at the hospital. He dressed me down for not being at my post earlier in the afternoon. He went on and on about a CO never leaving his men at crucial times, even about relieving me of duty if something had gone wrong at B-Med while I was away. He backed away from further talk of disciplinary action, though, possibly remembering that Tisdale was my CO, back in Di An. Buswell was the Division Surgeon, and I was only indirectly part of his responsibility. But he was a superior officer so I had to listen. He got madder and madder as he went along, really blistering me about running off "in foolish pursuit personnel adventure" and "trying to play soldier." I said nothing at all. I was simply too exhausted to comment.

As things turned out, there *were* some casualties seen at B-Med that afternoon, and nobody died. I never heard a word about what happened to the soldier who allegedly had been holed up in the bunker on Highway 13. The medics gave me strange looks when I asked about it, like I'd lost my mind or something. I found out that one of our ambulances had picked up some men from that bunker. I never got anything more specific than that. I seriously doubted B-Med had ever been unattended. Ira Cohen was in the field substituting for a battalion surgeon on R & R, but

Joe Callanan, the ablest medical officer I knew, had to have been there.

The precise source of the fire was never determined. An official inquiry concluded it did not occur as a result of contact with Charlie. Obviously the brass had a dog in that fight. To conclude that the VC was behind our losses in munitions, property, and possibly manpower would lay the blame at the feet of the commander ordering the investigation. Calling the fire an accident, or an act of God, was a better way out.

13.
JUNGLE CAPITALISM
AND A HOLLYWOOD
CHRISTMAS

I n late November Reb Rebholtz, one of the Dust Off pilots who spent four or five nights a month with us, caught up with me after sick call one morning. He informed me he planned to take his chopper up for a test run following some mechanical adjustments. Rebholtz was a tall, blond, sun-bronzed former halfback at Miami of Ohio who was very supportive of B-Med, particularly our medical officers. Since my experience five weeks ago in a helicopter that almost fell from the sky after taking off from the 24th Evac, I'd pestered pilots about the mechanics of helicopters and the principles of flight. To my delight Reb suggested it was good time to brief me on the instruments and controls in his cockpit.

He had me take the copilot's seat, then pointed out how the "collective," the lever arising from the floor to my left, varied the pitch of the overhead rotor, facilitating lifting and lowering the aircraft. The "cyclic," the instrument in front of me, moved the chopper forward, backward, sideways, and tilted the nose upward and downward. The cyclic was key to banking and rolling actions. With the foot-pedals coordinating the tail rotor with the main rotor, flying a helicopter was a dizzying prospect, involving both hands and both feet simultaneously. I was curious about aeronautical principles all right, but I would limit my own flying to kites on windy beach.

I watched him closely as he lifted us off the chopper pad and swept north over the swimming pool, then banked sharply into a southerly route, climbing to a cruising altitude of three thousand feet. That put us safely out of range of all but the luckiest of AK-47 shots. Then he told me to engage my set of controls and "get a feel for things."

Almost immediately the ride turned shaky and bumpy. "Hey, what's going on?" I said.

"You tell me, pal. You're flying now." He was lighting up a cigarette, gazing out the left side of the cockpit. "Relax. Just feel it."

In a few minutes the flight evened out a little, and I began to see what he was talking about. After a turn or two I can't say I got a taste of the exhilaration and joy of flying, but it was a lot different from being a passenger.

After a while, we turned back north and eventually Reb directed me on a course back to B-Med. I couldn't believe this was happening. The landmarks were not always easy to identify as we turned west for our final approach, but he pointed them out with patience. As we descended toward the swimming pool he spotted Callanan and Stan Riveles sunning themselves in lounge chairs. I glanced down at the pool, but couldn't make out anybody, then quickly refocused on what I was doing. I wasn't going to land the aircraft but still—we were getting closer and closer to the ground! Just as the first pangs of panic set in, Reb took over and set us down like a giant hawk landing on aching feet.

•••

A week later Reb invited me to fly down to Bien Hoa with him. It was a clear and reasonably quiet night so he let me fly most of the way. At one point the air-traffic control officer squawked an order over the radio to change course thirty degrees to the left. I muttered an uncomfortable "roger" when Reb nudged me, reminding me the controller expected a response, then I eased into a long, slow turn. Seconds later the controller repeated his order with some urgency.

"What's eating him?" I mumbled.

"Nothing much," Reb replied, activating his controls with a chuckle, then tilting us to the left and dropping us into a roll. "He's a little concerned because you're flying us into the Bien Hoa artillery pattern."

Suddenly I had had enough of flying. That was my last escapade as an amateur helicopter pilot.

•••

Having Dust Off crews bunking at B-Med from time to time gave us access to opportunities we wouldn't ordinarily have had. One of the crew-chiefs had purchased a pet from an infantry unit in the field for a hundred bucks. He was due to rotate back to the world in a few weeks and wanted to leave it with us until then. He was dead set on taking it home with him, admitting he planned to sell it to a zoo.

It was a snake, an immature python, almost ten feet long.

It proved to be perfectly harmless, sleeping most of the time in a corner of our hooch. I can't believe now that I was able to get to sleep with a python hardly a body length away, but it was truly the most docile animal I could imagine, sleeping away most days and every night. It was fully awake only when we took turns posing for photographs with it draped around our necks and outstretched arms. No one wants to be photographed with a dangerous animal unless the danger seems to be removed. Then the photograph becomes a passion. I had heard of a python constricting a man's life away, then wedging him into its massive, double-jointed throat and swallowing him whole: clothing, shoes, and all. That is a scary thought.

Exactly how were we going to keep this snake alive? Consensus around the chow table was that pythons lived on birds, pigs, dogs, cats, and primates. Since they devoured their prey whole, digestion typically took at least a week. Rarely hungry for weeks after that, most pythons ate only once a month. For pythons held in captivity the trick was to know when to serve.

An enterprising enlisted man understood that American boys of a certain age thrive on games, the more cruel and heartless the better. Accordingly he purchased a chicken off the local economy and rigged up a coop of chicken wire. It was roughly twenty-by-four-by-three feet. After drawing up a calendar for the month of November and dividing each day in half, he sold twelve-hour chances at the jackpot for $2 each. Word spread quickly throughout the company area and beyond, and the entire calendar was subscribed within hours.

The snake and the chicken were introduced to each other, and set up as temporary housekeeping partners. The chicken did its best to ignore the danger it faced, and over time became resigned to its fate. The snake simply bided its time, sleeping up an appetite.

They lived in perfect harmony for days, then a week. A daily topic of conversation became: did the chicken make it through the night again?

Midway in week-two the snake's thoughts turned toward dinner, and by noon on Wednesday a specialist-four medic claimed the $96 prize. The remaining twenty-four bucks went to the guy who had scrounged up the chicken wire and collected the money. No doubt he, before leaving the Army to buy and sell cars, real estate, or mortgages, would learn to demand more than twenty per cent up front on a sure thing deal.

By early afternoon the chicken became a bulging mass immediately behind the snake's head. Over the next three days the lump gradually diminished in size as it progressed southward. Daily we tracked the chicken's transit, and ultimately the remains of the chicken began to appear. What shall we call it? Snake-shit? Chicken-shit? The excrement included of assorted bones, feathers, an intact beak, and one scrawny foot. The other foot was never recovered. The snake hardly moved for days. Growing into a giant python on one meal a month required a lot of rest.

The Dust Off crew-chief processed through Ton Son Nuit Air Base a few weeks later. We got word that the snake was coiled into a canvas carry-on bag. Of course the crew chief was required to open it and surrender its contents. What had be been thinking? He would have had a better chance of smuggling an AK-47 back to the world. At least a rifle could have been disassembled and packed as separate parts. In 1967 there were no x-ray machines in airports. The guy went home with a story to tell, all right, but at considerable expense. It proves once again that it's the middle man who makes the real dough.

We never heard what happened to the snake.

...

In early December I got a letter from my wife saying she was in the hospital with vaginal bleeding. We were aware of her pregnancy when I left home, but I only kidded myself thinking complications couldn't happen. It was a real blow. I needed to call home in the worst kind of way.

I had heard that selfless amateur radio operators around the world went out of their way to patch telephone calls from Vietnam to the States. Soon after dark I was in a line with enlisted men outside a tiny wooden shelter in the middle of a clearing on the eastern edge of the base camp. There were only seven or eight of us, but I found that the patching process could be lengthy. Minutes after midnight a ham operator in Australia explained that he had established a connection with a colleague somewhere in rural Georgia and who was preparing to dial the phone number I'd given them. I was tingling with excitement as I heard the first ring at 141 Mills Avenue in Spartanburg, South Carolina.

On the second ring two mortar rounds crashed into the trees some eighty yards north of us, then two more closer, in the clearing around us.

Instantly we left the impromptu radio shack, three of us, including the young sergeant who had been last in line, spreading out and running for cover.

Two days later, just after noon chow, I was summoned to the orderly room for a telephone call. Thinking it was LTC Tisdale, who had contacted me by phone once, I was shocked to be speaking to my wife! She sounded like an angel, seeming so very near. She assured me she was fine, but that she had had lost what would have been our second little girl. She went on to tell me she had been home from the hospital several days when she found herself speaking to a ham operator in the middle of the day. He explained he had lost his connection with Vietnam. She told me it was almost 5:00 a.m. in Spartanburg, that she was going to wake up the kids to talk to me. It was a wonderful moment.

Spurgeon Green had found out about my misadventure of two nights previously, and had the call initiated by guys in the B-Med radio shack. He amazed me, seeming always at his best behind the scenes. He admitted I'd embarrassed him, standing in line in the middle of the night with enlisted men. He told me I needed more dignity than that! I had thought about speaking to the guys in our radio shack but concluded I had no business making an entirely personal phone call to the other side of the world on the government's dime. The ham radio guys, on the other hand, were just there for us. They were humanitarians who got a kick out of providing a service to soldiers. They were as popular in Vietnam as the Red Cross.

•••

The following week I took a different kind of call, one patched through from the ER via the radio shack. A LRRP (pronounced "lurp," for long range reconnaissance patrol) was seeking to speak to a doctor. A recon patrol consisted of four or five men functioning under the most secret and dangerous of circumstances. I was informed that the guy I would be speaking to could be almost anywhere, within a few miles to as far away as Cambodia or Laos. LLRPs desperately guarded their whereabouts. Their survival depended on equal parts stealth, balls, and good luck.

There was intermittent static, but the communication was distinct enough. I listened to a young, steady voice in little more than a whisper, giving me the idea he was in a jungle somewhere right under Charlie's nose.

"One of my buddies has been stung by a scorpion," he whispered. "What can we do for him?"

A scorpion? To the average GI a scorpion's sting was believed to be deadly, and I knew nothing to refute that idea. In almost three months the subject had not come up. I didn't know the first thing about scorpions, certainly no idea how to treat one's sting. I must have dozed off the afternoon they were discussed at Fort Sam. Now, my incompetence was sending a shiver up my spine.

"Your buddy's been stung by a what?" I stalled, needing time to think.

"A scorpion." Then he spelled it.

"Are you certain it was a scorpion?"

"Affirmative."

I continued to rack my brain for a solution, at least some semblance of a plan. The few books we had on hand contained nothing about scorpions. I'd read them all from cover to cover.

"What's the victim's condition?"

"Pain mainly, at the moment. He was stung just twenty minutes ago."

"Where? What part of his body?"

"His elbow."

It could be worse. Certain snake bites to the face or neck could kill a man in minutes. Poison introduced into an extremity had farther to go to the brain.

"Is he conscious? Can he talk to you?"

"Affirmative. He's talking like crazy, out of his head. Hysterical. Says he's gonna die."

"Can you get him to us?" One of the other docs would know something about scorpions. If not, we could call somebody at the 93rd. They might even take this guy themselves. Insist on Dust Off over flying us.

"Negative. Extracting him would blow our mission. Can't do it. No way."

"What have you got in your first aid kit?"

"Bandages and morphine. That's about it."

Morphine was a staple in Vietnam. It was used for everything from gunshot wounds to snake bites. If nothing else, it allowed a soldier to die in relative comfort.

"Morphine can help." I was only guessing. "It will calm him down. Keep him quiet."

"Roger that, Doc."

I continued to scroll frantically through my memory, but kept coming up empty. There had to be something more specific to do.

"Listen, soldier," I began, thoughts finally falling into place. "Your buddy may get very sick for a while, a few hours, even a few days, but he will recover. I repeat: he will not die. I am certain of that. Tell him that. It's important. Whatever you've heard about scorpion stings is not true. Do you understand?" Positive thinking had a role in just about everything. I believed that, anyway. It just might be the difference.

"Roger, Doc."

Then he was gone. I never heard another word from him.

I hardly slept that night. I had rolled the dice with a soldier's life, purely because I was ignorant. I'd even lied to him. He could be dead by morning.

It haunted me for days, then weeks. That none of the other medical officers knew anything definitive about scorpion stings didn't help much. It would be months before I found that less than 2% of healthy adult males died from single scorpion stings. Hundreds of scorpion species existed, but only a handful were deadly, even in Southeast Asia. The recommended treatment was supportive—pain control, sedation, bed rest.

Sometimes a doctor needs a little luck.

...

The day before Christmas Eve was like any other—hot, bright, muggy. Nothing even resembling a fir tree or a holly bush grew in Southeast Asia. One might imagine Santa's sleigh and flying reindeer, but only back in the world, where the hopes of children are paramount. Vietnam was about stark, cold realism.

But we still had expectations. Santa Claus might not be coming, but Bob Hope was. And he was bringing a planeload of Hollywood honeys with him! They would arrive tonight, and put on a show for us tomorrow. I couldn't imagine gathering thousands of soldiers in broad daylight. It was based on Charlie having no concept of what was coming. The VC could not pass up so many distracted Americans in one place at one time. Well placed mortar fire could wreak havoc.

But who was I to question bringing Hollywood to Lai Khe? Hope and his group were coming, and they were being welcomed by the highest of the brass. Hope and company would face the same risk we did every day. But still, how could I question the magic of Christmas? The VC might just take the day off!

At mid-morning the group visited our inpatient ward at B-Med. You can't believe the looks on those guys' faces as Hope, Raquel Welch, Barbara McNair, and others swarmed around their beds. Hope was in top form, eyes twinkling from a perfectly straight face, brazen one-liners rolling off his tongue.

Miss Welsh, far and away the supreme American sex symbol of the day, had awoken with diarrhea. We gave her medicine, but she couldn't have been comfortable. Nevertheless, she smiled her way through her adversity. She was perfectly stunning, far more beautiful in person than in her photographs and movies. For a nineteen-year-old GI, a kiss on the cheek from Raquel Welch could cure malaria and typhoid fever simultaneously, plus anything else that bothered him. I watched them take her in, exuding pure joy and wonder. Tanned, smiling, in a blue-and-white miniskirt, she reeked of intelligence too. Raquel Welch with brains? It was unimaginable.

Captain Spurgeon Green (center) with singer/dancer Elaine Dunn (black dress) and singer/actress Barbara McNair. Two dazzling attractions with Bob Hope's visit to Lai Khe. Christmas 1967.

The man at her side could have been a body guard, but he didn't seem quite the type. He was hesitant, plain-looking, almost meek, and not quite as tall as Raquel. On his tan and turquoise tie he wore bits of the scrambled egg he'd had for breakfast. It was the only necktie I ever saw Vietnam. I was informed later that he was her husband. Maybe opposites really do attract.

Barbara McNair, the beautiful singer and movie star, was equally engaging, but in a different way. She seemed a little older than Raquel, and maybe a touch more real. But the real sweetheart was Madeline Har tog-Bel, the 21-year-old raven-haired Peruvian beauty who was the reigning Miss World. Her rudimentary English was not at all limiting. Her playful grins and the sidelong glances insinuated her into the hearts of everyone. Her unaffected charm placed her in every GI's dream of the perfect girl next door.

While Raquel may have been the most popular with the troops, Hope himself was a close second. His commitment and energy were hard to miss. Phil Crosby, one of Bing's twin sons, a former Army medic, was unpretentious and humble, and Les Brown, the band leader, was equally engaging. Although Hope cracked risqué jokes about hot women in Hollywood, the stars he brought with him oozed femininity at its best and purist. They teased and bantered but always in good fun.

Hope ran the operation with an iron hand. He never engaged any of his cast in small talk, rarely casting a glance their way. Though polite and engaging with bird colonels and general officers, he clearly preferred the enlisted men, repeatedly making gentle eye contact with them as he popped

Bashful, awe-struck author with Madeline Hartog-Bel, from Puru, the 1967 "Miss World," at Christmas, 1967.

off jokes about their home towns and favorite football teams, all the while diminishing himself.

Hope said no to the Army's offer of engineering support for his show. He even brought his own sound crew. Stationed back stage among them at the early afternoon performance, I had an insider's view of all that happened.

Hope's opening line was, "Here we are in Lai Khe, and I no like-ay." A barrage of jokes followed, rapid-fire, spiced with sexual overtones or poking fun at the anti-war crowd back home. Many were lame or corny, but the GIs laughed anyway. Hope understood they wanted to laugh, actually *needed* to laugh.

The stage was an inverted T-shaped affair, with a long runway projecting into the thousands gathered on a hillside in fresh fatigues and polished boots. Hope fell into a fast-paced monologue as he strolled back and fourth across the stage immediately in front of the curtained backdrop. His only prop was a golf club, a driver, which he sometimes brandished like a sword.

Twenty minutes into the show, the sound system went dead!

At first Hope ad-libbed a joke or two about incompetence, one, about how a green second lieutenant could screw up the simplest military operation. I could imagine his cynical grin as he strolled out the vertical boardwalk toward the troops. The farther he went the less we could hear, the ever-present prompter-cards flashing him the option of the intended script as he neared the end of the runway. Not once did he lose his swagger, alternating waggling his golf club with propping it on his shoulder like a rifle, still seeking to make eye-contact with guys in the front rows and immediately beyond. No one else could hear him.

When he reached the end of the boardwalk, he posed with a hand on his hips, another extended in front of him, tilting the head of the driver at his feet. Then he turned, and began to retreat, facing us backstage, now suddenly dark and sinister, his voice vicious and mean. He hurled malignant epithets and threats at the sound crew who were scrambling mightily with a maze of wiring, fuse boxes, and monitoring devices. Just as Hope seemed to exhaust his prodigious store of four-letter words and blasphemies, he turned again and faced the crowd with calm serenity.

At that very instant the sound system was restored!

I had no doubt that the only look the GIs saw was impishly angelic. They went wild, tossing their headgear into the air. They seemed to think the snafu was part of the act, and I wasn't so sure it wasn't myself. In any case, it was clear we were being treated by one of the truly great showmen on the planet.

After the show I asked Hope in his dressing room if he would consider visiting the guys at B-Med one more time. He was obviously exhausted, but seemed to take energy from my request. Once again an enthusiastic smile flooded his face. But Colonel Krause, Division's chief-of-staff, butted in crisply, announcing that the flight schedule was tight, that it must be adhered to for tactical reasons. General Hay backed him up. I backed down, of course, and Hope seemed crestfallen.

Bob Hope was the real deal. He was a generous patriot. That afternoon he brought joy to thousands of American boys who had been forced into manhood ahead of their time. It was a joy to witness. Today those guys revere his memory.

•••

Colonel Blazey threw an informal dinner at his villa the night of Christmas Eve. Remembering the piano in his living room, I hoped a few Christmas carols might be on the menu. But it was not to be. None of his staff could play, and neither could I. Some weeks later, though, when the 11th Armored Cavalry Regiment moved into the area, its commander,

Colonel George S. Patton, IV, commandeered that piano. I can imagine it swinging from a giant Chinook helicopter ascending over the rubber trees. Patton was rumored to be the same kind of heroic, larger-than-life figure as his World War II father. If he didn't play that piano himself, he was quick to find someone who could. Did the Cavalry really trump the Infantry and Medical Corps for musicians?

The Army outdid itself to set a festive, Yuletide tone. On Christmas Day the entire Division, including thousands in the bush, was served a Christmas dinner rivaling the one we'd had on Thanksgiving Day. We enjoyed turkey and all the trimmings, including shrimp cocktail, cranberry sauce, cornbread dressing, mashed potatoes, glazed sweet potatoes, and buttered mixed vegetables. Then there was fruit cake, mincemeat pie, pumpkin pie with real whipped cream, and assorted fresh fruit and candy.

Christmas goodies came from all over the United States: decorative holiday cards and small gifts such as wash cloths, combs, soap, cigarettes, even a box of chocolate chip cookies that somehow seemed fresh. They were baked by a dear lady from Indiana. Notwithstanding the news I'd gleaned from *Time* and *Newsweek*, somebody back home cared about us.

For me, though, what truly made my Christmas came from home in the form of a tin of beaten biscuits, an old Virginia specialty championed by my wife's grandmother. I'd witnessed the process once, beating the dough until it blistered in an antique machine that had been in my wife's family for generations. The result was crisp and delicate and light. At family dinners I'd been scolded for helping myself to more than one or two, but this Christmas I ate the entire tin of them in a single afternoon. Sharing them was out of the question.

The greatest expression of love that Christmas came in the form of audio-tapes made by my children. They sounded nothing like the little characters I'd left just months ago, particularly the five-year-old who chattered on and on like he was on TV. It was sometimes difficult to make out exactly what he was saying, but it didn't matter. The weather and the circumstances were unlike any Christmas I'd ever experienced, but it was still Christmas. There is no such thing as a so-so Christmas. That night I sent up a prayer for those thousands of American soldiers out in the boondocks, trusting God to show up for them too, and serve them the same kind of joy I felt.

14.
THE MEDICAL CIVIL ACTION PROGRAM

Winning the Hearts and Minds

In order to encourage local civilians to resist VC overtures the Army developed the Medical Civil Action Program, establishing "winning the hearts and minds" of the South Vietnamese as an important strategy. How could families not be affected by seeing American doctors minister to their sick, particularly their children? Tenderly caring for a trusting toddler in the presence of its mother could be a powerful tool. Psychological warfare had many forms. Even more important, freeing such a child of illness could have a profound effect not only on mothers but entire families and communities. The VC could hardly supply the locals anything near as dramatic as the miracles of modern American medicine.

At first I was a little reluctant about being a "political missionary," but I got used to it. In many cases we actually did render service to needy people. It wasn't always about show. But good medicine required rigorous follow-up treatment, including the keeping of careful records. With a war going on around us I couldn't see that happening. But the Army didn't insist on my approval of its MedCap. My job was to see that B-Med did its part to implement it, and the brass didn't care how we went about it.

We were told that American charitable organizations supplied medicine and supplies, but most of it flowed through the supply channels of USARV on Washington's nickel. Judging from the medicine and equipment we employed, I'm confident the U. S. government spent some real money on the MedCap.

We conducted a MedCap (Medical Civil Action *Patrol*) to the village of Ben Cat twice a week, hardly fifteen minutes south on Highway 13. With the village rumored to be teeming with VC and communist sympathizers, we traveled by armed convoy: at minimum a jeep, an ambulance or two loaded with supplies, and a gun-jeep of heavily armed MPs. An M-60 machine gun was mounted on the rear platform. Typically a MedCap consisted of two doctors, a dentist, and a pair of medics, the officers with side-arms, and the medics armed with M-16s. We all wore steel-pot helmets and flack-jackets, at least in transit.

Our trip to Ben Cat on January 12 was a typical one. Rolling down Thunder Road that bright morning we enjoyed the agrarian surroundings. Local farmers worked their fields steadily with primitive gear and water buffalo. Stan Riveles, one of our dentists, a handsome New Yorker with a wry sense of humor, out of the blue made a crack about "that cute little farm girl over there getting ready to lob a hand grenade our way." Everybody laughed, but every single head swiveled to make certain he was joking.

Entering Ben Cat we crossed a temporary bridge, the old one having been destroyed the previous week. A new bridge was under construction nearby. Moving into the village on the narrow main road, one couldn't help being impressed by the industrious villagers pushing carts of produce to bustling stalls in the marketplace. Gangs of children, spotting the red crosses on our ambulances, waved and screamed as they ran behind us. They knew we carried as much candy and gum as medicine. I couldn't help wondering how many of their fathers were VC. Even the kids weren't exactly harmless. Weeks earlier I had walked through a crowd of laughing and reaching children, ages of six to ten or so, dispensing candy and bubble gum from a paper sack. When all the goodies were gone, I noticed my wrist watch was too!

As we entered the village square, we steeled ourselves for the exhibit we had been warned about. Several days earlier the VC had decapitated one of their own who had declared his allegiance to the ARVN-USARV alliance. His head was said to be fixed to a post, with a nasty inscription beneath it.

But it had been replaced by evidence of ARVN terrorism. The local commander had retaliated with a vow to display a fresh VC corpse daily. We almost ran over the body as we crossed the square. The back of his skull had been blown away by a rifle round, exposing an amorphous mass of brain tissue. Nineteen thousand flies buzzed in and around the wound, inspiring equal measures of disgust and pity, along with a deep sense of foreboding.

My distress intensified when I noticed that the sign identifying the local dispensary where we were to hold our clinic had been taken down. The entire compound was surrounded by a new eight-foot chain-link fence topped with barbed wire. One of our hosts, a local practical nurse, explained the sign had been riddled with bullets, that a new one was in the works. Slowly we began to unpack our gear as the MPs scanned the area for prime observation sites and fields of fire, a fairly simple task once they confirmed there were no signs of vulnerability in the fence. The only entrance was the front gate.

The fact that Sergeant Chuong was a favorite with Ben Cat's nurses was crucial to our success. He was an ARVN on loan to B-Med as our primary interpreter. His family, including two toddlers, both girls, lived in Lai Khe. Chuong was always in uniform, but he never carried a weapon. A twenty-five-year-old graduate of a Saigon equivalent of high school, he had an excellent grasp of common illnesses and how to elicit pertinent information from patients and mothers. He interviewed them before I saw them, then concisely presented the positives and negatives of their medical histories, leaving me to focus on follow-up questions before examining them. Chuong was an invaluable assistant.

He was also a good intelligence man. More than once he had advised against going to Ben Cat on certain days, and we always cancelled without question. Instinctively he formulated bits of gossip into real meaning. Being aggressive observers was key for South Vietnamese nationals trying to stay alive. Chuong faced more danger than any of us. Rumors were the VC placed bounties on the heads of all Vietnamese assisting Americans. Losing him would be a crippling blow to B-Med.

My first patient was a 40-year-old woman Joe Callanan had seen previously with a nine-month history of coughing up sputum that was sometimes tinged with blood. I read his note on the page she handed me. Our records were simple but effective, proving that my original skepticism was unwarranted. Every new patient was asked to write their name and age at the top of a fresh sheet of paper when we saw them initially, and we made appropriate adjustments as we went along.

With a presumptive diagnosis of pneumonia, Callanan had started her on antibiotics and arranged for her to have a chest x-ray at B-Med. Unfortunately I was the bearer of bad news about that x-ray. She had a nasty-looking mass in the hilum of her left lung which was almost certainly cancer. I told her the x-ray had revealed a curious lesion in addition to her pneumonia. It would require additional x-rays in the coming weeks to determine exactly what it was and how it should be treated. Obviously, that was an overly optimistic view of her condition, but I would go out of my way to avoid admitting impossible circumstances when it would hinder hope. The truth would come out soon enough. What purpose did snuffing out one's hope serve? I gave her a smile and a hug and another bottle of tetracycline along with a slip of paper requesting another chest x-ray at B-Med in a week. Her outlook was terrible. Judging from her weight and general health, I assumed she had hardly months to live. Patients with lung cancer in the U. S. who had been coughing up blood associated with such a mass on x-ray rarely benefitted from surgery, which we were in no position to offer anyway. Operations only increased most lung cancer patients' suffering.

I understood that some MedCap clinics in Vietnam were different from ours in that they were held monthly. Doctors sometimes saw a hundred patients in an afternoon, most of them not even sick, only curious about what American doctors were like. Our doctors rarely saw more than a dozen patients a day because our patients understood we were only there to help individuals with illness. We did give candy to every kid we saw, though.

We claimed no ownership of our system because it had been established through the ingenuity and foresight of the doctors preceding us. We only strove to maintain what they had started, make it even better when we could.

My second patient was a filthy sixty-year-old woman I had seen previously with emphysema and bronchitis. She had a dry, hacking cough and the typical physical findings of chronic lung disease. Despite the heat she wore three layers of clothing, which she shed layer by layer with some ceremony. Like most Vietnamese women, she exhibited little reluctance to exposing her body, a good thing since our examination room and waiting room were one and the same. The waiting rooms and exam rooms at the old French hospital in Lai Khe were more in tune with Western preferences. This woman had been on a standard chronic lung regimen of expectorants and intermittent corticosteroids for a long time, and came in regularly to be examined and have her medications renewed as necessary. I'd seen a fair amount of chronic lung disease over the preceding months, particularly in women, and wondered if the dustiness of the dry season might not be responsible for it. Few of the Vietnamese I saw had picked up the cigarette habit.

Next I saw a twenty-one-year-old ARVN soldier whose face was deformed by an old shrapnel injury. His left zygomatic arch was essentially missing. I reassured him that his wound had healed nicely, and that his deformity would not worsen over time. But I had to admit we couldn't help him. He'd been fortunate that his problem was only cosmetic. He could easily have died from a compound brain injury. Had he been an American soldier he would have qualified for a dramatic facial reconstruction at Brook Army Hospital in San Antonio where the maxillofacial surgeons had international reputations. Almost daily I saw women and children with pronounced limps and various deformities, usually amputations, all direct consequences of war thrust upon non-combatants.

Then I saw a courtly sixty-one-year-old man with a short, neatly-trimmed white beard. He had chronic emphysema. He seemed a classic example of oriental paternalism. The Vietnamese were quite solicitous of their elders, presumably from the Confucianism rooted in their Chinese heritage. Chinese had lived in Vietnam for centuries, and if this old gentleman was not a direct descendent, he at least was influenced by the culture. Although I didn't say so, I was eager to demonstrate to him that even though I knew little about Confucianism, I had been influenced by Moses and my mother to honor my elders.

A number of infants and toddlers came for examination. I relished holding them in my arms, showing off my magic trick of pulling candy from their ears, and counting their ribs, almost always finding ticklish spots. I was fascinated by the kids just learning to talk, how they looked at me as I spoke. My words were dramatically different from what they heard at home.

I was saddened to examine a screaming eighteen-month-old boy who had been brought in by a teenaged neighbor. The child's mom had a job that kept her from accompanying him. I only hoped she was not a prostitute, a thought I quickly put out of my head. I made it a point not to ask about the nature of her employment.

The child was dehydrated and burning up with fever. Listening to his lungs confirmed rip-roaring pneumonia. He was in urgent need of hospitalization, which, of course, was impossible in Ben Cat. The hospitals in Saigon were full of kids like this one, like those I had visited months ago with LTC Tisdale. B-Med was no option either since our medics had no training in taking care of infants. I instructed the girl who brought him about the importance of hydrating him and giving him the antibiotic elixir I gave her. But I doubted this desperate child, with no blood relatives to care for him, would live out the week. He was yet another shattering example of the innocent victims of war.

Although a number of the children we saw were dependents of the First ARVN Division, which was based in Ben Cat, no doubt some of their fathers were VC. It took some discipline, but I refused to think about that as I examined the sick kids.

Next was a forty-six-year old woman with an upper respiratory infection accompanied by two small children with the same problem. She was probably their grandmother. I couldn't make myself ask about their mother. One's upper respiratory infection was already complicated by an ear infection. But I knew we could help them. All three would recover, and the child with the ear infection might not if we hadn't come to Ben Cat that day. Then there was an elderly gentleman with a chronic cough, night sweats, and weight loss. We initiated a skin test and arranged for him to come to B-Med in three days to have it read. He would also get a chest x-ray then, and almost certainly begin anti-tuberculosis medications. He would need close follow-up for months. My very next patient was a man of roughly the same age with chronic TB. I gave him a new supply of medicine.

Toward the end of the clinic I saw a seventeen-year-old boy with chronic epilepsy who had been seizure-free for almost a year. He had been on Dilantin and phenobarbital. His age all but ruled out a brain tumor as the basis for his epilepsy. His long-term outlook was good if he continued to take his medicine every day. An older sister had stolen his phenobarb some months earlier to sell on the black market, but it seemed we had nipped that problem in the bud. She had a new baby, and I promised her no more free medical care if she continued to steal from her brother.

Of course no doctor's afternoon clinic is complete without examining an elderly woman with a million complaints, no combination of which suggested known disease or treatable condition. This had to be true in every society. I sympathized with her and reassured her that her symptoms would not progress to serious illness. Then I loaded her up with aspirin and vitamin tablets, especially red ones and bright green ones. I'd seen some that day who, for varying reasons, would not make it to our next clinic, but I knew this faithful soul would not be among them. Driving rain and a hail of bullets would not keep her away!

My last patient was a child with pyoderma, a relatively common problem among GIs and Vietnamese civilians alike. The little girl was in agony. Her skin was red and swollen from infection around her eyes, ears, and mouth, extending to her trunk and both legs. I gave her mom a bar of American soap, a small tube of steroid ointment, and a bottle of tetracycline syrup. She would be much improved when I would see her on Saturday.

After seeing the last patient, our hosts treated us to Coca Cola in tall glasses with ice. The cola was bottled in Saigon, but there was no telling where the ice came from. Ice was a precious luxury for the Vietnamese, but they knew it filled a real need for Americans. Normally I was careful about what I ate and drank outside the base camp, but it was hot and I was really thirsty. More importantly, how could I turn down our hosts' generous hospitality? After packing up our gear and shaking hands around the room, we loaded up our vehicles for the trip back to Lai Khe.

The gentle breeze felt good as we headed up Thunder Road. The Coca Cola had hit the spot, influencing me to have a little fun with Chuong. He sat immediately behind the jeep driver.

"What do you think about dropping by the orphanage on the way home?" It was near the French hospital in Lai Khe. Brigade intelligence had warned us to avoid it this week.

Chuong looked away, then mumbled something that sounded like, "not a good idea."

I turned to face him. "Why not? We missed them last week. Remember?"

"Many VCs in houses behind orphanage," he said finally. "More than last week. Today not good time to go."

Somehow I kept a straight face. "But if I go, will you go with me?"

He mumbled something unintelligible so I repeated the question.

"Yes sir," he replied with clear reluctance.

I laughed as I reached for him and slapped his knee. "I wouldn't go to that place today for a million dollars and a truckload of ice cream."

Soon all four of us were laughing.

We stopped briefly to photograph some children skinny-dipping in a swimming hole just outside Lai Khe, then pushed on. I knew everyone was relieved to get back home without incident. Nobody said it aloud, though.

Within days the Medical Civil Action Program died a quick death, at least for a while. A major enemy offensive was in the works. Even the brass were convinced that psychological warfare wasn't worth the risk of American life.

15.
TET-1: THUNDER 4

The Beginning of the End

As 1967 drew to a close the general feeling among Americans under arms in Vietnam was that the VC and NVA regulars were wearing down, that a turning point in the war was at hand. Hope and anticipation was in the air with the approach of Têt Nguyên Đán, or simply "Tet." The celebration of the lunar New Year was Vietnam's most important holiday. 1968 had been designated the "Year of the Monkey." January 30 through February 5 would be a time for giving thanks and worshiping heaven, nature, and one's ancestors. Families decorated their homes with flowers, prepared holiday food, and participated in ancient customs.

American forces prepared for a surge in enemy activity with the coming of Tet. A brief truce had been vaguely agreed upon, but whether it would last thirty-six hours or four days remained unclear. Recent history and current intelligence suggested that any truce would be limited at best. The 1st Infantry Division, out of respect for the national celebration, was committed to no offensive activities for the duration of the holidays. It went on "gray alert" early in the second week of January, with orders to fire only if fired upon after January 29.

Lai Khe was under mortar attack for the first time in weeks on January 14. There were no deaths, but the assault served as a wake-up call. Direct hits split tree trucks and destroyed a latrine, and fragments damaged vehicles and caused minor casualties.

Six days later, at dusk, I was lifting weights with a few enlisted men in B-Med's open-air gym behind the mess hall when mortar rounds began to land in the vicinity of the barracks for enlisted personnel, two exploding within one hundred feet. As we raced for the bunkers, whistling shrapnel ripped into the walls of the mess hall and the sandbags fortifying the rear of the radio shack, all before the siren sounded "red alert."

As I entered the bunker, a mortar round crashed into the roof of the hooch next door, sending fragments and debris in every direction. Within seconds the bunker telephone sounded, with a message to come to the hospital ASAP. An ambulance had been dispatched for casualties east of the landing strip.

In helmet and flack jacket, carrying an M-16, I worked my way on foot through the growing darkness to the hospital. Red-alert prohibited flashlights, but I was confident I could get to the hospital with my eyes closed. Another shriek overhead preceded an explosion behind me, soon engulfing me with the smell of cordite.

In five minutes the shelling stopped. Over sixty incoming rounds—eight or ten in the B-Med area—yielded no deaths or life-threatening injuries. We'd been lucky. The roof next door had taken a direct hit, splattering cots and personal gear with dust and debris. Elsewhere in the compound, door and window screens were shredded, three ambulance tires flattened, and a jeep lost a windshield and suffered cosmetic damage. Again, no medics or medical personnel were injured. The next morning I found a splintered tree trunk near the motor pool, giving me an idea of what that kind of force could do to a man's head, steel helmet or no steel helmet.

Another mortar attack came on the night of January 25. Lai Khe had not faced such destruction for months, dating to before my arrival. This time there were deaths, and serious casualties were evacuated to the rear by Dust-Off choppers. We couldn't escape thinking that if Charlie could create such havoc in the Division's command post, we had real reason to worry.

But I have no details to report about the January 25 attack. I missed it altogether! That morning I received an order to send Captain (Pete) Kelly, a medical officer recently arriving at B-Med, to the field as a temporary replacement for a 1/16 battalion surgeon who was scheduled for R & R. Captain Bill Thomas, who was to be replaced, had left Thunder-4 in the morning for a night in Lai Khe, then one in Di An before proceeding to Hawaii. In recent months he had seen his share of combat accompanying the command group on "battalion minus" search-and-destroy missions. I'd met him a few weeks earlier. He was a quiet, almost shy sort from Mobile, Alabama, where he had done his internship following medical school at Ole Miss.

On an impulse I got Tisdale on the phone and convinced him to let me go instead. In a few hours I was on my way to Thunder-4.

...

A single company of the 1/16 was dug in at Thunder-4, an NDP (night defense position) just west of Highway 13, twelve miles north of Lai Khe. It was supported by an artillery battery. Thunder-4 served also as the command post of LTC Cal Benedict, the 1/16 commander. I had never met Benedict, but I'd heard about him. A member (with Colonel Blazey) of the West Point class of 1946, he was regarded as an outstanding battlefield commander. Very tall and bald-headed, he moved with the loose, rhythmic grace of the former All-American and captain of the Army soccer team he had been.

Here and there, mainly through a couple of platoon leaders over the next few days, I would gain some information about our tactical situation. It went straight into my journal, however limited my understanding was.

An NDP is essentially a circular clearing created by leveling burned-off jungle with bulldozers and tanks. Thunder-4 was essentially two hundred meters in diameter with another one hundred meters or so beyond, cleared away in every direction, providing fields of fire for the heavy machine guns placed at intervals around the perimeter, just inside surrounding loops of concertina wire. There were at least four. A short walk from the eastern perimeter was the tent I shared with two medics. It was enclosed by a three-foot wall of sandbags. The open end faced a shallow dugout, also surrounded by sandbags.

Thunder-4 was equipped with a helicopter pad, 105- and 155-mm howitzers, a tank or two and other tracked-vehicles.

Assorted sizes of flexible radio antennas sprouted from the vehicles. High protein, high-caloric hot breakfasts and evening chows were prepared on site, and noon chow generally consisted of sandwiches and canned fruit to suit the needs of daytime patrols through surrounding terrain.

NDPs were dedicated to the nighttime defense of infantry elements engaged in daytime patrols, offensive operations, the *sine qua non* of any infantry unit. But with Tet fast approaching, the First Division was committed to a defensive posture. The 1/16's mission was limited to "road operations," patrolling a segment of Highway 13 in order to keep it clear for local produce traffic and convoys resupplying the string of NDPs along the route. Artillery shells and other ammunition, certain kinds of food, and fuel were transported by land vehicles, while medical supplies, perishables, mail, and other light items arrived by helicopter. Under normal conditions Charlie's initiating a fire-fight in broad daylight on Thunder Road was almost unthinkable, but at Tet all bets were off. At Thunder-4 we had to be prepared for anything. But still, considering our fire power and air support advantage over the VC, I couldn't help thinking that the worst thing likely was for a GI to lose a leg to a VC land mine. It began to dawn on me that I probably wouldn't be of much use at Thunder-4. My presence was to cover unlikely contingencies, like a fire extinguisher in a public building back home, or on a bus. An experienced medic could handle what casualties we would likely encounter. Wounds of significant magnitude could be evacuated by chopper to B-Med or the evac hospitals in Long Binh or Bien Hoa. My job would be to lie in the sun all day and read. But, hey! I could live with that.

I had arrived at dinner time, and by dusk I was as settled in as I was going to get. Feeling a vague call of nature, I was informed that the latrine was just beyond the concertina wire. With no wish to manage my business beyond the perimeter in the dark, I headed in the appointed direction only to be called back immediately. "Do you know the password?"

Password? What was he talking about?

"The guy with the machine gun will be quite interested in everything going on out there. You can bet he's going to challenge you, and you won't hear a peep from him before you're in his sights and his machine gun is ready to fire."

The explanation was not given to alarm me, only to advise me of the standing procedure. But, after rethinking my condition, I concluded I didn't need to go to the latrine after all, with or without the password of the day.

...

We were scores of men huddled in black-out-enforced darkness, some of us fully awake. One of my tent-mates finally began to snore, and the other one only stared into the darkness outside, which was interrupted sometimes by the flash of a cigarette lighter.

The conversation-buzz from surrounding tents shut down when a machine gun opened up. The first time the gunner had had no target. He was only checking to see if his weapon was still functional. How green does that sound? But I preferred a machine gunner on the perimeter who was a little jumpy over one who was a touch sleepy.

Getting to sleep with the sounds of supporting artillery from a firebase at some distance, possibly Lai Khe, was much different from having big guns hammering out-going rounds from as close as a few hundred yards. I managed it, though. The howitzers inside Thunder-4 woke me up a little before midnight the first night, and again three or four hours later, but I was back asleep within a minute or two. It was a trick I'd picked up as an intern, fielding phone calls all night.

...

On the morning of January 26, I saw an assortment of cuts, scratches, and headaches at sick call—something any medic could have handled. After that, unless something terrible happened out on Thunder Road, I was confident my workday was essentially over.

I picked up where I'd left off in my mildewed paperback copy of *All Quiet on the Western Front*. Being in sunny South Vietnam was a better deal than being in World War I Germany. Even the boredom was different. I would choose a warm night at Thunder-4 over a freezing night in a trench within earshot of one full of Germans in a heartbeat.

The courier chopper arrived at mid-morning with bad news from Lai Khe. Charlie had inflicted havoc there during the night, leveling the officers' club to the ground, killing at least eight (including Major Gerz of Division staff) and injuring sixteen, two seriously. A birthday party had been in progress at the time of the attack. Spurgeon Green had compiled a typed report of the activities at the hospital. Both

GIs with serious wounds were evacuated to Long Binh. One was unconscious.

Colonel Blazey's villa was also hit. He had recently returned from the 93rd Evac, and as of this morning, Green had not yet accounted for him. It gave me a hollow feeling. Losing Blazey would be a personal blow for me. He was a decent and talented man, and his presence had a stabilizing effect on many of us.

One of the chopper crew had heard that attack had been orchestrated from the Lai Khe village, inhabited by many Vietnamese we saw every day and assumed were our friends. They consisted of laundresses, PX employees, interpreters, and the like. Prior to the early days of 1968 the perimeter defense of Lai Khe was not a high priority. Locals living in the village came and went at will. On the night of January 25, VC living there had only to creep through the darkness and set satchel charges of high explosives against the foundation of the officers' club. Others went to Colonel Blazey's villa and elsewhere throughout the base camp. Sites seemed to have been hit simultaneously, as part of a well thought out and executed operation. Rumor had it that the attacks were in retaliation for casualties taken by a rifle company of 1/16 surrounding the village two weeks earlier in an attempt to intercept VC returning to their homes in the village after a night operation.

I remembered that night well. One of the bodies turning up at B-Med early the following morning with a bullet in his chest was quite familiar. He had been my barber, cutting my hair at intervals for months. He always insisted on lathering up the back of my neck and around my ears, then finishing off his work with a very sharp, single-edged folding-razor. He could have slit my throat from ear to ear before I understood what was happening! After that I never allowed a razor-wielding Vietnamese anywhere near me.

I also received two letters from home. I'd assumed I'd not get mail from the world as long as I was at Thunder-4 so I was surprised. I made a mental note to give the mail clerk at B-Med an enthusiastic thumbs-up when I returned.

Green had sent a hand-written note about another loss that would affect me particularly. General Hay's tennis court had been destroyed on January 25, presumably beyond repair. Suddenly playing tennis seemed far away, in another time. I doubted I'd miss it. I definitely wouldn't miss Major Luce's blistering serves and dynamite forehands.

...

Minutes before midnight, the very last of January 26, the darkness gave way to a blinding flash at the edge of the wooded area beyond the southern perimeter, lighting up a circular sector a hundred meters in diameter. Machine guns began burping out converging and crisscrossing fire into the adjacent jungle. Charlie had tripped a flare, delivering himself and whoever was with him into a world of trouble. Soon M-16s and M-79s joined in.

Then artillery from Thunder-5, two miles north, reinforced the trip-flare illumination with star shells, arching over our heads, descending hundreds of feet after detonation by small heat-resistant parachutes. Suddenly the entire area was lit up like a high school football field on Friday night. Illumination fire was followed by high-explosive shells from the same fire base, wreaking destruction on jungle hardly a hundred meters from our southern perimeter. I could imagine a twenty-two-year-old second lieutenant making, and hopefully double- and triple-checking, his calculations. Just thinking about it left me a little queasy. Even a slight miscalculation could make my wife a widow.

Later a gunship appeared overhead and began flying in circles of increasing diameter, apparently searching for targets of opportunity. But no shots were fired.

Finally things calmed down, and most guys inside Thunder-4 went back to sleep, including me. But I kept my boots on and a .45 beneath my air mattress.

...

On January 27 I woke up sick—aching all over plus a vague sense of malaise. As the day wore on I was more easily fatigable than normal, but by late-afternoon I still had no chills or fever. Finally I was confident I didn't have malaria. Vivax malaria was probably preventable by the Primaquine we were supposed to be taking. I had to admit I wasn't as conscientious with the "malaria pills" as I should have been.

Colonel Blazey showed up early in the afternoon to see LTC Benedict. He dropped by my tent to let me know he was much better than when I'd seen him last. It wasn't clear if the doctors at the 93rd had changed his tetracycline to a different broad spectrum antibiotic, but at least they had confirmed my presumptive diagnosis of typhus. An internist specially trained in tropical diseases would beat a surgical-type like me any day of the week. B-Med's textbook on tropical diseases could take me only so far.

Blazey explained that the dining room I remembered in his villa was no more. And much of the second floor had caved in. He'd had late night VC visitors from the village. He had been sleeping at the time, and was speckled with flying glass but had no serious wounds. He informed me the Lai Khe perimeter was now patrolled by two rifle companies, not the single-company nighttime defense recently established. Coming to grips with the problem of the village would be a day-by-day project.

He indicated that his leaving the 3rd Brigade was imminent, and that he wasn't happy about relinquishing command. His assignment at III Corps would present challenges, but soldiers like Blazey thrived on being in charge and in on everything. Rumor had him on the cusp of becoming a general officer, but even a shiny new star wouldn't compensate for the heat of battle. Real soldiers saw their duty as whipping up on the VC.

...

That night every NDP for miles was attacked but ours. Preliminary reports squawked in by radio. Elements of 1/26, two miles north, engaged and defeated one hundred VC, and 1/16's B-company, another mile farther north, took on seventy VC. C-company faced a similar number west of us. The Tet offensive was in full swing, but enemy body counts in the area soared, and American casualties were light. Finally Charlie had come out to fight, and was getting mauled. Amassed VC were no match for American fire power.

But back in the States, according to the national news magazines, anyway—*Time* and *Newsweek*—would suggest otherwise. We saw the Tet attacks as pure desperation, not at all sustainable. To us victory was in sight, while many at home were anticipating defeat.

•••

As the sun rose on January 28 I was still sick, but the absence of significant fever by late afternoon indicated no other doctor needed to be notified. I loaded up on aspirin and fluids and waited to feel better.

LTC Benedict wasn't above a "John Wayne moment" from time to time. His aggressiveness and aplomb packaged in the body of an athletic giant was impossible to ignore. After sending out four ambush platoons and giving his artillery-liaison officer some last-minute instructions, he climbed into an APC (armored personnel carrier) and roared down Highway 13 in the dark at top speed, daring Charlie to come out and fight. The area, like the NDPs nearby last night, had to be crawling with VC.

When B-company engaged a VC recon patrol three miles south, Benedict was on hand to focus fire power and pour havoc on Charlie. When the dust settled, he stacked seven VC bodies into his APC and sped back to Thunder-4 to ask me with a smug grin if there was anything I could do for any of them. After sorting through the pile of arms, legs, and grimy faces, I came up with one live VC. He was filthy, exhausted, and scared witless, but he had no need of medical care. There was little question he'd had an opportunity to exact revenge behind an unsuspecting Benedict on the trip back to Thunder-4, but he couldn't figure out a way to take advantage of it. A five-foot four-inch Vietnamese thinking about taking on a man like Benedict without a weapon faced a real problem. Possibly he had been momentarily unconscious, but it was equally likely he'd become resigned to his fate at the hands of the fiery Benedict. A lieutenant bound the VC's wrists and led him off for questioning.

...

The morning of January 29 was quiet, eerily so. For nearly a week Thunder-4's Vietnamese interpreter had been desperately seeking leave, claiming special family obligations. When he still hadn't been granted leave by mid-afternoon, he simply vanished, going AWOL. It was a bad sign. He knew something we could only suspect. With tomorrow being the first official day of Tet, he was probably positioning himself to join his VC pals, at least to avoid being in a caught in a crossfire when they attacked. We couldn't see his absence any other way.

On the other hand, the enemy dead collected over the past few days had been carrying limited amounts of ammunition, rations, and supplies. Intelligence officers identified them as members of the 165th NVA Regiment. Presumably they were not massing for an offensive, only trying to slip back into Cambodia for sanctuary and resupply.

Late in the afternoon I took advantage of the Australian shower rigged up near-by, a simple device to store heat from the sun. It was the first hot shower I'd had since leaving Oakland. It made me feel a lot better. I'd also had a breakfast of fresh eggs (who knew where they came from!), creamed beef, hot biscuits, and coffee. Finally I could begin to see the end of my illness.

At dinner time Sergeant Sims, my right-hand man at Thunder-4, a Texan from Houston, presented me with a couple of souvenirs: a VC medic's field kit and a sleeping hammock. They were collected from the VC bodies of the preceding night. I was delighted. There were no trees from which to string the hammock so I would have to wait until I got back to Lai Khe to try it out. Unfortunately, considering what happened over the next couple of days, I completely forgot about Sergeant Sims's booty. For all I know, the hammock and field kit may still be out there, a few hundred meters west of Thunder Road, twelve miles from Lai Khe.

...

On the night of January 30, after positioning myself to within listening range of a radio, Delta company reported taking small arms fire at the NDP immediately south of us. The proposed truce was only hours old, and already Charlie had broken it. I listened to Benedict's calm, measured response, "Okay, boys. They fired first. It's on them now. Let's give it to 'em."

Delta-company opened up with machine guns, mortars, and everything else they had. They had engaged an estimated force of fifteen. When the VC withdrew, and their direction of retreat was pin-pointed, LTC Benedict's eyes glowed as he assembled a party to join him on another trip down Highway 13. Even I was invited to the party. "I don't know how much good you'll do us, Doc, but we need every weapon we've got firing. You can't help us much sleeping, or listening to us kill VC."

What else did I have to do? If Buswell questioned me later, I would say I took Benedict's invitation as a direct order!

Within minutes I was sprawled on my ass against the front of the turret of a tank, my heels scrounging for purchase against the front deck. I had an M-16 in the crook of my right elbow—it was pointed at the stars and a round was in the chamber—as my left hand grasped for traction at the base of the turret. In that position, with my throat parched and eyes bulging, I hung on for dear life as we "thundered" south on Highway 13. Every pocket was jammed with clips of ammo.

Our convoy consisted of two tanks and two APCs. Highway 13 made for a bumpy ride at any speed, but the tank-driver drove like a starving man late for dinner. At forty miles-per-hour we were arrogantly not looking to sneak up on anybody, our tracks churning with a loud clatter. My biggest challenge was to stay perched on the speeding and bucking forty-nine tons of steel. I knew this particular driver wouldn't even slow down if I fell off.

In ten minutes we reached our destination, a stretch of brush and undergrowth to the right of the road, now lit up by illumination shells. We turned off and rumbled forward, winding toward a patch of jungle, some seventy-five or one hundred yards wide. Finally we took a position abreast of the other tank (both equipped with 90 mm guns) and a pair of APCs (each armed with a mounted heavy machine gun).

Still seated on the tank but now stretching forward over flexed knees, I poured round after round into that stretch of jungle. Others were firing M-16s or M-79 rocket launchers. The noise was deafening. Why we didn't rip the jungle into tiny pieces I would never understand. There was never a visible target, but if Charlie was in there he was as good as gone. (Yet, the following morning only two bodies were recovered. The rest had, somehow, escaped, probably before we'd fired our first shot.)

After what seemed like twenty minutes and a large chunk of our ammunition supply expended, we backed out and headed back to Thunder-4. For me the trip back was even scarier. It was very dark, no moon in sight, and the tank driver was out to prove he knew only one speed. I couldn't stop thinking about falling off unnoticed, and having to fend for myself until daylight. I still had one last clip of ammo tucked into my breast pocket.

Later, with the thrill of battle still on his face, LTC Benedict slapped me on the shoulder and said, "How did you like that, Captain Rogers? Tearing down the road like that you can't help feeling that if you run into somebody, you just can't help but whip him good." I had no ready reply, but I scribbled that sentence down word for word before I went to sleep that night.

One thing LTC Benedict and Colonel Blazey had in common was that the language of neither contained much profanity. I can't recall hearing so much as a "damn" from either of them. I wonder if this was a leadership trait ingrained in them at West Point. They were oriented toward killing VC, but cussing was beneath them. It seemed to have an effect on the men around them. Fighting was about commitment and flexibility, not expressing one's emotions.

Before I drifted off to sleep some time later, I realized I was feeling really good for the first time in days. Whatever "bug" I'd had had run its course. Or had "shock therapy" done the trick?

...

On January 31st I was returned to Lai Khe, late in the afternoon. Sergeant Carr met me at the landing strip in his jeep and took me back to B-Med by a route that was not familiar to me. Halfway there I heard a serious shriek overhead, followed by the cracking sound of shrapnel ripping into the bark of a medium-sized tree hardly twenty feet away. The suddenness and the proximity of the blast left me breathless. On a second glance I was struck by how unnatural a tree split up the middle really seemed. I stared at it helplessly as Carr swerved to a stop on the opposite side of the road. We rolled out and scrambled for cover beside the jeep.

But what were we doing? Taking cover from mortar fire may have been a natural reaction, but why the hell did we think we were safer than we would have been rolling down the road at Benedict speed?

Exactly where was safety, anyway? Without a word we got up simultaneously and climbed back into the jeep, then rumbled down this road I'd never seen before at forty miles per hour.

The idea that I was returning to the safety of my home away from home, as it had seemed for four months, was no longer valid. Charlie's "Tet Offensive" was only beginning. Already proved was the fact that no place in our sector was safer than any other. We would get used to it. We had to. Beginning in mid-January fifty-nine out of the next sixty-one nights Lai Khe would receive at least in-coming mortar fire. Don't think I was the only one counting. Soon mortars weren't the only worry. Within a week or so we would witness the devastation and destruction of an in-coming rocket. The Russian-made variant of its World War II 122 mm Katyusha rocket made a distinctly different sound as it whistled through the air, and it carried a bigger payload, yielding a louder explosion, leaving a huge crater behind. Life in the base camp over the following weeks would be distinctly different for everyone.

16.
TET II: LAI KHE

It's a Hell of a Way to Lose a War

For almost a week B-Med was on C-rations, water, and soft drinks at room temperature. Our main generator had taken a direct hit, knocking out mess hall refrigerators for a day and two nights. When power was restored, the mess hall took continual mortar hits on successive days, disabling the kitchen first, then blowing out the front door and adjoining wall. Nothing was more disheartening than seeing familiar tables and chairs splintered. Where we had gathered three times daily had become a symbol of brotherhood and normalcy we didn't recognize until it was taken from us. We had no choice but to close down the mess hall. Somehow Charlie had delivered a surgical strike, eerily understanding how taking away hot food and iced tea might affect us. To the VC we were a pampered, sheltered lot, but they couldn't imagine how taking away our common comforts would galvanize our focus against them. We would live out of tin cans for however long it took, and learn to like it.

When casualties began to flow in day and night, all three medical officers moved into the hospital. It only made sense. Being at our duty-station 24/7 ratcheted up our readiness, and the sand-bag-supported stucco walls made the hospital a virtual bunker. Only the roof was vulnerable. Like the structures at the 18th Surg, the weight of layered sandbags overhead could not be supported. We were committed to taking our chances there. Medics, lab techs, and x-ray techs worked in shifts, all with a new intensity.

The hospital bunker for ambulatory patients took a direct hit before dawn on the second day, but it absorbed the blow in good shape. No one was inside. We were encouraged that deep holes and layers of sand bags, defensive mainstays from the dawn of modern artillery, were still effective.

The men of B-Med proved to be resilient. To a man they managed under the confusion of the unexpected, even, over time, coming to make light of it. After the first few days, pale faces and muffled speech turned to pranks and banter. Each man seemed to possess a strange confidence he would not become one of the dead or maimed. That attitude helped. But some days were tough for everybody. The strain was wearying at times, but our casualties were primarily mental and reversible. For weeks we experienced few physical wounds, and none were mortal. Sergeant Crane, B-Med's all important supply sergeant and senior non-commissioned officer, bumped his head and fainted getting into a bunker on February 2 but nothing came of it. A large, roly-poly, red-faced man from Wisconsin, he joked that his brain was iron-clad.

Early in the first week we were initiated into the terror of an in-coming Russian rocket. Its approach was signaled by a low-pitched whistle, then a perfectly shattering explosion. It blew our chicken wire python-lottery-cage to smithereens, leaving a hole large enough to hide in. The sound of the explosion and the size of its crater had an indelible effect, one we learned to live with.

Structural damage was considerable. Within a few weeks virtually every building in the compound had absorbed at least one mortar shell. The motor pool joined the mess hall as a popular target. Early on, a two-and-a-half ton truck was destroyed by a rocket, launching door handles, glass, and windshield wipers hundreds of feet. Four ambulances were disabled that night, but two were up and running within days.

...

By mid-January Colonel Blazey was in command of five of the eight First Division infantry battalions giving it to the VC moving south toward Saigon. The 2/28, now under LTC Lou Menetrey, and the 1/16, under LTC Benedict, were prominent among them. Later, Blazey, with the First Division's Armored Cavalry Battalion, was called on to rescue local Vietnamese civilians surrounded by VC south of Lai Khe. Following that operation he met John Vann, whose Vietnamese experience and stunning views would be detailed in the best-selling 1988 book by Neil Sheehan, *A Bright and Shining Lie: John Paul Vann and America in Vietnam*. Several weeks later Blazey was reassigned to II FFV (II Field Force, Vietnam), the CORDS (Civil Operations and Rural Development Support) office led by Vann.

In the base camp we were aware that our infantry battalions were part of the fighting in and around Saigon, but we had little information about what success they met. Decades later I would run across a Silver Star citation describing the heroism of my friend, Major Al Maroscher, of Colonel

Blazey's staff. In summary, late in the afternoon of January 31, his reconnaissance force met intense automatic weapon and machinegun fire from a reinforced platoon of VC concealed in abandoned houses in a Saigon suburb. Ignoring the peril he faced, he organized his men in covered positions along the street to lay down maximum suppressive fire on the insurgents, then he directed another rifle company from an adjacent street to attack. The insurgent force was caught in the resulting crossfire and liquidated, some elements escaping through back streets.[15] Al's leadership and courage had been on full display. Silver Stars aren't awarded for trivial acts. He was proving himself to be a special soldier. I would see him weeks later, and he denied any specific actions or close calls, only saying that things had been intense in Saigon.

...

On February 1 we took mortar fire and rockets day and night, presumably from North Vietnamese Army regulars. I was informed that only the NVA had the ability to transport and arm rockets. We reasoned that Charlie, on foot in pajamas and sandals, could carry only a limited number of mortar rounds. Taking on regulars was new. They were disciplined, equipped, and possessed of a capacity to inflict real damage. They could elude 3rd Brigade daytime patrols we knew were out there protecting us. Even in groups they had a knack for melting into the scenery, reminiscent of what the VC, in twos and threes, had been doing for weeks.

---

[15] http://www.ohioheroes.org/inductees/2009/maroscher.htm.

I wondered why the NVA high command had suddenly decided to employ more conventional techniques, rather than the guerrilla methods that had been their staple for so long. Not only did sending battalions of troops deep into South Vietnam expose them to our superior fire power, it had to be expensive too, particularly with respect to logistical support and matériel. Maybe we were seeing the first of a last ditch stand for them.

By February 3 we had taken mortar shellings four straight nights, and had seen rockets twice, a total of six or seven of them. The intelligence people had information that the NVA types would be retreating to Cambodia any day now. So far we'd seen little evidence of that. On Feb 4 two officers, both lieutenants, were killed inside the base camp, and we got word that the 18th Surg and D-Med, west of us, had already been evacuated. The 18th Surg had left their inflatable buildings in place, taking only their personnel and equipment with them. So much for my plan to join them as a surgeon. I had all but forgotten about the 18th Surg.

Delta company going to Long Binh surprised me. We had heard that they hadn't taken any fire at all. LTC Tisdale must have been nervous about them for some reason. Our taking only three incoming rounds on February 5 seemed a reason to celebrate. Maybe the worst was over.

I made an audiotape that night to send home to my family. In it I mentioned seeing a tape aired on the Vietnam network of a recent Sunday TV news program, "Meet the Press." I had been disheartened by its negative tone about the Tet activities. We were feeling stress at B-Med and elsewhere, but at no point did any of us worry about the possibility of the enemy's campaign resulting in lasting strategic consequences. We were sustaining far fewer deaths and injuries than they were. But the folks back home were ready to throw in the towel? That was shocking. It hadn't dawned on us yet that we might be among the first Americans to lose a war. Nobody in the First Division expected to defeat the VC without loss of life and blood, but the guys in the Big Red One were dedicated to total victory.

By February 7 we entered our second week of living at the hospital. We still spent a lot of time cutting out shrapnel, controlling bleeding, and trimming dead tissue from wounds. Late that afternoon we admitted Colonel Blazey with a narrow sliver of shrapnel in his neck. There was no significant bleeding, swelling, or signs of respiratory distress, but his voice was different, slightly hoarse. My stethoscope picked up rushing sounds over his lungs. The fragment was wedged into his windpipe sufficiently to create sounds of air flow disruption as he breathed. But he still grinned as he tried to talk. He had no idea what a close call he'd had. A larger fragment, or even the same one placed an inch in either direction could have nicked a carotid artery, placing him in real trouble.

The fragment came out as a single piece, and his hoarseness cleared up immediately. He laughed and started for the door before I had a chance to apply a dressing. I convinced him to allow me to cover his wound with a medium-sized band-aid, but I knew he would take it off as soon as he was out of my sight.

On February 8 Charlie eliminated our favorite recreational outlet and number-one reminder of life back home when he blew up our TV antenna. Television was a real morale booster even though programming was sometimes sporadic. Not many guys had much time to watch TV, anyway. Everybody fantasized about the bubbly blond Red Cross girl who brought us the local weather, plus news and sports from the states. She and another cutie took turns teasing us, presumably from a Saigon studio. They rarely gave the slightest hint a war was going on. On weekends there were basketball games and golf tournaments, sometimes an action show or a drama on weeknights. "The Fugitive" was a big hit in early 1968. All three TV-screens at B-Med were silent for nearly a week.

...

The next day I bumped into five guys huddled around a board game in the "officers' club." With no TV I expected to see a card game or two, but this was Monopoly. Our mess sergeant, supply sergeant, a dentist, and two Dust Off pilots were in full focus, barely breathing, avoiding eye contact all around the table. The only sounds were dice rattling inside a cardboard cup, then bouncing and skidding across the board. Nobody looked up as I walked in.

Stacks of cash were guarded by each player. The numerals and borders of government scrip were gray, against a background of an odd shade of green, almost blue. It was clearly not play money. This game had nothing to do with play. The piles of tens and twenties had to add up to at least five thousand dollars!

It was not good. In college our football coach outlawed penny-a-point gin rummy on long bus trips to away games.

His thinking was that the effect of winning and loosing even modest amounts could wreck the camaraderie required to win football games. He was dead serious about it.

My tendency was to deal with problems right away, but exactly what could I do? The stockpiles of treasure were nowhere near uneven, essentially winners and losers already established. Breaking up the game now would create more problems than it solved. I chose to let matters run their course, have Green post a gambling policy tomorrow. No harm seemed eminent. It wasn't a matter of forty-five-year-olds taking advantage of the inexperienced. Randy Radigan's winnings were twice that of both sergeants' combined! He had probably set up the game, even lured the old guys into somebody else's club, a killing field, where he would teach them a lesson! I couldn't help grinning.

...

On February 10 a rocket exploded some two hundred yards away from the mess hall as nearly eighty men sat down for noon chow. It was Saturday. Not one guy made the slightest move for a bunker. Food was good at B-Med but nowhere near that good. I found myself up and barking a "clear out" order myself. Some carried plates and forks as they headed for the exits.

Two days later, when another rocket hit in the road directly in front of the mess hall, hardly twenty-five yards away, the mess hall cleared out in record speed, chairs overturning and tables shoved askew in the process. It was a matter of proximity.

The 3rd Brigade change-of-command ceremony was sandwiched between mortar and rocket attacks on the afternoon of February 10. It was held in a clearing surrounded by rubber trees, with troops in fresh fatigues, flack jackets, helmets, and freshly-shined boots. They alternated between attention and parade-rest as a gentle breeze rippled the stars-and-stripes at the flag pole. In a short speech General Hay commented that the current campaign could easily become the decisive battle of the war, that each of us was participating in history. We dared to hope that was true. If the enemy's deaths continued to exceed ours by ten-to-one, as we had heard, victory might come sooner rather than later.

On February 11, at noon, a rocket landed in the village, killing or crippling dozens of the locals and terrorizing the rest. Every home there was of flimsy construction, and there were no adequate bunkers. Four ambulances were dispatched. Even if some of their fathers were VC, it was tough to even look at five- and six-year-olds with intestines spilling through open belly wounds. We evacuated some to the 93rd, but surviving such wounds was all but impossible. Sights of parents struck dumb from the deaths of their children were etched into every observer's memory. Kids' blank looks, their eyes spent from crying as they milled about in confusion as the bodies of their parents and neighbors were covered in the streets, were even tougher. Medics and doctors went about their work like zombies, not a dry eye among them.

I had the opportunity to do a heel cord repair for a Vietnamese nine-year-old. Shrapnel had severed the tendon cleanly, leaving him in intense pain and rendering his foot weirdly unstable. Under local anesthesia with a little morphine I managed to achieve a reasonable repair by plantar-flexing his foot (forcing toes and forefoot downward). I planned to maintain that position in a cast for four weeks before gently stretching the healing tendon bit by bit each week and applying a new cast. I planned to get some advice from one of the orthopedic surgeons at the 93rd Evac about that because I'd not done that operation before. I'd only seen it done once. Sending the child to the 93rd for an operation would have been ideal, but civilian transfers were not typically authorized for non-life-threatening injuries and some mothers would not consider allowing their kids out of their sight.

Back in the fall a little girl from the village came to B-Med with a fever. Somehow, she was mistakenly placed on a chopper

full of South Vietnamese injured in a firefight headed for the 93rd Evac. Her mother became hysterical, fixing me with looks of hatred, leaving me no choice but to go to the 93rd myself. It seemed the entire village expected me bring her home. I couldn't go the next day, but I went the following, a Saturday. She was not to be found at the 93rd and no one remembered such a child. My only option

A joyful return! The author with a Vietnamese child lost in Saigon after mistakenly being placed on a Dust Off evacuation helicopter in the confusion created by mass casualties. She returned unharmed days later, thanks largely to her own wits and winsome ways.

was to tour the orphan hospitals around Saigon, searching each ward by ward and bed by bed. I had only the child's name, age, and a general idea what she looked like. I never found her. With a heavy heart I boarded the chopper back to Lai Khe late that afternoon. The little girl's mother was desolate when I gave her the news. But all was not lost. The child showed up a few days later on her own—smiling, happy, no trace of fever or other sign of illness. I was never informed how she had gotten back home, but her mom did bring her around to see me, even allowed her to pose for a photograph with me. The experience left me leery about sending any child away from its mother.

I never saw the child with the Achilles repair again. I never understood why, possibly the initial surgical experience was too traumatic for mother and son. Sergeant Chuong had explained to the mother that it was crucial that she bring the child back in two weeks to have his cast changed and his wound examined. Without careful follow-up he would have a deformed foot for the rest of his life, or even worse. Failure to recognize a wound infection could lead to an amputation or death from septicemia.

In the late afternoon of February 11 three rockets struck within a fifty-yard radius in hardly a minute, all three blasts visible in the woods and high grass beyond the Dust Off chopper pad, leaving me resolved to never remove my flack jacket and helmet again. Then mortar rounds shrieked from the sky down oval road, toward the lair of the Black Lions, the 2/28. For all the fireworks, though, we netted only eight casualties, none life-threatening.

The next day engineers bulldozed a huge crater adjacent to our orderly room, then lowered an eight-by-eight-by-ten foot steel Conex container into it which had a door and a tiny window. After stacking sandbags around it and over it, B-Med possessed a brand new, underground orderly room. I had no idea where the idea originated, but I never understood it. The heat and ventilation made it a virtual tomb. I never set foot inside.

...

On February 14, Valentine's Day, a rocket landed in the ammunition dump, setting off another fire. Fourteen were killed, and two of us spent hours in the ER that afternoon and early evening. Spurgeon Green dropped by to tell me Colonel Buswell had inquired about me.

"What did he want?"

"Nothing. He just asked if you were out chasing fireworks again."

...

By late February the rockets and mortar fire began to lessen. Attacks no longer came during daylight, only periodic barrages at night, mainly mortar shells. One night the Red Cross supplied us the movie, "The Sound of Music," in multiple reels.

I was among several dozen gathered in the courtyard outside the south wall of the B-Med hospital for the first night's showing, the First Division premiere!. A bed sheet was hung on the stucco wall as a screen. Mid-way in the movie the siren sounded and the area was bombarded by incoming shells. The movie continued while we made for the bunkers.

Thirty minutes later, I was among the first to slip back to see the rest of the movie. It was still running, and one guy had stayed behind, unwilling to miss a single frame. He was a tall, skinny PFC who had grown up near Boulder, Colorado. He explained that the music and the mountain scenes made him feel safe enough. He had no intention of leaving. For him, those "hills" were truly "alive."

...

Typically mortars and rockets came early in the evening, within two or three hours of maximum darkness. On one evening in late February there were no in-coming rounds as 2300 approached, giving us all hope that Charlie had had enough. We had been under attack of some kind for every night for weeks, but tonight there was nothing. It was eerie.

But well after midnight they came. There were no rockets, but mortar rounds, twenty or twenty-five, came over a period of fifteen minutes. Several landed in the village, causing the kind of civilian devastation we had come to dread. For over two hours all medical officers were at work with shrapnel wounds in the ER. There were no deaths that night, even few truly life-threatening injuries, but there was much carnage and suffering.

At a little past 0400, as ER activities began to wind down, there were the sudden sounds of automatic weapons fire from immediately outside the ER. Only a windowless stucco wall, possibly a foot thick, separated us from whatever was going on outside. The shooting waned suddenly, followed by loud shouting in English. In a few minutes there was nothing.

Very carefully I went out the exit facing the chopper pad. As soon as I passed the corner of the building, I saw the glare of flashlights moving up and down the external side of our ER wall. American soldiers, four or five, were conversing. Two carried M-16s in a relaxed manner, and other weapons were standing against the wall. Whatever had taken place there was now over so I moved toward them.

Four VC were crumpled at the base of the wall, lifeless, splattered with blood. What had been going on here? An execution?

As I drew nearer, I saw the satchel charges against the base of building. Explosives were stacked three feet high at the center of the wall.

The soldiers wore Black Lion patches on their shoulders, members of 2/28. One of them recognized me as a medical officer.

"Doc, what's on the other side of this wall?"

"That's our emergency room," I replied, "where we've been treating fragment wounds for hours."

"Looks like these bastards had plans for you tonight," he said casually, glancing at two corpses, one on top of the other, then two more within six feet, one with much of his face blown away.

Slowly I took a deep breath, trying to manage a sudden wave of dizziness. We had just witnessed a well planned and almost perfectly executed operation, aimed specifically at B-Med. No doubt it was an inside job, planned by people who knew us well. First, maximum mortar fire on the base camp, with any luck at all, would send casualties and medical personnel to the hospital, where these four VC would meet us with their bomb. They had breached the perimeter with enough explosives to blow up the entire west wing of the building and whoever was inside. Surely the shells in the village were mistakes.

•••

After that night we beefed up security inside the B-Med compound. This required assigning all enlisted men to pull guard duty shifts through the night, when we were most vulnerable to Charlie breaching the perimeter. It was serious business, and each guard was duty-bound to observe strict protocol.

Within a week, on a very dark night, as I made my way from the hospital to the company area, I was challenged by a guard.

"Halt!" came the loud, clear command. "Stand to identify yourself."

Guards were required to have their targets clearly in their rifle sights, with a round in the chamber and the safety off before issuing a challenge.

I froze, focusing on making not even the slightest movement. I didn't have to see the young soldier to know his weapon was aimed at my head and that he could legally shoot me if I didn't come up with the password. Suddenly, my mind scrolled through a list of recent passwords, most girls' names or cities back home, but I couldn't determine which was current. And there was no time to think. I had to say something, quick!

I decided instead to bank on my Southern accent. Quickly I shifted my Carolina-speak hundreds of miles south, to Mississippi or Alabama. With my heart in my mouth, I drawled my name and my address back home. "I've got a wife and two kids. Calm down now, y'all. I can't remember the damn password. Please don't shoot me!"

There was no sound for a moment, then the soldier laughed. "Relax, Captain. I know who you are. I'm just doing my job."

I breathed a sigh of relief. His voice was vaguely familiar, but I couldn't assign it a name. In the dark I could not make him out. He sounded close enough to hit me with a rock. I imagined him supporting his M-16 against the trunk of a nearby tree. I had served on guard duty at Fort Bragg in ROTC war games, but never for real. Yet I knew enough to understand that guard duty could be boring one minute and terrifying the next. This soldier had found a way to carve a little fun out of it, and at my expense.

...

Later Spurgeon Green pointed out that we had a problem with our guard duty roster. It had to do with conscientious objectors (COs). By law any young, healthy American could be drafted into the service, but there was no requirement he be a combatant if it conflicted with his personal or religious principles. Green had discovered that several COs agreed to stand guard with deadly weapons but to a man they stated they would not kill anyone if the need arose. They had no qualms about dying themselves, but they weren't going to shoot anybody.

At first I didn't believe what he was telling me. As much carnage as we had seen in recent months, I couldn't imagine anyone having a problem with defending himself and his comrades. Back in the world one's stated beliefs could vary, depending on the company and circumstances, but here reality forced a different mindset. I didn't volunteer to come to Vietnam to kill anybody, either. Green suggested I question some of the COs myself.

I interviewed two. Both were handsome, clear-eyed young men with firm beliefs about their responsibilities as human beings. I asked them basically two questions.

"If you encounter an armed VC intent on killing you, would you shoot him?"

"No sir," both responded. Their explanations varied a little, but each seemed to have thought the matter through.

"But in the course of standing guard, if you see VC approaching an area where your buddies are sleeping, you would do nothing? I almost held my breath as I waited for the answers.

One solider responded in the affirmative, and the other said he would fire his weapon into the air to sound the alarm. Neither would kill anybody, no matter who or under what circumstances.

Our only course was to excuse all COs from guard duty. I was frustrated because filling two-hour shifts from dusk to dawn already required assigning each enlisted man to guard duty at least once a week. But I was impressed with what the COs were telling me. I couldn't imagine dying myself or allowing any American to die without a fight, but I couldn't help respecting these young men. After all, they had agreed to serve, and they were serious about doing their duty. A number of them, some former college students, were among our very best medics, another was our top lab technician. They were good men, facing the same risk we all did. They had not fled to Canada to avoid the draft. I was a long way from understanding them, but I did respect them. They were solid human beings and fine soldiers.

···

Ira Cohen was a quiet, almost shy medical officer whose gentle nature seemed to predispose him to stress, particularly during January and February as the Tet Offensive unfolded. I couldn't imagine how he'd managed his two-week stint in December as a general medical officer in an infantry battalion. In Lai Khe he spent his quiet hours bent over a guitar in our hooch, picking out catchy, fast-paced melodies with three fingers. He went out of his way to deny any expertise as a musician, professing to be only a beginner, teaching himself to play. I admired his patience as he played the difficult parts over and over, seemingly for hours on end. Over time, he became quite proficient. I enjoyed his music.

He was particularly close to Joe Callanan, with whom he shared the Anthony & Cleopatra cigars he received regularly from home.

On the second Friday in April, Cohen took his turn lecturing the new troops at the end of their "jungle school" orientation. We'd had no daytime mortar attacks for weeks so when the mortar rounds came it was a shock. Midway through Cohen's presentation, a series of four or five mortar rounds exploded just down the road from the radio shack, One, possibly two, arched through the leafy "ceiling" of his open-air "classroom."

Recognizing the proximity of the blasts from the hospital, some seventy yards away, I left immediately, heading toward the company area. In the distance a very tall soldier approached, coming up the hill from the oval road. He was hysterical, screaming desperate oaths and epithets, and his face was a mass of blood. I stared at it intently. Its features were mangled beyond recognition, fully amorphous. In the distance I couldn't make out eyes or a nose. Wearing blood like a mask, he seemed to have little difficulty seeing or breathing as he approached, his arms swinging easily at his sides. His injury seemed to be limited entirely to his face. It was an incredible sight! I could not take my eyes from it.

He was breathing rapidly as he drew near, coughing at intervals, spraying blood into small clouds through parallel vertical openings in the center of his face. His eyes, deeply recessed beneath his forehead, were wide—panicked, pleading, terrified. His tongue wriggled wildly inside his mouth, slurring words beyond recognition.

The soldier had no lips, and no sign of a nose. In fact, *he had no face*. It had been blown away, only swollen, bleeding infrastructure remaining.

Blood from his forehead seemed to obscure his vision at intervals, causing him to rake the back of his hand across his eyes from time to time. Only his ears and eyelids remained intact. His black, disheveled hair was devoid of blood.

A piece of flying shrapnel had struck him tangentially, slicing away his face from ear to ear like the work of a misaimed blow of a faulty 15th century guillotine, or an executioner's ax.

When he was hardly fifteen feet away, he hesitated, then staggered in a small circle, finally facing me, looking at me expectantly, screaming something I couldn't make out. I was speechless and momentarily unsteady on my feet. Finally the soldier turned and continued toward the hospital. He had been in Lai Khe hardly a week, but he seemed to know where to seek medical care.

Finally gathering myself, I followed him, gradually picking up speed. I had never even imagined such a wound.

Suddenly I was overcome with unsteadiness, then an all consuming nausea as Pete Kelly and a pair of medics came out to meet the faceless soldier. I continued past the hospital entrance and proceeded around the corner of the building, where I became very sick.

Later I entered the ER to find that all was under control. The soldier was supine and seemed to be sleeping, no doubt from the effect of morphine. Two bags of blood hung at the head of the table. I backed away and watched as Pete slipped a narrow catheter through the soldier's exposed ethmoidal sinus and into his trachea and began suctioning away old blood and mucous. Bleeding appeared to have stopped. Then he began lining raw tissues that once had supported a human face with Vaseline strips, then applied layers of dressing sponges, finally wrapping the soldier's head with cotton gauze, leaving only his breathing spaces free and exposed. Pete Kelly was a quiet and gentle man, famous at B-Med for his efficiency. To the sound of beating rotor blades outside, he and the medics carried the soldier to the chopper pad. I followed at a distance.

Minutes later, standing in the chopper's down-draft, my mind churned, wondering what would come next. Doctors at the 93rd Evac would probably perform a tracheotomy first, then cleanse and redress the entire wound—nasal cavities, eyelids, everything. Next would come split-thickness skin grafts, and countless revisions over weeks and months. It may take years to construct a satisfactory nose and reasonable lips. I assumed the soldier would be evacuated for specialized plastic surgical care in Japan or at the burn unit in San Antonio. The chances seemed good he would be on a jet within hours.

If the soldier survived, I couldn't imagine the life he would face. His was different from any other battle wound I would ever see. Other than his face, he was intact, as healthy as a horse. His vital signs were normal. With timely air evacuation and the kind of medical care I thought he would receive, he would survive. But his appearance to the world, his very identity, would always be hideous. Plastic surgery could help, but it could go only so far. To many he would be reduced to a curiosity or a source of pity. Even from his friends and family he would suffer unguarded looks. I couldn't begin to imagine the adjustments required of him.

There were other casualties and two dead GIs. Two of the wounded would also be evacuated. I never questioned myself about not holding up the chopper that evacuated the faceless soldier. That guy needed every break he could get. For him every minute counted. We called another chopper for the other two, once we had completed our preliminary treatment.

Later, I went down the hill to my hooch, my mind still consumed with the image of the faceless soldier. I knew I wouldn't be able to talk about it. I didn't even want to think about it.

I found Cohen sitting on his cot, his ankles crossed, Indian-style. His guitar was nowhere to be seen. He didn't acknowledge my presence, and I said nothing to him. We did not make eye contact. He had to be even more shaken up than I was. At close range he had seen two men die, and the others wounded. For all I knew, he had been an eye witness to the soldier's face being ripped off. I hoped he hadn't seen that. I couldn't imagine such horror.

For a moment I considered embracing him and holding him in my arms. I rejected the idea, but I wish I hadn't. It would have done us both good. Cohen and I never discussed that afternoon.

•••

Days later I witnessed an even greater desecration of humanity. Someone had mistakenly directed specimens to

B-Med rather than the Graves Registration collection point. A single litter was piled high with unrecognizable body parts, interspersed with remnants of damp, soiled fatigues. It was delivered to the orderly room. Graves Registration was charged with assigning names and serial numbers to remains. In 1968 the primary tools of GR were dental charts and finger prints. DNA matching was over a decade in the future. The pile of flesh before me—weighing perhaps 170 pounds—could have come from dozens of GIs. What appeared to be the work of a crazed butcher was likely the result of exploding rockets and mortar shells. No remnant seemed even remotely anatomical, only formless flesh and bone. There was nothing resembling a man's limb, chest, or abdomen. Only one—with a row of three or four teeth—identified a distinguishable function.

...

During Tet, from late January through February, I learned what was going on in Saigon and other cities targeted by the NVA and VC throughout South Vietnam only in bits and pieces. A decade later Dave R. Palmer, in his book *Summons of the Trumpet*, put those events in perspective for me. Palmer was both a West Point-trained professional soldier and dedicated scholar. At the end of his career, as a Lieutenant General (three stars), he returned to West Point for five years as superintendent. In his book he focused on military realities while other historians saw the war from other perspectives. Palmer deemed 1968 as "the climactic year of the Vietnam War. It was the turning point which saw the virtual elimination of the Viet Cong as a viable movement, the apex of United States involvement in South East Asia, the final North Vietnamese attempt to gain a military victory in the face of American ground forces, the uniting of South Vietnam, the emergence of the ARVN as a mature fighting force, and a shift in the entire thrust of the conflict."[16]

Nevertheless the Tet Offensive, in which Americans and the South Vietnamese, Palmer emphasizes, were clear *military* victors, it was also the turning point in, ironically, strengthening the communist cause *politically*. Nevertheless, thirty thousand VC would lose their lives in the fist ten days of Tet. Losing so many insurgents so quickly put a strain on the strength of the VC effort in South Vietnam. Communist leaders in North Vietnam had to scramble to recruit and train replacements, placing them clearly on the ropes.

...

Palmer describes the initial attack on Saigon, occurring between 2:00 and 7:00 a.m. (Vietnam time) on the second day of Tet.[17] Twenty heavily armed VC blew a hole in the wall surrounding the U. S. Embassy and crawled into the compound. But quick thinking guards bolted the entrance to the Embassy itself, denying the VC entry. They could only fire into the lobby from the outside for the hours that followed. At dawn Military Police reinforcements arrived, and all

---

[16] Dave R. Palmer, *Summons of the Trumpet: U.S.—Vietnam in Perspective* (Novato, CA:Presidio, 1978) 210.

[17] *Palmer 190-191.*

twenty VC were killed. Five Americans did lose their lives, but the attack on the Embassy was repulsed. *It was never in enemy hands.*

"Confused and inaccurate wire reports (of the incident) reached the United States just in time for the evening news on television." Unable to confirm anything, TV newsmen put out the word that communists had captured the U. S. Embassy! A shocked Walter Cronkite, the venerable CBS newscaster, allegedly uttered, "What the hell is going on? I thought we were winning this war." Cronkite voiced his quick interpretation of information he received that night to millions of Americans and never looked back. America would awaken the following morning committed to backing out of the war. Fortunately the brave young GIs defending Saigon at that moment, undoubtedly shocked and fearful for their lives, kept their cool and fought savagely until rescued by the five American battalions dispatched to save them. Within hours what few North Vietnamese not yet killed were driven from Saigon and its surroundings. But that story was neither aired quickly nor with clarity.

The president of the United States and commander-in-chief of American forces, Lyndon Johnson, while watching Cronkite live that evening, is reputed to have said, "If I've lost Cronkite, I've lost middle America." He understood that Americans on the home front were in the process of losing their will in Southeast Asia. It was a hell of a way to lose a war. The North Vietnamese high command and had placed all its eggs in a single basket and had rolled the dice. The folks back home never got the message.

17.
AFTER TET

Incredible Events

As Tet wound down, B-Med settled into an uneasy routine. We knew the absence of casualties and mortar attacks would not last, but for the first time in months we had time on our hands. After sick call—dealing with an again rising incidence of gonorrhea and the odd respiratory infections and headaches—we were left to while away the hours reading paperbacks. Almost overnight they were in short supply. One I read was a dusty, yellowing copy of *The Man*, a novel by Irving Wallace, a ridiculous tale of racism and politics. And it wasn't Wallace's only clunker.

Another had been the basis for a 1962 film, "The Prize," staring Paul Newman and Edward G. Robinson. My wife and I had seen it when I was an intern, on a rare Saturday night away from the hospital. The movie portrays Nobel Prize winners assembled in Stockholm to collect their awards. When Robinson's character, the Nobel laureate in physics, is stricken with a heart attack in a hotel room, the quick-thinking Nobelist in medicine rips the power cord from a table lamp, separates the wires and strips away the insulation with a pocketknife. Then he tears open the dying man's shirt, places the wires in strategic places, and has a colleague re-plug the cord into a wall socket for a brief second. Instantly Robinson's body lurches and his heart returns to a healthy rhythm and he's all set to live life happily ever after.

It was pure science fiction, of course, totally impossible technically. Saving a life by simply plugging and unplugging a lamp cord trivializes medical technology. I did the best I could to forget that movie. Storybook medicine gives me the creeps. But I was to find that some ridiculous stories refuse to die.

•••

In late March, when rumors of the My Lai Massacre first drifted into Lai Khe, my first thought was that it was a gross exaggeration. I was in Ben Cat leading a MedCap when the news reached me. My Lai (pronounced Me Lie) was two hundred miles from Lai Khe, northeast of Pleiku, on the South China Sea. Hundreds of Vietnamese civilians were allegedly murdered by Charlie Company, 1/20 (1st Battalion of the 20th Regiment) of the Americal Division. Most of the victims were said to have been the elderly, women, and children, even infants. Women and girls were raped.

It couldn't possibly be true. American soldiers did not abuse Vietnamese civilians, ever. My personal experience made the news from My Lai inconceivable.

But what if . . . Could it have happened? How? Why? I could understand a mentally disturbed GI, driven to the brink of fear and despair, flipping out and using his weapon to achieve misguided retribution at the expense of an imagined enemy. But nothing like the stories we had heard, not hundreds of helpless victims. That kind of slaughter amounted to pure evil, from the mind of a psychopath like Adolph Hitler.

Or could drugs have been at the root of the slaughter? In Lai Khe we had seen evidence of drug use only by the enemy, an NVA regiment on a suicide mission some weeks earlier. The entire unit had been wiped out. Over two hundred NVA troops died that night. One after another they charged American machine gun positions. The first wave went down, and others in succession, leaving bodies stacked up like cord wood. The carnage was complete in an hour.

But My Lai *did* happen. The details were made public in 1969. I believe it now, but I'll never understand it. Twenty-six soldiers were tried, and one was convicted. One man was responsible for the deaths of over three hundred? How? First Lieutenant William Calley, a platoon leader in Charlie company, was sentenced to life in prison. The My Lai Massacre cast a blot on the entire American effort in Vietnam, an unimaginable tragedy.

...

More surprises followed. On the evening of March 31 President Johnson announced he would not seek re-election. I heard the speech live by radio, late in the morning (Vietnam time). I couldn't imagine the political turmoil that announcement might inspire back home. I'd assumed the anti-Vietnam sentiments were limited to college students dead set on not serving, plus their kooky professors and assorted hippies. It had to be more than that. And more bad news was on the way.

Later the news magazines reported that Bobby Kennedy was the front-runner to be the Democratic nominee for president. He was said to support the cessation of the bombing of the Ho Chi Minh Trail. That would be bad for us in and around Lai Khe. The Ho Chi Minh Trail, the route of new troops, munitions, and supplies into South Vietnam, was the lifeline of any continuing Communist effort. That was a fact. It must be destroyed. It *could* be destroyed! Back home people were supporting the VC, not us?

And the news from home only got worse. On April 4 Martin Luther King was assassinated in Memphis, jacking up racial unrest to a fever pitch. Riots broke out swiftly in Washington, D. C. to within blocks of the White House. Heavily armed police were pitted against incensed demonstrators. A score of them died, and a thousand buildings and homes went up in flames. Suddenly our nation's capital was more dangerous than Lai Khe, by far.

Robert F. Kennedy was assassinated on June 5. For twenty-four hours the Vietnam TV network was silent, airing only Kennedy's photograph on screens at military installations throughout the country. Nobody openly disparaged him—we, of all people, had learned to respect the dead—but one by one, every TV set in Vietnam was turned off. RFK couldn't have *bought* a vote in Lai Khe that spring.

In August the Democratic National Convention convened in Chicago: more vitriol, hate, rioting, death and destruction. The war had spread to America.

...

On the afternoon of April 21 Albert Maroscher, while directing artillery fire near Lai Khe in a light observation helicopter, was shot down by ground fire. He was dead when he arrived at B-Med. I recognized him immediately. His cold, pallid face was finally devoid of the vast energy and commitment that had made him such an impressive officer. He had wounds of entry and exit immediately above his knee. His bubble-type, two-seater observation chopper was armed with lead beneath the seats but not sufficiently. The bullet's trajectory had to have been perfectly vertical to enter Al's thigh. He had bled to death. Had I the slightest inkling that it could happen, I could have prompted him how to save his own life. Compressing the easily found artery in his groin would have done the job, or applying a tight tourniquet at mid-thigh.

I was told later that Al had to beg the brass to let him fly that afternoon. It was a battle he did not want to miss. I'd never met anyone like Al Maroscher before. Born in Romania, he became a naturalized American citizen when he was in college. A man of unusual character and dedication, he told me how blessed he felt to be an American. He wanted to serve in the worst sort of way. His death remains a personal loss for me and a big one for all Americans.

...

A few afternoons later, while sorting through sundry items in the equipment room adjacent to the ER, I searched for extra forceps and hemostats to replenish our out-of-date cut-down trays. I was shocked to come across an electrocardiogram machine. It was brand new, probably never used. The Army prided itself on being prepared for any circumstances, but anticipating the need for emergency heart tracings in our population of soldiers—almost all in their late teens and early twenties—seemed extreme, even wasteful. I expected an EKG machine or two in an evac hospital, possibly even a cardioverter to treat rare rhythm abnormalities. Of a half-million-plus Americans in Vietnam, only bird colonels, general officers, and a few non-commissioned officers were in their forties. General Westmoreland, commander of American forces in Vietnam, was fifty-four.

I had no idea I would soon need far more than a simple EKG machine.

The need came in the form of a pudgy staff sergeant in respiratory distress. He had a frantic look, his face a deathly gray, but most of all he was struggling to breathe. His medical record indicated he was forty-four, but he seemed ten years older. He was clearly the oldest looking soldier we'd admitted at B-Med during my time there. He was bald, and soft looking, mainly his belly and throat.

His chest heaved mightily, and even his hands and fingers were dusky. He was doing his best to die.

As a medic tore away the guy's fatigues, he commandeered a crumpled pack of Lucky Strikes from a breast pocket. Another covered his face with an oxygen mask, another hovered over the back of his hand, starting an IV, and still another wrapped a blood pressure cuff around the opposite arm and snapped down the Velcro.

His respiratory rate was approaching forty per minute, so fast I didn't bother to count it. With my stethoscope I could hardly hear any breath sounds anywhere. He was not moving any air at all! It was acute asthma! Nothing else looked like this.

Stateside physical exam screening was aimed at keeping asthmatics out of Southeast Asia, but somehow this soldier had slipped through the cracks. Something in the air had set it off. Possibly he'd had childhood asthma he had failed to report. Maybe he had assumed he'd outgrown it.

After infusing high doses of medicine intravenously, he seemed slightly less agonal but his respiratory rate continued to race at a dangerous clip. I'd had little experience with asthma, and I'd never seen anything like this. After twenty minutes I had given him massive doses of theophylline and prednisone, and there was no sign of improvement. If anything, he was worse. And I didn't know what else to do!

Suddenly his face went from gray to blue, and his eyes seemed to bulge dangerously. Then they rolled back in his head, and he lost his carotid pulse.

A medic looked up from across the table and said, "Blood pressure is thirty!"

This soldier was going to die, and there was not one thing we could do about it.

"Get that EKG machine in here," I snapped to nobody

in particular. The EKG machine had become a conversation piece, with medics taking turns running rhythm strips from each other, calculating their heart rates from it and trying to figure out what QRS-complexes and T-waves meant.

Someone had anticipated my direction because the machine was already at the bed side, and extremity leads were being applied.

The soldier's QRS-complexes were bizarre-looking—swollen, with elevated ST-segments. Then, before my eyes the pattern deteriorated into a weary-looking wavy line. He was in ventricular fibrillation, the electrical signature of a dying heart. He was getting away from us.

We needed a cardiac defibrillator in the worst sort or way. Without one, we would have little alternative but to stand by helplessly as the soldier died. I could only stare at him in frustration, his face focusing in and out, becoming blurred, seeming to turn to paste, his features subtly changing. Faint jowls appeared and his eyebrows darkened, taking on bushy mass. They were familiar eyebrows, arising from deep in my memory.

It was the face of Edward G. Robinson!

In an instant I became very calm. If we, as a team, could hold together for a few minutes, there just might be a way. I forced myself to nothing but positive thoughts.

Even the smallest of rural hospitals back home would not be without emergency power. The idea was a long shot, maybe even crazy to consider. But we had to do something. Suddenly I was aware I had become engulfed in a huge shadow.

"Tank, don't we have an emergency generator around here someplace?" I asked the man towering over me, not even looking up.

"Yes sir." His jaws rippled as he looked down at me.

He was a giant of a man, with steely gray eyes set well apart and a stern face that only rarely crinkled into a smile. He was said to have been a farmer in Mississippi before being called for Vietnam. He was popular among the medics for his easy-going nature and his endless collection of country stories. Rumor had it he had once played for the Steelers. Really? It wasn't important now. At the moment we were in a big enough game ourselves. Tank was an E7, but calling him Sergeant didn't sound right. Around B-Med he was simply Tank. It was an affectionate name. We all knew we could count on him.

"You know how to crank it up?"

"Yes sir."

"Get it. Now!" My words were barely audible.

Without a miracle in the next two minutes, this soldier's brain would turn to mush. But I had to force myself to slow down. Hurrying would lead us nowhere.

Ignoring the seconds ticking away, I made myself concentrate on the needle cups on the countertop across the room. Stainless steel needle cups had been a mainstay in every general practitioner's office in America from as far back as the 1930s. Nowadays, almost all suture is swaged onto tiny curving surgical needles by machine, and packaged in sterile envelopes, but for generations individual needles were stored in an inch or two of alcohol on the bottom of metal containers the old-timers called dishes. For decades suture was threaded manually, one at a time, through the eye of each needle. Military medicine didn't have to be state-of-the-art, just certain. Without a word I dumped the yellowish-green alcohol and a dozen or so needles onto the floor.

"I need some goose grease," I said calmly, sending a medic across the room for a tube of the lubricant we used for rectal examinations. Then I squeezed a glob of it on the soldier's sternum, and slathered it in circles, gradually covering the left side of his chest to beneath his armpit.

"I need two strips of copper wire, five or six feet long, and an arm-board," I announced to the group of gathering medics. There were at least four. One of them rushed to the storage room, another to the hallway.

The arm-board came quickly, and the wire almost a minute later. It was radio antenna wire somebody had rigged to a short wave receiver. Medics on the night shift listened to early season Major League Baseball on the Voice of America. The arm-board was roughly three-by-fifteen inches, padded with foam-rubber and adhesive tape. We used them daily to immobilize wrists and forearms by winding them with tape to secure IVs. It would be fine for what I had in mind. Wood does not conduct electricity.

I had finished threading the wires through each of the pair of tea-cup like handles of the steel cups, and twisting them down, when I heard the heavy, rumbling wheels of the gasoline-powered generator behind me. I glanced back at it. It was a huge, bulky contraption, vaguely resembling the lawnmower I'd spent Saturday mornings with as a kid. Tank needed no prompt from me. In seconds he secured the opposite ends of the wires to appropriate generator posts.

I placed one cup, bottom side down, immediately to the right of the soldier's sternum, and the other, some eight or nine inches to the left, at the beginning of maximum rib cage convexity. Then I bridged them with the arm-board, trapping each cup against the soldier's chest wall. Perhaps, with a little luck, the padded plywood would protect me from the jolt. It was a more or less self-designed defibrillator paddle handle, about to be tested.

"Okay, Tank," I said, noticing a squeak in my voice, and for the first time aware of beads sweat forming on my forehead. "Listen carefully. When I count to three, crank that baby up. Then, at the instant I say, 'cut,' turn it off. Got it? The 'turning off' is as important as the 'turning on.' It must be quick, like swiping an apple from a produce truck." Defibrillators back in the world would cut off automatically. Who knew how much current this contraption could generate and how quickly, even if it would work at all. But it had to! If it didn't, this soldier was a dead man.

"Yes, sir."

I glanced at Tank: his face was as still as stone, his steely eyes fully focused, as though he were preparing to assist me to lance a boil on some GI's backside.

Controlling the steel cups with the arm-board firmly against the soldier's chest, I took a deep breath and began, "One . . . two . . . THREE."

The generator growled to life behind me, and hardly an instant later the soldier's body leaped upward from the makeshift table as no telling how many amps or volts or whatever else surged through him. His movement knocked the arm-board from my hand, and sent the steel cups clattering to the floor in different directions.

"CUT—CUT—CUT!" I screamed, startled, even though it was obvious the circuit had already been broken.

Instantly the sound of the generator was no more.

"Click on the EKG," I snapped, now very excited.

It hummed to life and a narrow strip of paper rolled beneath the stylus, etching a perfect sinus rhythm. The abnormal segments were still present, but the rhythm was normal. Suddenly the soldier had a fighting chance.

"Well, I will be damned," I said softly, hardly believing what I had just witnessed.

There were other things to do, of course: replenish the theophylline drip, give him more prednisone, and increase the oxygen flow, for starters. But the soldier's color had improved, and he was breathing more easily and efficiently, his respiratory rate dropping to the low twenties within fifteen or twenty minutes. His blood pressure climbed to ninety, and, most importantly and most incredibly, his heart beat continued, now firm and steady. He was also moving air through his lungs. His expiratory phase was a little prolonged, but I could finally hear him breathe. We had given him a ton of theophylline and prednisone, and finally they had taken hold.

Over the years I related this story to colleagues from time to time, but I finally stopped. Their rolling eye balls and looks of disbelief were frustrating. But I did not blame them at all.

I got to be an Edward G. Robinson fan. I saw all his movies. I can't say I took any notes or memorized any lines, but I did pay close attention.

18.
MURDER, CONFUSION, AND MOVING ON

pril 27, a Saturday night, found me in the ER waiting for an ambulance to return. A fight had broken out in the village, and a soldier had been shot. Fights in the village were nothing new with battalions pouring in from the bush at intervals for much-needed down time, but the usual injuries were broken hands and broken noses.

However battle-weary, a soldier with too many beers on board had a way of reverting to the warrior he had been trained to be. What soldiers did best was fight. Mixing restless GIs, scantily-clad Asian beauties, and plentiful alcohol could turn the village into a crucible, making tragedy inevitable. Jealousy, an old grudge, or a perceived slight too often led to a senseless misunderstanding, then bedlam. Throw in a weapon or two, and young lives were at risk. Yet it was a part of war.

The victim was long and lean, with blond hair and a bullet hole squarely in the middle of his chest. He might have been the life of the party an hour ago, but now he was fighting for his life. He was pale and sweaty, and had no obtainable blood pressure. That he was alive didn't seem possible. How could a bullet in his heart not end his life in minutes?

But it hadn't. He was unconscious, but he was not dead. His carotid pulse was weak and thready, but it was clearly present. Positive thinking was a requirement at B-Med, but it also could be a two-edged sword, blinding one to truth.

The bullet wound was small, extremely small, definitely not from an M-16, or even a .45. But still it should have been lethal. My first thought was that the path of the bullet had pierced the covering of the heart, then the muscle itself, resulting in blood flooding the pericardial space, and, somehow, being trapped there, reducing the heart's pumping capacity. Cardiac tamponade was the medical term. Or maybe the bullet had struck the heart a glancing blow. Either way, the soldier could have a small but real chance to survive. I wanted that to be so, anyway. A cardiac surgeon in an ideally equipped hospital could open his chest and decrease the pressure gradient by opening the heart's fibrous covering, then stuffing a finger into the source of bleeding. With luck he could control the bleeding a minute or so, enabling him to place a purse-string suture around the site of the bleeding. It could save this soldier's life. I'd never seen it done, but I had seen good heart surgeons work. I knew how they did things.

But the only surgeon for miles was me, and our instruments were rudimentary at best. For one thing, they weren't long enough to allow working that deep in the chest. And our lighting system was nowhere near adequate for heart surgery. There was no time to intubate the soldier, and no heart-lung machine to back us up if things didn't go well. All kinds of things could go wrong.

What else was I to do? Just watch the guy die? I thought about it a few seconds, then waived the chaplain away. He'd been waiting as long as I had.

I sloshed alcohol over the soldier's chest, then donned a pair of gloves. "Get some blood, guys, and make sure we have at least two IVs. Three would be better. We'll also need two suction machines. And tell that chaplain outside to start praying. Tell him to pray his ass off! And one more thing: get that self-retaining thoracic retractor somebody pinched from the 93rd weeks ago. We'll definitely need that."

Was I really going to try this? Had I lost my mind?

Medics scurried in various directions. Sergeant Ramos, a new medic, taped the diaphragm of his stethoscope to the soldier's back to listen to his heartbeat, then settled into a seat beside the soldier's groin to monitor what was left of his femoral pulse. There was no backing down now.

I slashed a long incision beneath the fifth rib and continued through the intercostal muscles. Removing a rib was not an option. We didn't have that kind of time.

"We've got no heart beat, Captain, and he's no longer breathing," Ramos said calmly.

Ignoring him, I fit the retractor blades against the soldier's exposed ribs, and cranked his chest open to the crunching sounds of splintering ribs.

"This guy's dead, Captain," Ramos was insistent, demanding. "Not breathing, no heart beat, no femoral pulse. Nothing."

Speckled pink lung swelled from the wound. With an open hand I swept it away and covered it with a laparotomy pad. Then I cranked the retractor again. I found myself staring into a chest full of swirling blood. This may have been cardiac tamponade at some point, but it was way beyond that now. The GI's was chest was full of blood. I stared at it a moment—watching its eddies and flow—and slowly began to calm down.

"It's got us beat, guys," I said finally. I had been a fool. We had never had a chance. I'd been a damned fool.

...

If I thought things were about to get easier, I was wrong. Some things were worse than death. Thirty or forty minutes later a pair of MPs brought in a clearly inebriated GI with an injured hand. He had two weeks' growth of beard, chestnut in color—wet, nasty-looking—and he clutched a paper towel between his fingers. It was spotted with blood. One MP hurried through the ER and into our supply room, seeming in search of something, possibly another exit. When he returned, his partner announced they would wait in the hallway, reminding me to sing out if there were problems.

"What's he done?" I couldn't help asking.

"A shooting in the village," was the clipped response. "Murder suspect, we've been told. Who knows?"

The soldier showed not the slightest reaction.

His injury was a simple laceration. It extended from opposing surfaces of the index and long fingers of his left hand, crossing the web space between them. The wound was far from complex, but I had never seen a laceration quite like that before.

"How did this happen, soldier?"

"Don't know, Doc. Been to a party," he said with a nutty grin.

Bleeding was minimal, leaving me only to cleanse the

wound and close it with interrupted sutures. The soldier kept bragging that he never required "deadening medicine for stitchings." He definitely wouldn't need it tonight. He was as drunk as a coot.

He continued chattering as though he hadn't a care in the world. It really bothered me. If he'd just killed one of his buddies, in a few hours he would wake up to unimaginable pain.

As I tied the last suture, he gave me a chilling look, then asked, "Is the bastard dead?"

I stared at him, speechless. He gave me a clear-eyed look, like he'd somehow swallowed his drunkenness, or had blinked it away.

"Say that again, soldier?"

"You treat a guy a while ago with a bullet wound? Pretty fella, six feet, yellow damn hair." His speech was crystal clear, and did not waver. He didn't sound like the same soldier. What should I say? What *could* I say?

"We did have a young blond soldier die nearly an hour ago," I said.

"Good." It was a simple statement, delivered without a trace of emotion. He seemed as sober as a priest.

"You? You shot him?"

"You bet I did, Doc. He had it coming."

Really? Was this a confession I was hearing?

But coming from a man with multiple beers in his system, it probably wouldn't mean much. And did the Army consider doctor-patient communications privileged information, inadmissible in court? I'd been sworn to the Hippocratic Oath: to keep my patients from harm and injustice. How did that change things? I wasn't working for individuals any more. I worked for the whole damn Army.

I didn't know the first thing about law, but I assumed the Oath would be the issue in civilian life. However the Uniform Code of Military Justice (UCMJ) looked at it, I had a moral obligation to a dead soldier too.

I spoke to an MP a few minutes later, but he had no idea what was required of me under military law. He took down word for word what the soldier had told me, and said a JAG (Judge Advocate General) officer would be contacting me.

I felt sick, and went outside for some fresh air. There were no more patients to see. It seemed a peaceful night from the narrow terrace at the west end of the building. Had this really happened? A soldier was dead, and another one's life was as good as ruined. Did they even know each other? Fighting over a dancing girl or a prostitute that neither of them knew? It was a staggering thought.

I stared at the stars for a long time, thinking, tears beginning to work their way down my cheeks. Then I put my head down on the stucco rail and wept.

···

It would be years before I would see how medicine interfaced with the civilian justice system, but what I'd heard in the ER would seem to boost the charge from possible manslaughter to something more serious. The soldier with the grimy hair seemed to have personal issues with the dead kid. Had they had a previous history? What happened may have been more than the result of a drunken rage. Were JAG officers in Vietnam qualified to handle a case like this one? I assumed they were all young guys like me. I'd spent four years in college, then four in medical school and two more in postgraduate training. I had just been guilty of beginning a heart operation, one I was in no way qualified to perform, but that was in a life-and-death situation, an urgent emergency to give an innocent kid what slim chance he seemed to have. Trying a young man for murder was never an emergency situation. Did the skill and experience necessary to try murder-suspects rise to the level of performing heart surgery? Maybe the Army flew in special legal experts for the difficult cases. I could understand suspects not being sent home for trial. Cases had to be tried where the witnesses were. Maybe murder convictions were reviewed by a special board, and outcomes could be overturned. It was necessary to have a mechanism to keep things fair. I might have missed some UCMJ lectures at Fort Sam, but did they expect me to learn so much from a lecture or two I would never have to ask questions if circumstances arose? I needed to talk to somebody.

Weeks passed, and no JAG officer had contacted me. In a way I was relieved, but still I worried about what might lay ahead. I assumed that any witness would be prepared before appearing at a court martial. If I were to be a prosecution witness, the prosecuting officer wouldn't try to influence my testimony, but he would see that I understood what I might be asked so I wouldn't be making snap judgments in court. And shouldn't someone be informing me how to conduct myself, and something about the routines and procedures? I'd never been in court in my life. Wasn't it reasonable for witnesses to be comfortable in court?

...

Additional time passed and still no JAG officer appeared to brief me on the process and about the possibility of being questioned about information given me by a soldier under my care. Was it my personal responsibility to refuse to answer such questions? Refusing to answer a question like that could buy me legal problems of my own.

I was surprised a few days later when Green informed me an order had arrived commanding me to appear at a general court-martial the following week. Still, no JAG officer had contacted me.

I was uneasy on the morning I was scheduled to appear. I had yet to see a JAG officer. I concluded I had no choice but to limit every answer to precisely what I had been asked, no more, no less. Possibly I would be permitted to refuse to answer until I'd been advised by the court of my own rights and restrictions. Surely that would protect me from violating any doctor-patient confidentially obligations I thought I had.

...

I entered the courtroom a few minutes past 1100 hours. The trial was held at the quarters of a nearby infantry battalion. The room was not small—certainly we didn't have a room that large at B-Med—but it was filled to capacity with fresh fatigues and serious faces. Mess halls would have made better courtrooms but for their screen walls, which limited privacy and confidentiality.

Five officers sat stern and stiff-backed at the narrow table at the front of the room. A full colonel was in the middle and two of the others were captains. I didn't recognize any of them. As a matter of fact, no one in the room seemed familiar.

I gave my name, rank, and duty station, then my questioner, a captain with a sonorous voice and a brisk manner, turned and faced the table before asking me to give the name of the defendant.

The name of the defendant? Really? I had anticipated dozens of questions, but certainly not that one. I had no idea what the soldier's name was. I could easily have gotten it from our records at B-Med, even as late as an hour ago—possibly it was on the order Green had supplied me—but I had no idea anyone expected me to know the guy's name. How was that germane to anything? I expected to have to confront him, and I knew I would recognize him. If I didn't, I would say so. I was shaken by that question. I even tried to match faces with name tapes, but the distances and angles in the court room made that virtually impossible.

Every eye at the table was focused on me when I had said nothing for almost a minute after the question was repeated. With my ears and the back of my neck on fire, my only answer could be, "No, sir."

Suddenly I had a serious need for a drink of water. My questioner, presumably the prosecuting officer, ignored my request, only twisted his face into an incredulous look. He seemed on the verge of rolling his eyes. Finally he looked down, studying the floor for long seconds.

"Captain," he said, feigning patience, "can you identify the defendant in this room? Can you point him out?"

I began scanning every face I could see, all eyes still on me. My perspective of almost everyone present was in profile. The closer to the table they were, the tougher it was to see their faces. None of them offered me eye contact. In my rising panic, I didn't think to ask if I could approach each of them or have them turn to face me. Why didn't the prosecutor suggest that? Wasn't my testimony to support his argument? The court stenographer, a young sergeant to the left of the table, furiously scribbled in his notebook. I had not seen the defendant for weeks. When I saw him last he had shaggy brown hair and an uneven beard. It dawned on me that not a single soldier had a beard, and virtually every one of them had had a recent haircut.

Finally my questioner, a sarcastic look on his face, sidled up to me from the opposite side, grinning at me in disdain.

"The witness is excused," he announced in his rich baritone voice.

I was more embarrassed than I'd been in my entire life as I stumbled toward the door and left the room, easing the door shut behind me. It would be days before it dawned on me that my testimony wouldn't have made any difference anyway. Surely the prosecutor had eye witnesses to whatever happened in the village that night. Several would have witnessed whatever argument had taken place, and probably the actual shooting. Convicting anybody on my testimony alone would have been absurd.

As big a fool I as had made of myself at the court-martial, I had at least avoided divulging information given me by an intoxicated soldier under my care. Did the prosecuting officer see that, and disqualify me as a witness to avoid addressing my doctor-patient confidentiality issues? It was a strange way to help me. I was *his* witness, and he was hostile toward me.

I assume that justice was done that day. I hope it was. I'll admit, though, I've harbored questions about the military justice system for decades since then.

···

When the rainy season (the southern monsoon in South Vietnam) ended in late September, there had been no fanfare of nature or any particular suddenness. Almost before we knew it days had passed without rain. Very soon the was quite predictable, and offensive activities resumed.

The *coming* of the rainy season, on the other hand, in early May, occurred with sensational climatic change. I was flying back to Lai Khe from Binh Hoa late one afternoon when I noticed the heavens were filled with ominous yet beautiful clouds throughout the northern sky. Within twenty minutes they darkened from shades of gray, beginning to take on the look of impending doom. One could almost feel moisture in the air. Simultaneously the temperature fell from the nineties in the early afternoon to the seventies by dusk. After dark the temperature would fall to almost sixty, making me wonder if one could freeze to death in Southeast Asia. I was truly cold. And, other than a few at the hospital, we had no blankets!

Our enterprising supply sergeant had traded our allotted two hundred blankets for something he deemed of greater value: probably food. I remember being surprised once or twice by better than average steak. I do not criticize his judgment, though, because I was cold only a single night of my four hundred in Vietnam.

Thunder and lightening came later, and rains poured throughout the night. The most startling aspect of the appearance of the monsoon was in evidence the following morning. I was awakened to the light-footed sounds of tiny frogs on the floor, hopping back and fourth in every direction. It was truly something to see. There were dozens of them. And I came close to crushing several when I tried to slip on a boot. For the rest of my life I would shake out my boots on hunting and fishing trips before putting them on.

···

A few weeks later I received a letter from Lew Flint, a former med school buddy. We had been med students, interns, and junior residents together. Somehow he had landed himself an assignment as a general surgeon at the 71st Evac in Pleiku. I had no idea he was in Vietnam, and couldn't figure out how he had known where I was.

The only thing stranger than hearing from an old friend out of the blue was the content of his letter. Lew was scheduled to rotate back to the States in a few weeks, and had discovered his slot at the 71st was not yet filled. He thought I might be interested in succeeding him. I read that part twice, realizing that this could be one of the most important letters I would receive in my life.

But there were things I needed to know before I accepted his offer. He explained that the surgical staff—the entire medical staff, for that matter—was well trained and experienced. He had been treated well and had gotten to do a lot of surgery. The caveat was that the style of living was not at all what we had been used to at Duke. He described the 71st Evac as much like a college fraternity, with weekend beer parties, the whole bit. That gave me pause. Socially Lew was more advanced than I was. Unlike me he had attended Duke as an undergraduate, and was quite comfortable with fraternity life. I was in a fraternity too, but Davidson College was a dry campus back then. For a student to drink beer within the town limits would buy him a hearing before the honor council and a one-way ticket home. One classmate, who was the son of a member of the Board of Trustees, was suspended an entire year for merely *possessing* a can of beer in his dorm room. I had had my first beer at age twenty-three!

Lew pointed out that to gain everything the 71st had to offer, I must go along with the social program, prove myself to be comfortable with it. He could offer no guarantees, but the chances were good I would move into his old room in the officer barracks. More conservative medical officers were quartered elsewhere, but living in FUB-1 (for, Frigging Unbelievable) could be a golden opportunity. He was vague about it, but assured me the experiences I would have would amount to an opportunity to meet people and do things which could change my life. I read those sentences over a couple of times. They sounded nothing like Lew Flint. He was never into hyperbola. He said he would leave solid recommendations with his buddies, but I would have to do the rest. He predicted I'd be invited to a Saturday night party soon after arrival, so they could check me out. It really did sound like a college fraternity.

He urged me to reply as soon as possible so he could get the paperwork started. I would be expected to arrive soon after his departure and must agree to serve until late October. My current obligation was a twelve-month tour, ending in September. To take advantage of a chance to work at the 71st Evac, I would have to extend my tour in Vietnam by five weeks.

It was a no-thinker. This was the chance I'd been dreaming of! And I could impersonate a frat-boy too. It was a dumb assignment, but I could handle it.

...

In June I met my wife for a week of R & R in Hawaii. We had a glorious time. Our financial situation had kept us from even dreaming of such a trip. We took in all of Honolulu and then some. We stayed at the Ilikai Hotel on Waikiki Beach. The Ilikai was where "Hawii Five-O," the police procedural drama staring Jack Lord, would be filmed. It opened its first season on CBS just weeks before I would leave Vietnam. One evening I wore my uniform to the formal dining room at the venerable Royal Hawaiian Hotel, where the maitre d' presented us beautiful leis and complimentary desserts. That gave me a special feeling, tempting me to believe such a gesture might be repeated when

I got back home. The only hiccup in Hawii occurred outside a movie theater. We had just seen "Guess Who's Coming to Dinner," starring Sidney Poitier. An automobile a block away suddenly backfired, creating a sound much like a mortar shell exploding. I found myself running for cover!

···

My return flight arrived at Tan Son Nhut Air Base at night, resulting in a trip to the officers' club and an overnight stay. At the OC I met another medical officer, a general surgeon with the rank of lieutenant colonel. As things turned out, we had more in common than medicine. He was an avid golfer, and we had a good time talking about Trevino winning the Open just days ago, and equipment, the new ultra-light aluminum shafts in vogue back home. I told him I'd grown up playing golf at Pinehurst. In time the conversation turned to my present duty assignment and future expectations. Then he asked if I might have an interest in spending a year at the Walter Reed Army Medical Center in Washington, D.C. He was scheduled to become the commanding officer of WRAIR, the Walter Reed Army Institute of Research. When I was skeptical that he could pull off such a plum assignment, he took down my name and social security number and promised me he not only could, he would! Beginning the following spring, we would spend most Saturday mornings together on the golf course at Fort Meade, a short motorcycle trip north from D.C. on Highway One.

Suddenly things were falling into place. The future was bright, and the wind was at my back!

19.
PLEIKU—
71ST EVACUATION
HOSPITAL

"The prettiest girl I ever saw was sipping bourbon
through a straw."
(From a World War II Army barracks song)

With two duffle bags of gear and my official personnel records I was one of a half-dozen to board an old C-47 one evening in third week of July. It was a starless night and beginning to rain. Brown plastic bags were issued as we boarded. When the spec-4 ahead of me asked what they were for, he was told, "Don't worry about it, soldier. You'll figure it out."

Qui Nhon (pronounced Quin Yon), an old seaport town on the South China Sea, was two hundred thirty miles north, but getting there required the longest flight of my life. Rain came in earnest twenty minutes after takeoff, and for nearly two hours we huddled miserably in darkness, punctuated by flashes of lightning. Our under-ventilated, non-air-conditioned aircraft was buffeted all over the sky by heavy winds and sheets of rain. But somehow the old boat held together. Without the barf bag, though, matters would have been worse.

The next afternoon, brightly sun-lit beneath clear blue skies, a courier helicopter took me an hour due west over green plateaus and sloping fields of coffee, rubber, and cashew trees to the ancient town of Pleiku. It was the terminus of the military supply route along Hwy 19 from the coast. Nearby was the home to the 633rd Special Operations Wing (U. S. Air Force) and the base camp of the 4th Infantry Division. A mile northwest lay the sprawling 450-bed 71st Evacuation Hospital.

Pleiku and its environs were populated by a strikingly different kind of Vietnamese. The "Montagnards" (from French, "of the mountains") were a fierce, industrious people of firm cultural roots who had lived in the Central Highlands for over two thousand years. They were primarily Christians, converted by 19th century French Catholics and American protestant missionaries of the 1930s. They quickly allied themselves with the American cause in hopes of achieving the autonomy they had sought for centuries.

The 71st Evac was spread out in a series of relatively new single-story buildings. Paved and covered walkways connected postoperative wards and OR buildings, insuring consistent working conditions in the rainy season. Other structures included a spacious, well equipped dining hall and a PX stocked with snacks, paperbacks, audiotapes, beer by the case, condoms, and hard liquor, with Chevas Regal selling for $2.40 a fifth. There was also a chapel seating several hundred, complete with a tall wooden steeple and a stained-glass window.

Arriving Saturday afternoon, I was assigned a bed in the barracks for male officers by a sergeant from the personnel section. The following day I was given a tour of the facility, then took in the protestant chapel service. Seeing American female nurses paired off with 4th Division soldiers and hospital staff, I was not shocked that the sermon was aimed at the joys of personal purity against the slippery slope of adultery. The chaplain seemed to understand he was preaching up hill.

Monday morning I assisted an impressive young, dark-haired surgeon who had been trained at Wayne State University in Detroit. He couldn't have been more engaging as he whisked through gall bladder surgery on a middle-aged Fourth Division officer who had developed acute pain during the night. It was an operation I never expected to see in Vietnam. Assuming I'd never done a gall bladder, he maintained a running commentary on what he was doing and why, without once seeming to talk down to me.

In the afternoon he assisted me with an inguinal herniorrhaphy, another case I wouldn't have expected in a war zone. He explained that most guys with hernias were evacuated to the States or Japan for elective surgery. He decided to operate himself since he worried the soldier would not be able to make the trip without a serious complication. He'd been having swelling and pain for two days. The following morning the surgeon from Wayne State was to assist me with a huge perirectal abscess, but left the OR as soon as I was underway. Abscesses anywhere near the rectum are not esthetically pleasing cases for some surgeons, but I was thrilled to be doing an operation of my very own. He returned during the final stages and seemed okay with what I'd done.

There was no surgery at all for the next two days, leaving me time to read and shoot baskets behind my quarters. Thursday afternoon I received an invitation to attend the "Hi and Bye Party" held on Saturday nights for incoming and outgoing staff members. They were held in a building adjacent to the row of officers' billets behind the PX. Across the top of the Xeroxed invitation was scrawled, "Urge your presence at after-party at FUB-1 next door."

Saturday night I found myself sandwiched among wall-to-wall people moving back and forth to truly loud music. They consisted of hospital staff of both sexes, including a few junior officers from the 4th Infantry Division. They were dressed in civvies, basically Bermudas and tee shirts for men and a range of outfits for the women. After a few beers, the people I had met became a blur of laughing faces whose names had gone in one ear and out the other. Names of the new and the departing were read from the front of the room, but to little attention or acclaim. Around 2200 hours the party began to wind down, with pairs and threesomes drifting off in various directions. As far as I could tell, I was the only one heading for the building next door.

FUB-1 was of identical construction as the other half-dozen residences on either side of a paved walkway. They consisted of steel siding and peaked roofs with wide eaves. There were no windows, and sandbags surrounded each building, stacked to a height of four feet.

A gregarious, roly-poly Italian-American introduced himself as Ray Parisi, who was in the process of serving up meat balls and spaghetti to the crowd spilling from the front yard to the side yard. He passed me off to a tall, lanky guy named Fisher, who made introductions to the ten or twelve gathered out front in folding chairs, all with beverages in hand. Some had female guests, including Fisher. His girl friend was tall and friendly and almost pretty. Fisher had a courtly manner but was close to being over the top, exaggerating almost every statement and gesture. His eyes bulged and twinkled, and his hands and arms were in constant motion. I couldn't decide if he saw me as someone worth recruiting or merely tolerating. It was obvious he'd been well served with whatever was in his paper cup. Neither he nor anybody else mentioned my old pal Lew Flint. It was curious. At the moment I was underwhelmed by my reception.

Parisi's spaghetti seemed to clear my head a little and possibly encouraged me to load up with another few beers. What else could I do? Standing and drinking seemed to beat standing and staring. People addressed me with wide eyes and happy faces, but nobody had much to say. Few offered me a name. I remembered Parisi and Fisher by their last names, but for a long time I couldn't figure out which one was Ray. The only guy I was much drawn to was a late-comer. He had dark, thinning hair and was pleasant. He looked me squarely in the eye, surprising me by calling me by my name. Somehow, that was intimidating. If he'd been drinking he didn't show it. He told me he was Dave and didn't give his last name.

As the crowd began to thin out around midnight, the FUB-1 inhabitants, plus me, migrated indoors. Fisher offered me some sort of punch which was very good. I knew I was approaching my limit, but I still felt the need of a drink in my hand. It made me seem less an outsider.

Inside, Fisher introduced me to Dave again, and I began to think that Fisher's first name was Dave too. The other Dave was in the process of leaving. He seemed to remember meeting me earlier but had forgotten my name! I got the idea he was as uncomfortable as I was. From the way he took the steps to the walkway, I knew he had not had much to drink. Fisher informed me Dave was the hospital commander.

When the punch was gone, Fisher hauled out a tub of iced champagne from his bedroom at the end of the hall. That was not good sign. I was tipsy enough. He handed me a paper cup of champagne with the comment that I looked sick, that this would make me feel better. "Trust me," he said. "I'm a doctor." Then he bent double, letting out a deep, goofy laugh.

For the third time since coming inside I headed for the bathroom. Halfway there, another guy stopped me, calling me Flint. I couldn't think of much besides my bladder, but I knew I had to stop and speak to anyone who even hinted of associating me with Lew Flint. We talked for what seemed like ten minutes, when we both were willing to give up on the idea of a conversation. If he had called me Flint as a slip, how could I bring up Lew's name without embarrassing him? Soon it didn't matter because I was desperate to get to a bathroom.

I found I was third in line. How did eight guys living in FUB-1 manage with a one-holer? I took a deep breath and forced myself to think dry thoughts.

When it was my turn, someone began banging on the front door, followed by the strident sound of woman's voice.

"All right, guys, it's past your bedtime. You might think tomorrow is just another play-day, but some of us have to work."

"Loosen up, Sandy," someone shouted. "Live a little! It won't hurt you.

"Somebody get her a drink," chimed in somebody else.

"Where's that new guy?" The voice was from the end of the hall. "Let him take care of this."

"Yeah. Lew Flint's pal," blurted the guy who had just left the bathroom. He was a big fellow, with an angry look on his face. "Get up there and take care of Sandy," he said, fixing me with his gaze at close range.

"Okay," I stammered. "In just a minute." My bladder was killing me.

"No, pal. Get your skinny ass up there, *now*." The big guy applied a vice-grip to my wrist and hauled me into the hallway. I had no choice but to suck up my agony and not even think about relief.

With no idea what anybody expected me to do, I scooped up some champagne empties as I staggered toward the front door, wedging two under each arm and gripping the other one in my right hand. I was way beyond the point of making any kind of sense, but my mission began to take vague form. Sorting it out seemed to help my bladder a little.

She backed away, seeming confused, but I kept on coming, elbowing the front door wide open.

She was tall, red-headed, and skinny, with an angular face and freckles. I was uneasy as I noticed the amber oak leaf patch on her collar. She was a major. Soon enough I would find she was the hospital's chief of nursing.

"Come on, honey, let's be reasonable," I heard myself slurring. "I think you owe these guys an apology. Shame on you for interrupting our little ol' party." Gradually I was warming to the task, and was buoyed by the shouts of encouragement behind me.

"You're drunk, soldier," she snapped, then turned and headed down the steps to the concrete path toward her quarters.

I fell in behind her, my confidence soaring. "I could be slightly drunk, sunshine," I roared, "but you, my dear, are rude." "Ugly too," teased my lips, but I managed not to go that far.

Sensing the FUB-1 crowd following me, I continued across the walkway as freckled-faced Sandy entered her hooch and slammed the door.

I dumped the champagne bottles I had clamped against my ribs on a patch of grass and began pounding the door. The sound of a shrill chorus followed, gushing unladylike epithets from inside.

I rattled the neck of a champagne bottle up and down the louvered door, ratcheting up the fury inside. Still the door remained closed. I backed away from the stoop and took aim at the door and let fly a champagne bottle.

It missed badly, clanging off the wall and landing on the shelf of sand bags.

The second one missed too, but the third and fourth hit spot on, crashing into the door but not shattering.

The guys behind me cheered. Then one guy yelled, "Incoming rounds!" and "All girl scouts to battle stations!" from another.

I leaned back and threw the last empty with every ounce of strength I could muster, and it struck high on the door jam at precisely the right angle, shattering into countless shards of glass. An instant after they'd rained on the concrete stoop, the door flung open.

The guys behind me broke into a rhythmic chant: "San-*dy*! San-*dy*! San-*dy*!"

Now with fire in her eyes, she planted her feet on the stoop and shook a scrawny fist at me, screaming, "You're destroying United States government property, soldier, and for that you will pay."

"Government glass! Government glass! Government glass!" The guys behind screamed.

Now out of champagne bottles, facing a menacing threat from a superior officer, my bladder could no longer be ignored. Even the cheering FUB-1 guys couldn't change the fact that I was beyond desperate, my options shrinking by the second.

Suddenly I had no choice. I made a critical wardrobe adjustment, then relieved myself, splashing onto the concrete in front of the stoop.

Sandy glared at me, speechless. Others peeped around her from the doorway, all shouting obscenities.

They were matched in kind by deep voices behind me.

After a full minute I was still in strong stream, finally beginning to sense relief, confident the danger of wetting my pants had passed. For a moment I considered stopping, but no, now with a crowd to please, I kept on pissing.

"You people are animals," Sandy screamed, her voice on the verge of failing her, "Every one of you. You will hear about this. You are pigs!"

"You're pigs! You're pigs! You're pigs!" screamed the chorus behind her.

•••

The next morning every FUB-1 resident appeared at my temporary quarters to help lug my gear up the hill. I moved into Lew Flint's old bedroom.

I didn't exactly avoid Sandy in the days that followed, but I didn't seek her out to apologize, either. I had found myself in a bad spot: drunk for the second time in my life, with a rapidly expanding bladder. I understood I may have offended her feminine sensitivities, but there was no way I was going to wet my pants like a child. My thinking had been too muddled to alert me to every possible social solution to my predicament. The incident happed so fast. I definitely was not proud of what happened.

•••

Paperwork demanding a court-martial was on Dave Green's desk the next day. He never mentioned it to me, or what happened Saturday night, but he got an eye-witness report from Fisher that afternoon. Apparently he shared the details with Colonel Birdsong later. Birdsong was commander of the base, the ranking officer in Pleiku.

I didn't witness it myself, but I was informed on excellent authority that Birdsong, after returning from a bomb run at mid-afternoon two days later, flew his A1-E (Skyraider) screaming over Sandy's hooch at treetop level. I could imagine the walls rattling. Possibly Sandy was not inside. Maybe nobody was. Possibly no one realized that the little serenade was meant for Sandy, or that it had anything to do with Saturday night. But it was also possible everybody understood everything. Suspecting the base commander was involved could have been the reason no one complained to Green about his inaction. There were all sorts of regulations against stunts or flying at excessively low altitudes over the base. No one on the base defied the local command. Only Colonel Birdsong could have been the culprit. Everybody in the hospital knew that Birdsong and the FUB-1 crowd were as thick as thieves.

•••

By mid-August I had my first opportunity to see how evacuation hospitals managed mass casualties. It amounted to the ultimate in discipline and teamwork. I would witness as never before what "to preserve the fighting strength" was all about. Late on a Friday afternoon a series of Dust Off choppers descended to the helipad outside the ER and deposited twenty casualties, some in really bad shape. Others followed during the night.

Gurneys of grimy, bloody GIs lined the ER walls, with nurses stripping away their sweat- and blood-soaked fatigues and muddy boots, tossing them to the center of the room as they scrambled to start IVs and draw blood for the lab. Medical officers, five or six, focused on small groups of GIs, searching for breathing problems and internal bleeding. They were upbeat, offering encouragement as they worked. GIs in shock were transfused with universal donor blood, type-O.

The triage officer hurried up and down rows of gurneys, prioritizing wounds. He paused from time to time to question colleagues, or to check critical physical findings himself. He was the center of the operation, the toughest decisions reserved for him. His qualifications were not necessarily seniority-based, but determined by his skill and experience. Typically the triage officer was the top surgeon on the staff, nevertheless one rarely seen in the OR during the busy times. Triage was key to everything. Military triage was different from civilian triage. The top priority was not always the most seriously injured. Medical Corps policy frowned on potentially futile operations, particularly if they meant delaying care of wounded soldiers more certain to survive. The mission was clear—first, last and always: to preserve the fighting strength.

In civilian practice doctors sometimes felt pressures to consult each other before making a crucial decision, but medical officers weren't about to make judgments by committee, not with the lives of soldiers on the line. Procrastination, second-guessing, and arguing could be dangerous with mass casualties. But just "going along" wouldn't cut it either. Other opinions were valued, but mutual respect was demanded. The chain-of-command was always central, from triage officer on down. It cut through egos, politics, and other forms of inefficiency. Every medical officer knew where he stood. If he couldn't figure it out, somebody would show up who would sure as hell tell him.

As a consequence, my youth and inexperience had me spending more time in the OR than in the ER. The chain-of-command worked there too. There was always a senior surgeon around to help the less experienced find his way.

My first case was to assist a senior surgeon with an operation for massive abdominal injuries. Surgery is ninety-nine percent mental, aimed at prioritizing actions, but even the best surgical mind is wired to a single pair of hands. In abdominal surgery typically four hands are required. Mine were controlled by my mentor's grunts and groans, or occasionally a cryptic phrase. I made it my business to need fewer and fewer directions. Within an hour or so I sensed I was succeeding. It was the way surgeons had learned their art for centuries. For me, that evening amounted to an amazing personal experience. Small successes morphed into larger successes and so on through the following day and night. When I finally got to bed I would be a different man altogether. It was exactly why I'd signed on for Vietnam.

My next case was also an abdominal injury but one of lesser magnitude, with less anticipated mortality and overall risk. This time I was the primary surgeon with a senior surgeon as my assistant. One of his jobs was to make me, the lowliest surgeon in the hospital, better. In the process I began to sense that only the sky was my limit. It was another lengthy case, working my way through my first bowel resection. To remove destroyed bowel, then connect adjacent functioning components efficiently and accurately for the first time constituted a benchmark in any surgeon's career. Managing it without spilling bowel contents into the peritoneal space where it could create serious havoc was a challenge.

By midnight a hot supper awaited me in the tiny room adjacent to the OR, and after that, another operation to perform, not necessarily a simpler one but one less likely to result in death or lasting disability if delayed. Again I was talked through the tough parts by a man who knew all the tricks. It dawned on me that I was seamlessly becoming part of the system. If Army policy didn't include the idea that strengthening young surgeons is crucial to preserving the fighting strength, it should have. Facing long odds, no man need stand alone.

When breakfast came over from the dining hall at 0700, I felt far more fulfilled then weary. Rushing adrenaline and achieving small victories had a way of minimizing fatigue and sleep-deprivation. Then we worked through that day, case by case, in the same manner, taking only bathroom breaks and catching snacks on the run. With no windows through which to glimpse the presence or absence of daylight distorts one's perception of time. Determining whether the time registered by the OR's wall clock was AM or PM was anything but automatic. It gave me an eerie feeling. Replacing scheduled meals with frequent snacks could also complicate one's sense of time.

By the time the last casualty was treated, the sun was peeping over the horizon on still another day. I was a little unsteady as I stepped outside, trying to remember when I had last slept. A light rain was beginning to fall on the covered walkway. But the sense of accomplishment and growth I felt trumped my fatigue. I had seen problems I'd never seen before: controlling bleeding from wounds of the liver, for instance, and repairing a leaking vena cava. Those cases were way beyond my skill level. But the two bowel resections I'd performed myself— one including a colostomy—did unimaginable things for my confidence. They were major milestones for anybody not yet three years out of medical school. In forty hours I had taken huge steps toward realizing the dreams of years. What I'd learned wasn't limited to surgical technique, either. Equally important was the knowledge I'd gained of myself, and a greater perception of what lay ahead.

...

There were fun times too, particularly at the informal dinner parties at Dave Green's home, a small house on one level at the far end of the hospital complex. There was one every week, and the FUB-1 guys had standing invitations. The dress code was shorts and tee shirts, and mentioning rank or using last names was off limits. Booze flowed freely and grimy jokes were told, some over and over. Gags usually centered around the base commander, a man simply oozing charm and charisma. Approaching fifty, he was a big brother to everybody. He seemed to have known Dave Green all his life.

Colonel George Purnell Birdsong, Jr. earned a football scholarship to Southwest Mississippi Junior College when he was seventeen, and afterward attended the University of Nebraska and Michigan State. Finally in the Air Force, he earned his pilot's wings in 1942, and was soon to be flying sorties with the 91st bomb group out of Bassingbourne, England. He regaled us with harrowing escapades in his B-17, "The Delta Rebel." A proud participant in the first daylight raids over Germany, he was later first to complete twenty-five combat missions in the European theater. He flew B-29s,

B-47s, B-52s, and B-58s in Korea and during the Cold War. Birdsong was all man, and all about winning and having fun. He was commander, hero, role model, and good friend to us all. There was not a pretentious bone in his body. To us at Dave Green's, he was simply, Buzz.

After a few drinks and poking fun at everybody in sight, then a World War II story or two, Buzz would commandeer Dave's guitar and gear up for some serious singing, always the same song. The first verse went like this:

> The pre-tti-est girl . . .
> I ev-er saw . . .
> was sip-pin' bour-r-bon
> through a *straw*!

His right foot tapping out the rhythm, he amped up the catchy melody, generating energy like electricity on fire, he launched into the second verse:

> I walked right up . . .
> I sat right *down* . . .
> I or-dered up . . .
> an-oth-er *round!*

From there the ballad proceeded through placing a hand upon her knee, then her thigh, then picking her up. and setting her down. Ultimately there was a wedding, a formal one, with her daddy present, sporting a white shotgun. Then finally:

> And now I've got . . .
> a mo-ther-in-*law* . . .

and four-teen kids . . .
who call me *paw*!

Then we would sing it again, with increasing enthusiasm. Buzz fell into making up new verses, moving the plot in a different direction. Some of us faltered as the verses mounted up, but Buzz never showed any inclination of letting up. If a new verse didn't quite work, he never dropped it, he just brought it back the next week.

Bill Fisher, the 71st's neurosurgeon and our fellow FUB-1-resident, seemed to enjoy at times playing the role of buffoon, which he clearly was not. He was tall, with a deep voice and a back-slapping laugh. He also had an appetite for manufacturing pithy new verses for Buzz's "Prettiest Girl

Major Bill Fisher, truly one-of-a-kind, after breakfast outside FUB-1 on the sprawling campus of the 71st Evacuation Hospital at Pleiku. Fisher was one of only two neurosurgeons in Vietnam in 1968.

Ballad." And he had a knack for getting Dave Green into the act. Fisher and Green came up with more lyrics with less, than anybody could have imagined. They sang their four-liners over and over, however silly or disconnected, then hee-haw deliriously. Their lyrics resulted from and depended on beer. One night Fisher's efforts turned vaguely pornographic, with a suggestion we serenade in my friend Sandy's backyard. But Dave put his foot down on that idea. We were too far gone to find the place, anyway.

Over time, working out new verses was the only way Buzz could assure himself of a solo. The only thing he liked better than the sound of his voice, was dancing, Mississippi-bayou-style, he called it. He moved in circles and tight spins, elbows high, extending Dave's guitar over his head with one hand, all the while shimmying his skinny butt. Dave put a stop to Buzz dancing with his guitar, though, the night Buzz tripped over a sofa and broke his coffee table.

...

Well into September, on a Saturday afternoon. Dust Off choppers descended to the ER at the 71st Evac. Within minutes every gurney-station was occupied as grimy fatigues and muddy boots piled up on the floor. Little could I know it then, but that afternoon that would shape my professional life. The lesson would be that observations prior to surgery could be as crucial as anything that happened in the OR.

The triage officer pointed me to a pale, unconscious GI midway down a row of gurneys. "He's going to the OR right away," he snapped. "Got a ruptured spleen." I glanced at the soldier. The triage officer had been with him hardly seconds. I never saw him even touch the guy. How could he *know?*

It was no time for questions, though. I was assigned to "work the kid up"— listen to his heart and lungs, get a blood specimen to the lab, then write a note in his chart.

I jumped at it right away. The soldier's blood pressure was hardly sixty, and his pulse rate was racing north of 110. The triage officer had ordered blood, and nurses were hanging the first two bags as I sat down with the chart, which at that point was only a few loose pages. I sketched a quick cartoon of the soldier's belly, indicating the wound of entry immediately below the left side of his rib cage. I had listened closely to the adjacent lung, and the breath sounds were fine.

His abdomen had been tight, with tenderness in all four quadrants, not unlike many of the abdominal wounds we typically saw. There were excoriations and bruises on both hands and forearms, but his extremities were otherwise unremarkable.

An anesthetist and an X-ray tech showed up almost simultaneously. Together they lifted the soldier into a semi-sitting position for an upright chest x-ray. A minute or two later the anesthetist rolled the soldier toward the OR, where the chest film would be read, still dripping developing fluid.

I took my time, trying to make my handwriting legible. When I finished, I began a similar process with another wounded soldier. Within twenty minutes, with work in ER beginning to wind down, I headed toward the OR, hoping to be assigned a case.

I met Bill Fisher on the way. He was heading in my direction, with an intense look on his face. I had never seen him quite like that.

"Did you see that spleen a few minutes ago?" he snapped, clearly upset.

"I did."

"Could he move his legs?"

Instantly I was numb all over. Move his legs? His legs were fine. "Sure," I replied, sensing the uncertainty in my voice. The guy was in shock, trying to die! The problem was in his *belly*! But all I said was: "He was moving his legs when I saw him." How pathetic it sounded.

It was also a lie. There was no way I could be certain of what I'd just said. I played back in my mind's eye what I thought I'd witnessed. I had not examined the muscle tone in his legs, or checked their spinal stretch reflexes. What was wrong with me? I was ashamed of myself. How could I have possibly missed paralyzed legs?

But it had happened.

"Are you sure?" Fisher asked softly, his gaze boring into me. He knew I wasn't.

"I . . . don't know," I mumbled weakly, my stomach in turmoil.

Fisher's eyes were clear and cold, now firing bullets at me.

"Damn, Bill," I stammered. "I didn't do a full neurological exam. There was no time! We were trying to get the guy to the OR." Scrambling for excuses was a sure sign of the lie I was still desperate to sell to myself.

"The same fragment that nailed his spleen knocked the bejesus out of his spinal cord." Fisher spoke slowly and softly, his face emanating a knowing look, even vaguely sympathetic.

I only stared at him, helpless.

"Okay . . .okay," he said, his characteristically goofy grin peeping at me. He explained he had examined the soldier before the anesthetic had been started, that he'd found both legs flaccid with paralysis.

His statement hit me like a fist to the jaw. What could I say? Who was I to tell a neurosurgeon he was mistaken about his neurological findings?

If the soldier's paralysis had appeared between my examination and his, there was a good chance surgery could really help the guy, may even have him up and walking someday. Under typical circumstances, though, with paralysis occurring with the entry of the fragment thirty or forty minutes ago, possibly longer, soldiers never walked again, whatever anyone did. I knew *that* much about spinal cord injuries.

...

Immediate abdominal surgery for a bleeding spleen would have taken precedence anyway. That was a life-saving procedure. But immediate spinal surgery afterward might have made a huge difference had the soldier's paralysis been only a few minutes old. If Fisher had believed my statement, he would have insisted on a temporary abdominal closure the instant the abdominal bleeding was controlled, then rolling the soldier over for a spinal operation. Finalizing the abdominal closure would come later. Neurosurgeons were aggressive people, and Bill Fisher certainly was.

Finally he was calmer. He understood I'd dropped the ball. But he couldn't get the idea of exploring the soldier's spinal cord out of his head. He still might be able to make a difference. I sensed it, and he admitted it. "Stranger things have happened you know, sometimes anyway," he said with a grin. "You want to scrub with me?"

...

He made a long incision in the center of the soldier's back, then meticulously began stripping wide straps of muscle from either side of vertebral elements. He normally worked alone so I hoped I could make things a little easier for him, anything to rid him of the bad taste I'd left in his mouth. I worried that my presence would increase his frustration, but I was determined to do my best. The splenectomy had taken hardly twenty minutes, and stripping the bowel and closing the wound little longer. Time was no longer crucial, but Fisher reminded me that recovering lost movement and sensory function wasn't the only reason for surgery. Eliminating the possibility of a spinal fluid leak or meningitis could be life saving.

"Hey, listen," Fisher said as he finished packing muscle away from bone behind cotton sponges. "Don't beat yourself up about this. You just missed a sign. That's all. Nobody expects you to be perfect. You haven't been at this long enough to expect so much of yourself. This guy was paralyzed the minute he was hit. You can't change that, and neither can I. Of course that's what happens ninety-nine percent of the time."

I didn't say a word. He was trying to help me get through it, and I appreciated that.

Later he pointed out details as he went along. He explained the importance of controlling even slight bleeding from the very beginning. "The slightest trickle of blood high in the wound will collect at the bottom, where it will obscure our vision when we need it most."

The soldier was very fit, with huge back muscles. Fisher pointed out that freeing up muscle as widely as possible from the spinal column, dense bone surrounding the spinal cord, was crucial. Later, slowly and steadily he removed bone bit by bit from the midline outward. He used what looked like an orthopedic instrument, only it was sleek and delicate. He maintained a disciplined pace through the bone, never hurrying or even pausing. His hands seemed extremely strong, a characteristic I'd never considered of much value to neurosurgeons before. He removed bone quickly, seemingly with ease.

The dura mater—the tough, fibrous covering of the spinal cord—was intact. There was no sign of bleeding, spinal fluid, or torn dura. I suggested that might be a good sign, that the outlook may not be so bad, after all.

"Not really," he said. "The fragment probably entered the spinal canal from the other side."

I didn't say anything for a while, but finally I couldn't help myself. "But why are we going in from the back, then?"

He only chuckled, not saying anything for nearly a minute. "Going through the vertebral bodies, between the cord and the belly, might take us all night! Plus, then there would be the problem of reconstructing the spine, no small feat from the front. Vertebral bodies provide the bulk of the spinal column's stability. We don't want to make things worse than they already are, you know." I could sense him grinning behind his mask. "This is the only realistic approach. Nobody expects this kind of case to be easy, you know."

With a tiny, rounded scalpel blade he nicked the dura in the midline, encountering clearly bloody spinal fluid. Then slipped a narrow, delicate instrument inside and extended the opening by sweeping the instrument upward and toward the foot of the operating table, exposing a five- or six-inch length of spinal cord. It bulged through the opening: pale, with a network of dark veins spreading over its surface.

"The cord is really swollen." Fisher said. "Not a good sign, but about what we expected." His voice was matter of fact, seemingly devoid of emotion.

Carefully he extended the dural incision even farther, as far north and south as the bone exposure allowed. "This will release the pressure on possibly intact spinal cord," he announced. "Over time, days to a week or so, the swelling will begin to subside."

"You think he might get better?"

"Not really. This is a bad injury, probably beyond anything anybody could do. You never know, though."

I listened to him in wonder. I'd seen spinal cords as an intern and as a junior resident, and except for the bloody spinal fluid this one wasn't dramatically different. Fisher had mastered all the subtleties. At FUB-1 he was more or less a comedic figure, a little weird, off center. But he knew what he was doing in the OR. Tonight he'd been ready to move heaven and earth to give this soldier a chance to walk again. He'd also been more considerate of me than I deserved. We had been operating for almost four hours, and he'd not once lectured me about my ineptitude in the ER. He worked with authority and passion, even seeming to take an interest in teaching me something. I couldn't understand it.

He spent another forty-five minutes sewing a fascial graft to the exposed edges of dura. It would provide space for spinal cord swelling in the coming days, and almost certainly fend off a deadly complication.

We closed the wound in silence, Fisher placing sutures in muscle with curved needles, layer by layer, allowing me to tie them down, drawing muscles together in the midline. He stopped me after the first few sutures, though, saying, "Take your time! We've got no place to go. Square them down, four knots, every single time. Take pride in what you're doing. We owe it to this guy to make this case a work of art. It might not turn out so well, but at least we've gotta know we've done everything we can."

He meant it, and I would never forget it. Fisher was complex, and he had something I wanted.

●●●

The following week he treated a soldier who had lost the use of both arms and legs from a broken neck. He had placed tongs in the soldier's skull in order to reduce the fracture-dislocation with traction, then left him in traction in a contraption called a Stryker frame. Since the soldier's sensation was preserved only in his face, scalp, neck, and across the front of his shoulders, he had to be turned from front to back every two hours to prevent pressure sores from developing over the rest of his body. The weight of the body on skin that is unable to sense pressure or pain can result in tissue destruction that can heal only when the pressure has been relieved, and then only with difficulty.

The Stryker was a temporary solution, enabling the soldier to be turned from front to back and vice versa. Relieving his skin from pressure even part-time could keep it from breaking down. Pressure sores led to infection, which could result in all sorts of problems.

Fisher planned to evacuate the soldier to Japan, where surgeons would fuse the unstable bones in his neck, allowing the traction to be discontinued and initiating a vigorous rehabilitation program. He faced a long, difficult road ahead, but Fisher was determined to do everything he could for him. His primary concern was the soldier's breathing. Muscles responsible for lifting his chest were paralyzed, forcing him to depend entirely on his diaphragm for breathing. If the alignment of his neck was altered even slightly, he could spend the rest of his life on a respirator. For that to happen in flight, at worst to drop him, could be disastrous, even cause death.

I shouldn't have been surprised when I was approached hours later, asking if I would accompany the soldier with the broken neck to Japan. Apparently evacuating quadriplegic patients in Styker frames required the presence of a medical officer en route. I jumped at the chance. I hadn't been to Japan before and would probably never have another opportunity. I assumed Fisher was behind the assignment. For some reason he was taking me under his wing.

...

We left Pleiku in the early evening. Most of the seats in the C-141 had been removed, converting the aircraft into a cargo plane. It was the Air Force equivalent of the largest, fastest commercial jet airliner of the day. It could be equipped to seat over 150 passengers. As things turned out, there were only three that night. The soldier in the Stryker was stationed immediately behind the flight deck, with me in a seat to his right and to his left a male nurse to minister to the soldier's every other need. We arrived at Camp Drake and the 249th General Hospital at sunrise the next morning.

After hours of anxiety—sleeping had been out of the question—I was already dreading the return flight, which I assumed would be available within a few hours. Later I was informed there were no return flights scheduled that day, and was assigned a bed in the barracks, where I slept all day and half the night. The next morning, when I pointed out I needed to get back to Pleiku, the sergeant laughed. "Take a few days off, Captain," he said. "Nobody expects you back in Nam right away. They'll get by without you. Go see the bright lights in the big city."

The 249th was a thirty-minute train trip from Tokyo so I spent the day touring the Ginza and sampling Japanese cuisine. I assumed that few Japanese in downtown Tokyo spoke a word of English, and none of the words on signage had roots in the European languages so basic to English so I was truly alone in the presence of millions of people for the first time in my life. I was met only by smiling faces and unimaginable kindnesses in restaurants and shops. I doubted that Japanese visitors in New York were treated the same way. I had a fine time that day, but still I looked forward to getting back to Camp Drake. I could easily have gotten lost in Tokyo!

20.
BILL FISHER AND CHALLENGES AHEAD

Long Days and Long Nights

I'd been back at Pleiku for ten days before I missed Bill Fisher. He had told me he would be leaving for R&R the day after I left for Japan, but he should have been back almost a week ago.

And nobody knew where he was or how to contact him. If his girl friend knew, she wasn't saying. I wasn't surprised nobody else was alarmed. As much of a party boy as he was on Wednesday nights at Dave Green's, he was more a loner than one might expect. He and his girl friend were both quiet, choosing to while away their free time reading paperbacks at the pool. Neither seemed truly close to anybody else. Bill was clearly a ring-leader at FUB-1, but his relationships were never deep, or designed to be lasting. Most nights he cooped himself in his bedroom and read himself to sleep. Fisher read anything and everything: crime novels, history, science fiction, you name it. Some nights he read all night long, sometimes not seen again before almost lunchtime when he poured himself a glass of tomato juice and sat outside FUB-1, sunning himself. Only it wasn't only tomato juice. The drink was half beer.

Like any evacuation hospital in Vietnam, there were long lulls in the action. When Fisher worked, he worked, hard. When there was nothing to do, he dealt with it in his own way.

Before I'd left for Japan I had begun to think I knew him about as well as anybody, but he was still more mystery than a real pal. Dave Green didn't seem much upset by his absence. On second thought, Dave *did* know Fisher better than I did. As hospital commander, surely he was privy to whatever backup arrangements were in place in Bill's absence, and he didn't seem concerned at all.

It was my understanding that Fisher was one of only two neurosurgeons in Vietnam. The other one was at the 24th Evac, which seemed another world away now. I couldn't imagine how the 71st worked out backup call for neurosurgical emergencies. I assumed there was a floating naval hospital somewhere off the coast in the South China Sea to support the Marines in I Corps. I guessed it would be possible to send our neuro casualties out there, in a pinch, anyway. An alternative would be to transfer a neurosurgeon over from Tripler in Hawaii, even from Walter Reed, for a week or two of TDY (temporary duty).

When he hadn't showed up in another week, I gave up thinking about it. Maybe he simply got tired of military medicine and decided to check out, open a private practice back home in Louisiana. Only Bill Fisher could manage something like that without going to jail. Only he would even think of something like that.

Finally though, as soon as I managed to get it out of my mind, he appeared, as though nothing had happened. He showed not the slightest remorse or embarrassment about extending his R&R almost three weeks. He sported a deeper tan, a new pair of sun-shades, and a bag full of new paperbacks. He put himself into social mode and made exaggerated greetings to his buddies at FUB-1, then went back to his room to take a nap. I assumed he would look for his girl friend when he woke up.

He explained later that he'd had personal business in Honolulu and simply got side-tracked. Really? What kind of business could be so important for him to run the risk of being arrested for being AWOL?

He explained there were divorce papers to be processed and finalized, then some complications developed that demanded more time than he expected.

"Complications?"

"There was a wedding." He said it without batting an eye.

A wedding? Was he kidding me? Had he arranged to meet a brother or a sister in Hawaii? Another relative or a friend?

"Who's wedding?"

"Mine," he said, with a sheepish grin.

Suddenly I'd had enough. I didn't want to hear any more details.

"Then there was the honeymoon," he continued. "It would be a shame to get married in Honolulu and not enjoy the scenery. And we went over to Maui too."

"But didn't you worry about being arrested for not getting back here?" I couldn't help asking.

"But what could they do to me? Send me to Vietnam?" He leaned back and laughed from deep in his belly.

I couldn't help remembering how nervous I was about spending a couple of extra days at the 249th in Japan. Had

Fisher been in my shoes he might still be there. He might even have found himself a cute Japanese honey and melt into the society.

I made myself not ask anymore questions. I surely wasn't going to ask about what he was going to do with his girl friend at the 71st. The next afternoon I saw them in bathing suits heading for the swimming pool! I doubt he told her anything about his life elsewhere. I was certain I knew all I wanted to know.

...

One night in early October Bill had a guest, a civilian. Apart from the Bob Hope group, you just didn't see civilian Americans in Vietnam, even in a really safe place like Pleiku. I asked him what he was doing so far from home, but I never got a satisfactory answer. He and Bill had been drinking for hours. Bill introduced him as an old buddy from Dallas, but for all I knew it was somebody he'd just met. Fisher was like that. They did have things in common, among them a taste for beer and a penchant for "cutting the fool." His pal's name was George.

I assumed George was somebody Fisher met in Dallas when he was an intern. He'd been kidding me for months for trying to learn to play a guitar I'd purchased off the local economy. I was told it was constructed of match sticks. I wasn't so sure about that, but I recognized the Vietnamese to be a very industrious people. It had been mine for ten bucks.

George rolled his eyes when he realized how out of tune it was. I was only mildly embarrassed. Who would expect me to know anything about tuning a guitar? The smile never left his face, but his eyes turned serious as he twisted the tuning key back and fourth for each steel string, then struck a sound from each in different sequences, then finally fingered out a few chords. After a minute or two he became one and the same with my ten-dollar guitar. The sounds he coaxed from it were amazing.

After a few ditties he launched into another gear. He had a distinctive voice and mood: sad, but sad with a beat, and not always sad. The sound was clean and sincere. I would never forget it. With a few more beers under his belt he treated me, Bill, and a few others to some real country music. In no time a crowd assembled.

When he was done, so was my guitar. I'd been watching helplessly as he destroyed it string by string. Even when it was down to three strings, he still strummed music from it, somehow. Finally, when one of the three remaining strings unraveled from its tuning key, the concert was over. George handed the guitar back to me with a grin. There was no apology, or a feeble excuse. Just a grin.

"It's pretty much trash now." What else could I say? Where do you have a ten-dollar guitar repaired in South Vietnam?

"It's always been trash, Doc," George said sadly. "Pure T. trash."

Fisher laughed.

After that night, George was gone. I figured he might be a musician who had come to entertain the troops of the Fourth

Division, that he'd moved on to his next stop. On the other hand, he could have been one of a number of things. His name never came up again.

Years later, as I was rolling across the dial of my radio as I pulled out of a hospital parking lot late one night, I heard a voice that brought back instant memories. It was George! It had to be him. There couldn't have been another voice like that, anywhere. Soon the disk jockey informed me I'd been listening to the legendary *George Jones*.

I have not been able to confirm it for certain, but I believe Bill Fisher's pal was *the* George Jones. Who else could impersonate him? Jones was known within the industry for decades as "the greatest living country singer," producing fourteen number-one country hits between 1959 and 1983.

...

As time went on I scrubbed more and more with Bill Fisher. We did another spinal case one night, for a simple ruptured lumbar disc, then there was a compound brain injury from a depressed skull fracture, later a craniotomy for a gunshot wound. That GI might have been beyond salvageable, but Bill decided to operate anyway, since there was nothing better to do, and reminding me again that sometimes miracles did happen if you gave them a chance. He suggested I tag along since it would be an opportunity to see some real anatomy, brain anatomy.

It was a special time. It was the spinal cord injury I had overlooked in the ER two months ago that had jolted me in the direction of neurosurgery, but with this operation I was hooked. I carried images with me for days. Bill pointed out two of the three branches of the middle cerebral artery, the delicate-walled superior sagittal sinus, the wispy olfactory nerve coursing on the undersurface of the frontal lobe, even a glimpse inside one of the lateral ventricles. It was amazing! I knew I would never be the same again.

The social Bill Fisher and the surgeon Bill Fisher were different animals. In the OR he was quiet, sometimes bordering on morose. There were flashes of jubilation at other times, even in the form of a corny joke, or breaking into song once or twice, but most of the time he was all business, fully focused on the problem at hand. He did not permit chatter from nurses or the anesthetist. He insisted the entire team function as one in order that his patient got the chance he deserved. I liked that. I could be comfortable with that.

As an intern I had spent nine weeks on the cardiothoracic service at Duke. I was attracted to it because there were serious challenges, demanding everyone's best effort. While a neurosurgeon typically worked only with a couple of nurses, heart surgery involved larger teams, leading to distractions for a guy like me. By the time a team of nurses heart-lung machine technicians, a cardiologist or two, plus the occasional radiologist showed up with their opinions and suggestions, the surgeon was somehow marginalized, degraded more or less to one of many. Some surgeons were so skilled they would be at their best in the face of any distraction. I worried I might not have that capacity. I sensed I would need all the focus I could manage.

The more I thought about it, the more I leaned toward charting a different course. Did I really want to be a heart surgeon? I wasn't so sure anymore.

I brought up the subject after the craniotomy we'd performed for the gunshot wound. "How did you get into this, Bill?"

"The Army?" He flashed his best goofy grin.

"No. Neurosurgery."

"It was just something I was comfortable with. It presented some challenges, but I enjoyed them."

After a long silence, he gave me a sidelong look and said, "Do you have a confession to make?" His smile dazzled, and his eyes were warm.

"Yeah. I do. I think I'd like to go into neurosurgery. What do you think about that?"

"Well," he began. "There are a lot of long days and long nights. If you can handle that, you'll be fine. If you can't handle it, neurosurgery will sure as hell handle you."

Getting started might not be so easy, though. I worried about qualifying for a residency. Most guys entering a neurosurgical training had been moving in that direction for years, and had made some connections.

"It might be too late for me," I said. "Neurosurgery residencies are competitive. Certainly the one at Duke is. I might be aiming at the impossible."

"Oh, I don't think so," he said, flashing his goofy grin. It bothered me. I was dead serious.

"I'm behind. Most guys apply to a number of universities at the same time. I've got another year in the Army so I can't see how that will work out for me. I go to Walter Reed from here, where nobody will know me. Letters of recommendation are important, aren't they? I could go back to Duke for another year, I suppose. Maybe catch on in a lab. I'd had some experience in biochemistry research. But that could lead nowhere. I've got a family. I don't have years just to get to first base."

"I can write a letter for you. That should do the trick."

"You're kidding. How can that be?"

"I know a guy."

I said nothing. He was playing with me.

"Kemp Clark, in Dallas," he said finally, almost gloating, like he had magic up his sleeve. "He's chief of the neurosurgical service at Southwestern Medical School, part of the University of Texas"

"Parkland? Parkland Hospital? That was where they took JFK."

"Right."

Somehow, I couldn't quite buy it. This guy hadn't exactly proved he was the most trustworthy guy I'd ever met. I liked him, but still . . . My gut feeling told me I needed to apply to five or six residencies to increase the chances that somebody would take me seriously. I knew some of the faculty at Duke, but they had commitments for first-year slots years in advance. So I assumed, anyway.

Fisher told me Kemp Clark had business in Washington all the time. He told me to expect a phone call form him in late November or early December. He would invite me to meet him for dinner at the Willard Hotel. How could he be specific about something like that? He was having fun at my expense. Why?

He went further. He told me the most important thing I would do that night would be ordering a drink in the hotel bar. It must be a vodka martini, very dry, on the rocks with olives, at least two drinks. If I got that right, I would be on my way. It was crazy. Was Kemp Clark as nuts as Bill Fisher?

"Of course you've got to drink them," Fisher added with a chuckle. That gives him the opportunity to find out exactly who you are. He's not a man who tolerates much bull shit."

A martini? A full glass of vodka? Two of them, then make sense? Would that be easy or impossible? How many of the corporate types, when looking for a job, get drunk before the interview?

Fisher sounded sincere enough. He seemed to wish me well. But, actually, all he really knew about me was my screw up that day in the ER. I needed to think about it.

•••

On October 19, late morning, I boarded another C-47, this one for the first leg of my trip back to the world. There was a wait, but finally we taxied out to a runway. Within an hour I would be back at Qui Nhon and tomorrow night I would board a 707 for the long flight home.

The old boat made a final turn, at last facing down the runway, revving up its engines to take off. Suddenly the noise and vibration diminished, then slowed to an idle. Through a small window I watched a dusty old tan Chevrolet station wagon rattle across the tarmac toward us. It was bizarre, like in a movie. The old Chevy crossed in front of the aircraft, where I could no longer see it.

In a minute Buzz Birdsong appeared in the doorway and called my name, then came bouncing toward me when he spotted me in the last seat. He waved off my salute and shook my hand, a big Mississippi smile all over his face.

"Bye, Doc. Be good, now. Y' hear?"

It was a special gesture.

He had a word with the pilot on his way out, and soon soldiers scrambled in the front rows, making room for me.

I was leaving the Central Highlands in style. Next stop Qui Nhon, then home.

EPILOGUE

Bill Fisher came through for me. In January, two weeks before Nixon's inauguration, I met Kemp Clark in the bar of the Willard Hotel in Washington, D. C. and not only ordered two vodka martinis but managed to drink them. I can't say I remember much of what happened after that, but I ended up with a job as first year resident in neurological surgery. Later I discovered that Fisher was as storied at Parkland Hospital as he had been at the 71st Evac. One escapade concerned an elderly gentleman who had had three separate episodes of bleeding inside his head.[18] Fisher, a resident in general surgery, was then a temporary on the neurosurgery service. The patient recovered from all three operations, but no reason for the bleeding was ever determined. Repeated x-ray and laboratory studies had been negative. One night, with Clark out of town and Fisher not on call, the patient died. When Fisher came in the following morning and found that the body had already been released to a funeral home before an autopsy had been performed, he hopped into his rattle-trap old Chevy and raced to retrieve the remains. He knew that Clark would fire any resident allowing such patient to be released without an autopsy. With the funeral home staff standing by in shock, Fisher hoisted the body to a shoulder and carried it to his car. Knowing the funeral home director would have no choice but

---

[18] Kemp Clark, *Before the Indian Came: A Memoir of the Early Days of Parkland Memorial Hospital, 1982: Private publication, p 14.*

to report the body as stolen, and unwilling to have to explain a corpse in his trunk, he propped up the old codger in the front seat and placed a hat on his head. Then he drove to Parkland Hospital where an autopsy was performed. Fisher and his car disappeared for a few days until Clark had returned and cleared up the legal nightmare he had created.

...

With residency coming at me at warp speed what had happened in Vietnam was reduced to hardly a glimpse in the rear view window. I had chosen a special curriculum in medical school which allowed me to trade elective courses in surgery for a chance to focus on research in biochemistry my junior year. Those courses qualified me for the trade only if I committed to a surgical internship. For fifteen months I toyed with the idea of using my biochemistry background to pursue an academic career as a basic scientist. Choosing neurosurgery did not preclude that possibility, but it would be a stretch. As things turned out, spending a year at the Walter Reed Army Institute of Research was perfect for me. Focusing on brain function and its diseases, I designed a research project to evaluate the technique of monitoring the death of brain tissue with a pH meter. I spent my spare time reading volumes on neurology and neuroradiology, and attended weekly neurology conferences at the hospital and periodic neuropathology conferences conducted by the legendary Dr. Kenneth Earle at the Armed Forces Institute of Pathology, also on the Walter Reed campus.

I commuted from Beltsville, Maryland on a motorcycle which I parked daily in a garage across the street from the Walter Reed entrance. Throughout the freezing winter of 1969 I made it a habit to take short cuts through the ground floor of the hospital to minimize the long, freezing walk to my motorbike. Late one afternoon in December I was surprised how little traffic there was inside the hospital. Shoving open the door from the lobby to the north wing, I literally ran into the president-elect of the United States! Richard M. Nixon was en route to a conference with former president Dwight D. Eisenhower, who was a resident on the top floor of the hospital throughout his final illness. The Secret Service had cordoned off the entire ground floor, but, somehow, I failed to notice until too late. Nixon, taller than I expected, seemed terrified as I begged his pardon and continued toward two Secret Service men eyeing me coldly from end of the hallway. Neither of them had much nice to say to me.

...

I ran into Dave Green, who also had a Washington assignment, and invited him to dinner at our small apartment on Powder Mill Road in Beltsville. Most of the conversation that night had to do with our present duty assignments and plans for the future, but I couldn't resist asking him what happened with the court martial request that I imagined had sat on his desk in Pleiku for months. The words "court martial" brought our wives chit-chat to a screeching halt. Those words seemed to echo in the long silence that followed. Green only gave me a curious look and said, "Court martial? What are you talking about?"

Eventually conversations resumed, and Green told me quietly, "No doubt what happened that night has been told and retold. I'm confident Fisher embellished it as he passed it on to me the following afternoon, but he dressed it up even more when he repeated it to Buzz a few days later. We laughed and laughed. Buzz probably never said anything to you about it, but he told me it sounded like something he could have done when he was younger."

I grinned. So that's why he stopped my plane on the runway as I was leaving Pleiku.

...

In 1972 Spurgeon Green visited me in Dallas, and informed me he had been accepted to medical school. Bursting with pride in his accomplishment, I hugged him on the spot.

I lost track of him for decades after that. I imagined him as an internist or a family practitioner somewhere in the South, but I kept coming up empty in my periodic internet searches. When I finally did find evidence of him, in early 2010, I wished I had never tried. A year earlier he had been convicted of illegally distributing and dispensing controlled substances through his practice in Perry, Georgia, near Macon. At age seventy, he had been sentenced to thirty years in federal prison. I was stunned, and much saddened. He had been indispensable to B-Med, and to me personally.

But I did not like the smell I sensed.

His lawyer, whose name I got from a newspaper article, put me in touch with Green's wife. Over the telephone Dorothy Green was charming but obviously heartbroken. She had served as business manager of Green's clinic, and was convinced her husband had been let down by the criminal justice system. She assured me a vigorous appeal was in progress, which I assumed would probably exhaust what remained of their savings. Spurgeon and I exchanged warm letters but he refused to allow me to drive down to Talladega, Alabama to see him. I could understand that. I doubt I would want him to visit me in prison, either.

The last I heard from him was a beautiful Father's Day note over a year later. My most recent letters to him remain unanswered. I can only assume he is still incarcerated. Dorothy's phone numbers were disconnected and presumably she lives in another community now. I hesitate to initiate an exhaustive search in the interest of her privacy.

I am convinced Surgeon Green should never have been sent to prison. I have a good sense of the circumstances he faced. As a primary care physician in a small community, he doubtless had dozens patients with chronic pain, many indigent. I had had some myself in my own practice.

Doctors became aware of the risks of opioid drugs as early as the 1930s. In 1961 an International Narcotics Control Board was established to restrict the trade of opioids and protect patients from their indiscriminate use. Doctors of my generation were taught to prescribe them primarily for terminal cancer victims and patients with post-surgical pain, whose need would be restricted from days to a week or so, not long enough to run much risk of addiction.

By the 1990s attitudes had changed. In 1986 Dr. Russell Portnoy, a New York pain management specialist, presented a paper assuring colleagues that opioids were much safer than had been previously thought. A movement began. Doctors were not only encouraged to use opioids to treat patients suffering from many forms of chronic pain, but those who didn't were vilified in lay publications coming to my attention for being behind the times or insensitive to the suffering of innocent people.

Having been in practice for decades, I was very much alarmed. Nothing had happened in medicine or pharmacology that could possibly make narcotics safe for long term use. I couldn't imagine any doctor with gray hair thinking otherwise.

Frequently neurosurgeons are called on to evaluate patients with "failed back syndrome," many already addicted to opioid pain medications. Only rarely is additional back surgery of value. In the early 1990s I referred four such patients to local neurologists specializing in chronic pain-management. Within months two died under their care, a fifty percent mortality in the hands of the best pain-management specialists I could find!

In small communities like where Green practiced, certified pain specialists were uncommon if they existed at all. The poor, in particular, depended on non-specialists for care.

On December 17, 2012 an article appeared in the *Wall Street Journal* ("A Pain-Drug Champion Has Second Thoughts") which described Dr. Portenoy as rethinking his having recommended a more liberal use of opoid drugs for twenty-five years.[19] He admitted that his lectures and articles had not been supported by new research data, that he had not only overemphasized the benefits of opioids, he had minimized their attendant risks. The practice inspired by Portenoy and others led doctors like Spurgeon Green into the vicious trap of prescribing dangerous drugs without fear of complications.

Immediately I sent Green a copy of the WSJ article. The information could be argued to be an extenuating factor in whatever crime he had allegedly committed. He had already been in prison for three years. Was keeping him incarcerated for life truly justified? I have serious doubts about that. There was no response to my letters, and I have no other way to contact him.

...

Joe Callanan, my right hand medical officer colleague at B-Med, visited me in Washington, and we have more or less kept in touch since then. He lives in Nampa, Idaho (near Boise) where he has practiced allergy, immunology, and internal medicine for over forty years. He was a solid, clear thinking, and unflappable medical officer.

...

I ran into Ira Cohen in a Sears store in the Washington D.C. area soon after I had settled in near the beltway. His

---

[19] *http://online.wsj.com/article/SB10001424127887324478304578173342657 0.*

addressing me cautiously as Captain Rogers both shocked and saddened me. Recently I called the office of a physician by that name in Washington, D. C. but received no return call. Cohen and I were just different kinds of men. I value his service to B-Med and to our country. He was a good man.

...

Randy Gordon Radigan, a First Lieutenant in 1967 and 1968, went on to serve thirty-nine months in multiple tours in Vietnam as a Dust Off pilot, completing 1,597 air rescue missions and transporting 4,191 wounded soldiers. He was awarded a Distinguished Flying Cross, two Silver Stars, five Bronze Stars, and a Purple Heart. Following Vietnam he married, had two sons, five daughters (two dying in infancy), and four grandchildren. He was employed by the Alyeska Pipeline (Alaska) as a security helicopter pilot and served on the Copper River School Board. He died in 1998 at the age of fifty-two.

...

Buzz Birdsong retired from the Air Force in 1970 and died in 2004 at eighty-five. He, like Bill Fisher, was a true original.

...

Brigadier General Frank Blazey retired in 1975 to the mountains near Hendersonville, NC. Following his retirement he was employed by Toledo Fabrication Company, Conveyor Systems, Inc, and the Coca-Cola Company. For years he remained active in conservation projects in and around Hendersonville.

···

LTC Cal Benedict was promptly promoted to full Colonel, then to Brigadier General in 1971 as Support Commander at Fort Bragg, NC. He became Major General in 1974 then served as Commander of the 1st Infantry Division (1976-1978) and Berlin Commander (1978-1981) before retiring in 1981. He and Frank Blazey remained best friends until the time of his death in 2011.

···

For a long time, seeing America walk away from a war they were on the verge of winning seemed a tragic waste of the American blood already shed. But now almost fifty years later it is clear that losing even one more life would only have only made matters worse. History has confirmed that the perceptions of Presidents Eisenhower, Kennedy, and Johnson of the communist threat in Asia were flawed, however logical their instincts seemed at the time. Dominoes remains a parlor game, not part of a misguided political metaphor, however well intended. America had no business in Vietnam. College students, hippies, and their parents and friends—perhaps the media too—ironically, by driving public opinion against the war, however selfish their interests at the time, worked in their country's best interests, proving once again the miracle of democracy. Times had changed. What had seemed to be worth fighting for no longer was. With the gift of hindsight it is clear America was fortunate that its Greatest Generation had been correct during its day by choosing the opposite conclusion in its dealing with Hitler and imperial Japan. For many Americans, however, World War II was far from popular before it had been won and our heroes had returned home to normal lives.

The presidential election in 1968 reflected the political realities, and the number of American troops in Vietnam decreased from 550,000 in early 1969 to 24,000 by the end of hostilities in late 1972.[20] The war in Vietnam had finally come to an end.

Movies and books appearing in subsequent decades confused me. Tim O'Brien's *The Things They Carried*, a collection of metafictional stories, was published in 1990 to great literary and popular acclaim. Beyond the opening pages, however, the book reflected little of what I experienced in Vietnam, and neither did any of the movies, including "Apocalypse Now," "The Deer Hunter," and "Platoon," which I saw myself.

•••

Throughout 1969 I found myself confused and embarrassed by the talk I heard about Vietnam, particularly from various

---

[20] Dave R. Palmer, *Summons of the Trumpet: U.S.—Vietnam in Perspective* (Novato, CA:Presidio, 1978), 222, 259..

pulpits, where the morality of war, particularly the Vietnam War, was often a topic. More than once I found myself commenting to my growing sons and daughters that I hoped those men of the cloth knew more about the Bible than they knew about the world, certainly with respect to young men answering the call of their country. I never lost my faith, but I did stop attending church for a while.

...

The communists entering Ben Cat that steaming morning during Co Bay's childhood to execute her family and other village leaders weren't practicing politics. Those men were evil, pure evil. Sometimes I dream that Co Bay survived the American withdrawal from her country, but in all honesty that is hardly possible. That she was forced to choose sides so early in life amounted to her signing her own death warrant. I try to picture her now at roughly age seventy, physically wizened and worn like the Vietnamese women of that age I met and treated for sundry illnesses back then, but that image will not come into focus. She was on VC hit lists far too long. She and Sergeant Chuong possessed talents and resourcefulness that would have qualified them for leadership roles in their homeland. But that was not to be. Even if they survived through 1972, they would have faced martyrdom at the hands of the Ho Chi Minh regime.

Through Co Bay and Sergeant Chuong and others like them I learned to respect the Vietnamese people in ways I had not anticipated. They are a vigorous, industrious people, as evidenced also by the successful lives many of them have since carved out for themselves in America. In 1974 I was privileged to head a committee in my home town charged to adopt a Vietnamese family of four that two years earlier had escaped their homeland with makeshift paddles in a small boat in the South China Sea, heading in the general direction of the Philippines. One of my duties was to provide free medical care for the growing children. Within hardly a year the entire family was speaking passable English and both parents had found employment on their way to becoming vibrant citizens as Americans. I lost track of them when the kids were well into high school and their parents had procured a home more convenient to their places of work than the small house we had provided for them. I was so proud of them. They were another reason I felt that the time I spent in their homeland had been far from wasted.

I also encountered a dozen or so Vietnamese in my nearly three decades long medical practice. They were so positive and upbeat, whatever their illnesses or circumstances, each with a stunning story to tell. They were clearly among my favorite patients.

•••

I continue to think of the man who lost his face to flying shrapnel in chapter sixteen. Although life in any form is precious, I can't help thinking that some things must truly be worse than death. He had been in Vietnam hardly a week, and in the twinkling of an eye on a hot Friday afternoon an unimaginable sacrifice was demanded of him. My fervent hope is that he has found the courage and strength to live a rewarding and meaningful life. I doubt an ordinary man could achieve that. His injury quite possibly led to my darkest moments in Vietnam.

...

How did the United States manage to spend $140 billion and almost 60,000 American lives plus several times that many who were unspeakably maimed over a decade in the course of losing the war in Vietnam? Better yet, how are guerrilla wars to be fought more efficiently in the future? Scholars in the Social Sciences Department at West Point have tackled the latter question in recent decades, devouring countless books and studies on Vietnam-type wars. In his 2013 book, *The Insurgents: David Petraeus and the Plot to Change the Way of War*, Fred Kaplan aptly describes how a group of courageous, determined officers and civilians went about re-writing the book on fighting such wars based on the theories of counterinsurgency. According to Kaplan, such doctrine dictates, in part, that "winning the minds and hearts" of civilians by supplying money or needed resources and services is not to make host-nation civilians like Americans, or thank Americans, but to gain their respect and trust. Along with making the military goal less to kill insurgents than protecting civilians establishes a sure flow of reliable intelligence, a crucial element to winning any war. When recognizing that using unnecessary force is counter-productive to winning trust and cooperation, search-and-destroy operations become unthinkable. To engineer principles like these into Army field manuals in Iraq required both guile and guts, further solidifying General David Petraeus' legacy.

...

A soldier never goes into battle without being prepared to lay down his life for his county's cause. A politician never thinks that way. When faced with certain failure, a politician simply reinvents himself and looks toward the next election. Whenever young men and women are called to arms by their government, their sacrifices must never be marginalized by any American. This is also true of the brave men who fought in Vietnam.

APPENDICES

APPENDIX A

HEADQUARTERS & SERVICE BATTERY
2ND BATTALION 33RD ARTILLERY
APO San Francisco, California 96345

24 December 1967

SUBJECT: Recommendation for Award

THRU: Commanding Officer
2nd Bn 33rd Arty
1st Inf Div APO 96345

TO: Commanding Officer
1st Medical Bn
1st Inf Div APO 96345

1. I wish to bring to your attention certain acts of heroism on the part of Captain (Doctor) Rogers, Co B, 1st Medical Bn.

2. On the afternoon of 21 Dec 67 at approximately 1600 hrs the ammunition storage area at the resupply pad at Lai Khe base camp burned and exploded throwing shrapnel and live rounds of ammunition several meters for a period of approximately 3 hours. At the height of the disaster and with complete disregard for his personal safety Dr. Rogers preceded South on highway 13, by foot, amidst intense shrapnel and exploding ammunition, towards the scene of the disaster to render medical aid to injured personnel.

3. Dr. Rogers' heroic actions brought aid and comfort to many injured US soldiers and Vietnamese civilians and inspired and gave hope and courage to the many personnel trapped in the danger zone, and set an example of courage that has earned him the respect and admiration of his contemporaries. His personal bravery and devotion to duty were in the finest traditions of the US Army and the medical profession and reflect great credit upon himself and his unit.

4. I feel the Dr. Rogers' actions more than merit the award of the Soldiers Medal and do so recommend him for this award.

Peter K. Rallis
Cpt, Arty
Commanding

APPENDIX B

DEPARTMENT OF THE ARMY
HEADQUARTERS 1ST INFANTRY DIVISION
APO San Francisco 96345

5 April 1968

GENERAL ORDERS
NUMBER   3112

AWARD OF THE SOLDIER'S MEDAL

1. TC 320. The following AWARD is announced.

ROGERS, LARRY A O5313918 (SSAN 240-56-4729) CAPTAIN MEDICAL CORPS United States Army
Company B 1st Medical Battalion

Awarded:	Soldier's Medal
Date of action:	21 December 1967
Theater:	Republic of Vietnam
Reason:	For heroism not involving actual conflict with an enemy: On this date, Captain Rogers was serving as commander of a medical company at the Lai Khe Base Camp when a fire broke out in an ammunition resupply pad. There was a violent explosion and unarmed artillery shells were hurled several hundred meters in all directions from the pad. The intense heat of the fire detonated many rounds, bombarding the resupply area with flying shrapnel and debris. It also caused a large container of volatile aviation fuel to be ruptured, spilling hundreds of gallons of petroleum into a drainage ditch that led toward the blazing inferno. With complete disregard for his personal safety, Captain Rogers unhesitatingly braved the hail of flying shrapnel and debris and moved on foot into the extremely hazardous area to render medical assistance. He moved dauntlessly about the area giving medical aid to the many burned and wounded personnel. Working at a feverish pace, he remained at the scene and continued to treat the casualties until large scale assistance arrived and evacuation operations were organized and working smoothly. As a result of Captain Rogers' heroic performance, numerous friendly lives were saved. Captain Rogers' actions are in keeping with the finest traditions of the military service and reflect great credit upon himself, the 1st Infantry Division, and the United States Army.
Authority:	By direction of the President, under the provisions of the Act of Congress, approved 2 July 1926.

FOR THE COMMANDER:

OFFICIAL:

A. F. CROWLEY JR
Captain, AGC
Assistant Adjutant General

ARCHIE R. HYLE
Colonel, GS
Chief of Staff

ABOUT THE AUTHOR

Larry Rogers, father of five, practiced neurosurgery in Charlotte, NC for twenty-seven years. He is author of twenty-five scientific articles, author-collaborator of a neurosurgical textbook, co-editor of another, and a novelist, producing *Against the Grain*, a 2008 story of 1980s brain surgery, which is still available from most online vendors.